FOUNDATIONS
FOR A
PSYCHOLOGY
OF
GRACE

FOUNDATIONS
FOR A
PSYCHOLOGY
OF
GRACE

by

William W. Meissner, S.J.

PAULIST PRESS
(Paulist Fathers)
Glen Rock, New Jersey

Edi Potest:
James J. Shanahan, S.J.

Provincial, Buffalo Prov.

October 26, 1965

Nihil Obstat:
Robert E. Hunt, S.T.D.

Censor Librorum

Imprimatur:
Thomas A. Boland, S.T.D.

Archbishop of Newark

March 29, 1966

Library of Congress
Catalog Card Number: 66-24896

COVER DESIGN: Claude Ponsot

Published by Paulist Press
Editorial Office: 304 W. 58th St., N. Y., N. Y. 10019
Business Office: Glen Rock, New Jersey 07452
Printed and bound in the
United States of America

ACKNOWLEDGMENTS

Harper & Row Publishers Incorporated: "Love of God" from *The Art of Loving* by Erich Fromm, pp. 63-82. Copyright © 1956 by Erich Fromm. "Christian Perfection" from *The Divine Milieu* by Pierre Teilhard de Chardin, pp. 64-70. English translation copyright © 1960 by William Collins Sons & Co., Ltd., London, and Harper & Row, Publishers, Incorporated, New York. Reprinted by permission of Harper & Row, Publishers.

Holt, Rinehart and Winston, Inc.: *Pattern and Growth in Personality* by Gordon W. Allport. Copyright 1937, © 1961 by Holt, Rinehart and Winston, Inc. By permission of the publishers. All rights reserved.

Sheed & Ward Inc.: *Psychoanalysis and Personality* by Joseph Nuttin. Copyright 1953 by Sheed & Ward Inc., New York.

Yale University Press: *Becoming* by Gordon Allport (Section 21, "The Religious Sentiment," pp. 93-98, 1960).

Society for the Study of Psychological Social Issues, University of Michigan, and Dr. Isidor Chein: "The Image of Man," *Journal of Social Issues,* 1962, vol. 18.

American Catholic Philosophical Association: "Freud and the Image of Man," by A. Fisher, *Proceedings of the American Catholic Philosophical Association* 35 (1961), pp. 45-77.

Norton Publishing Company: *Insight and Responsibility* (pp. 111-113, 146-150) by Erik Erikson. Copyright © 1964 by Erik Erikson.

Theological Studies, Woodstock, Md.: G. A. McCool, "The Philosophy of the Human Person in Karl Rahner's Theology," *Theological Studies* 22 (1961), pp. 539-552.

Fordham University Press: G. Weigel, "Theology and Freedom," *Thought* 35 (1960), pp. 165-178.

P. F. Fransen, S.J.: "Towards a Psychology of Divine Grace," *Lumen Vitae* 12 (1957), pp. 165-178.

CONTENTS

Contents

I
PROBLEM
AND PROBLEMATIC

The Problem

We live in curious times. To paraphrase Dickens, it is the best of times and the worst of times. It is an age that has been called the age of anxiety, the age of automation, the atomic age. It is an age in which technology has become a dominant influence in shaping the course of history. At the same time, it is an age in which man's finest instincts for truth, justice, and charity have been activated on a scale never before witnessed in human civilization.

Ours is also, very decisively, an era of psychological concern. Mental health is a primary public health problem. Psychological testing in all its forms is big business. Beyond these superficial facts of contemporary life, there is a growing awareness and concern with the inner self. Insatiable human curiosity has in some definite way become introverted, has turned in upon itself in an inquiry that seeks to know more adequately, more precisely, more scientifically, what man is and why he behaves, thinks, experiences as he does.

Within the Church, of course, one is confronted with a variety of problems. The anguish of soul that accompanies the modern predicament often finds an answer in faith. The priest, in the confessional and outside of it, is confronted with the whole gamut of human problems and emotional disturbances. It is not a matter of deciding on the morality of this or that situation. It is rare, even in the confessional, that a priest cannot reach a moral decision. His problem is basically and universally pastoral. He needs a fun-

1

damental understanding of human motivation and the roots of behavior. More significantly, he needs to understand the role man's concrete religious existence plays in his life adjustment. He needs to understand, as he attempts to help particular penitents or parishioners, what influences the way they behave. The influences are multiple. They are psychological and sociological, and they are also theological. If the Christian life means anything, it means that God is presently active in the souls of his flock. This presence and this activity presumably make a difference. But the technical theological understanding of trinitarian processions and divine indwelling may tell us little or nothing about the impact of such realities on the inner workings of the individual soul. The priest, then, cannot rely much on such theological knowledge in his efforts to understand the influence of grace and to help the soul become more receptive to the influence of grace.

The guidelines for such understanding must come from a fully developed and profoundly meaningful pastoral psychology. But the mistake has often been made of thinking of pastoral psychology as a kind of application of psychological principles to pastoral problems. In the context of a Christian belief which accepts the reality of grace and the supernatural this is an incomplete view. The great resource of the Church is that through her sacraments and through her very life, she is the channel of grace. Her life is the life of Christ, and those who share in her life share in his mystical body. And grace is the vivifying principle of the body of Christ, giving it life and meaning. It is upon grace, above all else, that the priest must rely in easing the burden of troubled souls. To apply psychological principles, then, is not enough. They must be complemented by a psychology of the life of grace.

Another important area of concern is that of Christian spirituality in our day. The traditional approaches to spirituality have been almost exclusively theological. While the theological dimension of spirituality is undoubtedly the most important and significant aspect of this rich and complex area, it seems that the theological approach has missed something important, something perhaps more attuned to the needs and aspirations of contemporary culture. For Christian spirituality touches the soul at its most intimate and profound levels. The exploration of these depths is the work of a psychology of grace. It is a work that is essentially untried. A meaningful psychology of grace might make modern man realize the significance of the spiritual life for his own psychological development and maturity.

On a more theoretical level, moral theology in our day is undergoing a searching reorganization. The more or less juridical foundations of moral theology have proven, if not unsatisfactory, at least unpalatable. Moreover, it has become increasingly necessary to face up to the issue of the interplay between unconscious and conscious elements in the evolution of moral behavior. Attempts have been made here and there to reinterpret Freudian insights in more traditional terms [1] or to incorporate such insights into existing moral theory. The effort, I am afraid, has not been terribly successful for a number of reasons.[2] The difficulties are both logical and methodological. Traditional moralists simply asked quite different kinds of questions than do modern psychological inquirers. If one tries to amalgamate their approaches, one does so at the risk of distorting the meaning of both. The attempts have been noteworthy, however, in that they reflect a sensitivity to the need for understanding unconscious motivation in order to understand morality. It seems to me, however, that the more intelligent and reasonable — although plainly the more difficult — course, is to rethink both approaches. Modern insights have forced traditional moral theory to rethink itself in the light of the more recent data and theories. The converse is also true: Modern attempts to understand moral behavior run the risk of being incomplete if they ignore or discount the insights of more traditional approaches. But the important point is that both scientific psychology and moral theology or ethics must rethink the problem of man's moral activity, each on its own terms. To confuse the distinction between them is to give birth to a chimera.

There is no question but that an understanding of the unconscious dynamisms of man's psychic life can have a profound impact on the attitudes with which one approaches moral problems. But the moralist, particularly the Christian moralist, must approach

---

[1] M. Stock, O.P., "Thomistic Psychology and Freud's Psychoanalysis," *The Thomist* 21 (1958).

[2] A. Plé, O.P., *Vie Affective et Chasteté* (Paris: Editions du Cerf, 1964).

man in the fullness of his Christian life. An integral, and (on solid theological grounds, we believe) a major part of that life is due to the influence of grace. If a sound and adequate psychological understanding of man's Christian existence is to be achieved, it is necessary that we come to some understanding of the effects of grace. It is not sufficient merely to pick up some extant theory and transpose it into a theoretical framework that is quite alien to it. The great challenge to the Christian psychologist, therefore, is to shape a theory of man's psychological functioning which incorporates the data and insights of modern psychological understanding, and which is also fully consonant with the penetrating insights of the Christian tradition. It can be hoped that as such an integral view of Christian man under grace does emerge, we will grow in our ability to deal with Christian man in our day in meaningful psychological and moral terms.

These, then, are the kinds of problems which we are addressing. But it should be evident that behind any such aggregate of problems there lies a problematic. We are approaching the problematic of the psychology of grace here first of all to focus attention on the fact that there is a set of problems to which this consideration is related, and secondly to specify the terms in which the problematic should be stated.

The Problematic

The problematic of grace concretely involves a consideration of the methodology of the psychology of grace, the relations between such a psychology and the theology of grace, and the lines of thought along which such a psychology can be developed. We are not immediately concerned here to try to develop a psychology of grace. Rather we are concerned with what we have chosen to call the problematic of grace, with bringing it into focus and defining, if possible, the nature of the inquiry. Very likely these particular points cannot be successfully dealt with without our advancing some notions about various aspects of the psychology of grace. But at the same time any such observations need serious qualification. The development of a psychology of grace is a comprehensive and complex undertaking. The suggestions and indications we offer regarding the shape of such a psychological understanding or the lines of thought it might follow, are advanced here only as tentative formulations. They are intended to demonstrate merely that the psychology of grace can be structured in meaningful terms; we do not maintain that these particular terms are necessarily the right ones.

The first issue that must be faced in the problematic of grace is determining what the psychology of grace is not. Christian tradition has constantly concerned itself with the life of grace. The doctrine of grace over the centuries has undergone extensive development and Christian reflection has arrived at a profound understanding of the nature of grace. But the understanding has been couched in ontological terms. The questions which have been asked, and to a large extent answered, concern the existence of grace, the conditions of its possibility, its ontological nature, and the nature of its effects on man's soul. Christian reflection has also concerned itself with the theological dimensions of the relations between grace and the person of Christ, the incarnation, the redemption, the sacraments, and the Church. Christian theology, under the guidance of revelation, has developed a theology of grace which has far-reaching implications for the meaning and understanding of man's relations with God. Along with this rich theological elaboration have come many insights relative to the impact of grace on man.

In theological perspective, a *vulnus* or "wound" was inflicted on human nature in the fall and the action of grace is somehow directed to healing that wound. If the *vulnus naturae* consequent to original sin can be regarded as a loss of integrity, then the action of grace is directed toward the reintegration of man's nature. If the effects of sin can be spelled out in terms of a disordered concupiscence, then the influence of grace can be conceived of as contributing to an increasingly ordered concupiscence. Implicit in such formations is the presumption that grace is somehow psychologically relevant, somehow has an influence on man's psychological life. But this latter consideration remains a more or less latent and implicit element in the development of the theological meaning of the life of grace.

In all of this rich development the primary concern was ontological and theological. The changes that were wrought in man by the action of grace were defined in no more than theological terms or in terms of the ontological structure of man's nature. There was no concern with or extended attempt to penetrate within, to look within the reality of man and determine what changes were to be found there. But it is precisely this that the psychology of grace must try to do. If one can accept the proposition that grace is more than theologically operational, that it does have a psychological impact, then it should be possible to formulate that psychological impact. Grace does not merely change man's theological condition, changing him in reference to the supernatural, but it reaches into his very nature and makes contact with the deepest reaches of his psychic reality.

The question that the psychology of grace poses is the question of man's nature and what changes may occur in it under the influence of grace. It is important to realize that the inquiry into the psychology of grace, therefore, is not a theological inquiry. It is specifically a psychological inquiry and must be carried out in psychological terms. The psychology of grace, then, does not mean a transposition of theological insights into psychological language. It is an independent inquiry which must work its way to its own conclusions and state them in terms that are psychologically relevant. The psychology of grace must be definitively a valid psychology. Its language must be the language of psychology and its formulations must establish its connections with existing psychological theory. Moreover, its methods must be basically psychological. Its questions must be directed to man's inner subjective experience. It must explore the relations between grace and man's behavior, attitudes, emotional experience, values and ideals. This is not a theological or ontological investigation in any sense. It is rather an inquiry into the concrete and existential dimensions of the Christian life.

While the psychology of grace must maintain its methodological independence from theology lest it lose its scientific autonomy and become less than an authentic psychology, it is, however, true that the psychology of grace retains a certain specific and necessary dependence on theology. Grace is, after all, a divine activity, not immediately open to human observation. Further, whatever may be the reverberations of the action of grace in human experience (and this is a deeply disputed point), there seems to be no experience of grace which cannot be duplicated or mimicked in human experience without grace. Even in the most lofty mystical experiences of the great saints, the supernatural origin of what happens is ascertained on other grounds than the experience itself. The experience of "divine presence" which is frequently associated with the effects of grace is not of such a quality that it could not be simulated by psychological mechanisms operating independently of the action of grace. Consequently, the basic question of whether it is grace which is operative in a particular instance cannot be answered on psychological grounds alone. The elaboration of theological norms is necessary.

On another level entirely, it must be seen that the psychology of grace cannot take place in a vacuum. What grace is, what the conditions of its operation are, and what are its effects are all questions that require theological orientation. Thus the basic lines of inquiry, the directions of thinking about the psychological effects of grace, must be derived from theological reflection. It is really only theological reflection which can answer these questions. Not that the answers are going to be psychological, but they direct the course of psychological inquiry. It makes a good deal of difference, for example, whether grace is considered to be a sort of extrinsic force that coerces man's will, or is considered to be an inner process that depends on the exercise of man's free will. It makes a difference whether it is directing its effects to the will or to the imagination.

The point is clear. There must be some degree of antecedent theological formulation about the nature and effect of grace before a meaningful psychology of grace can become a reality. This consideration may be of decisive importance for the methodology of a psychology of grace. The methodology must be definitively psychological, as we have observed, but it requires by the very nature of the case a theological context. Thus the theology of grace must set the guidelines and indicate the proper focus of investigation, but from there on the investigation must be psychological. Never-theless, while the methods and concepts are psychological, the validity of any conclusions may be established only by crosscheck-ing with theological insights into the nature and operation of grace.

Within this context, then, some basic questions about the nature of grace must be considered. Grace is, first of all, a divine activity. Human existence, along with all other existence, is called into being by a creative act of God. God's creative act endows the human being with existence, and the continuous exercise of his creative power operates to sustain that existence. Human existence, how-ever, is an active, dynamic agency that extends its being into action. Just as the condition of existence is the definite existence of God, so the condition underlying the possibility of action is the infinite activity of God. Grace, then, is in the order of concurrent divine activity, sustaining and making possible certain kinds of human activity.

If the divine activity involved in grace is concurrent, it follows that the action of grace must be such as to respect the activity of the human agent. This is a basic maxim for the psychology of grace, as well as for the theology of grace. God respects his own creation. His concurrent activity works through the powers and forms of activity proper to such secondary agents. Man is a free agent and grace cannot violate that freedom. Yet grace as a divine activity is utterly gratuitous. There is nothing outside of God's own infinite love which could move him to extend the support of his divine activity. Grace is therefore a pure gift of love. Gifts cannot be forced, let alone gifts of love. In some ultimate sense, then, grace or the effects of grace depend on the exercise of man's free will.

Another way of formulating this basic principle is to say that grace perfects nature. This implies that grace exercises its effects in and through man's own proper activity. The force of this state-ment is to emphasize the fact that there is no effect of grace which is not at the same time a proper activity of man. This is not the same thing as saying that all the effects of grace are within man's unaided capacity to achieve. The common theological teaching is that man cannot over a long period lead a fully moral life without the help of grace. But leading a moral life is certainly a proper activity of man. Grace perfects human nature by making man more fully human and more perfectly human. If we accept the proposition that the life of grace has psychological relevance, it means that the psychological effect of grace is directed toward a fullness of personality development and maturity of function associated with adequate psychological growth.

Plainly, in adopting this approach to grace, I have selected a theological analysis which seems to me to be the most useful for illustrating my point. There are other analyses which are perfectly acceptable theologically. In any systematic analysis of grace, there are certain points of the Church's teaching that must be safeguarded — human liberty and the gratuity of grace. The rest is concerned with the ontological analysis of grace.

This inquiry into the psychology of grace is a major undertaking. I wish to repeat that our objective here is not to formulate such a psychology, and I think that this is appropriate conservatism. The full elaboration of a psychology of grace must mine from the rich sources of Christian theology a fuller yield of psychologically relevant insights into the nature and function of grace. This is a difficult and at the same time rewarding undertaking. Because grace is such a central part of God's salvific action, it has always been a focus of concern. Consequently, historical approach would have to return to a re-examination of scripture and especially the teaching of Paul and John. There would have to be a close analysis and scrutiny of patristic literature. To Augustine especially do we owe the traditional sensitivity to grace as pertinent to man's inner psychic needs. There would have to be a reassessment of the great theological tradition, of the middle ages, of the scholastic period, and of theological reflection on into the present day. But one cannot search aimlessly. There must be some direction, orientation, hypothesis, or tentative formulation to guide the search and suggest what is significant and what is not. If our present inquiry can contribute to this in some small way, it will have more than served its purpose.

The problematic of grace is wide-ranging and reaches to the depths of the Christian experience. It encompasses a broad theological spectrum and practically the whole of human psychology. The first step in approaching such a problematic is not altogether easy. It must provide a basis for psychological reflection and a meaningful point of contact with theology. It must be a focal point to which the insights of theology can be directed and through which such insights can be made psychologically relevant.

Our goal in this present inquiry will be the formulation of such a starting point. We will attempt to bring into focus an image of man. Some of the following selections give expression to a concept of man that is both psychologically acceptable and sufficiently broad to serve the demands of a psychology of grace. Other selections will concern themselves with the image of man in contemporary theology. Out of these various contributions, we hope to be able to bring into focus a more or less common image of man at once psychologically relevant and theologically sound. We can project only a limited success in this undertaking, since it involves so much complexity. But we can hope to establish the fact that such an image is quite possible. It may even be meaningful.

The formulation of a common image would, I think, provide a starting point for further consideration of the psychology of grace. The major difficulty in the development of a psychology of grace is making theological insights into the life of grace psychologically relevant. If the theological consideration and the psychological consideration both have a common reference point, in terms of which both can be interpreted, the way for further progress would be established.

We will attempt at the same time to lay down some of the lines of thought along which a psychology of grace might develop. The lines of thought involve both elaboration and implications derived from the basic image of man. While such formulations are necessarily tentative, we are hopeful that they will provide guidelines for future developments. At least, they will be advanced with the expectation that they will demonstrate the feasibility and possible richness of a true psychology of grace.

Questions for Discussion

1. What areas of general concern does the author mention as characteristic of the present era?
2. What must moral theology do if it is to successfully incorporate the insights and data of modern psychological theory?
3. What is involved in the problematic of grace?
4. What issue must first be faced in formulating a problematic of grace? What element has been stressed in the development of the Christian view of grace over the centuries?
5. What is the relation between the psychology of grace and theology? Why must they be kept separate?
6. Why is theology necessary here?
7. What does it mean to say that God's action in grace is concurrent? What conclusions follow from this?
8. What is the object of grace, psychologically speaking?
9. What are the limits and purposes of the present study?
10. What advantages would a "common image" offer?

II
WILLIAM JAMES AND THE
DIVIDED SELF

A. Prenote

It may seem strange that we begin this sort of inquiry with a passage from William James. But there are persuasive reasons for doing so. Whatever we may think about James's pragmatism, he stands forth as the principal figure in the history of American psychology. His *Principles* has taken its rightful place as the prototype of the psychological handbook. His approach to the reality of psychological man was marked by a breadth of understanding and a flexibility of perspective that was remarkable if not unique. James understood, as few psychologists since his time, the complexity and marvelous individuality of the human personality. It was he who spoke of "personal identity" half a century before it became the fashionable phrase. It was also he who spoke of the "spiritual me."[1]

For these reasons alone James would deserve consideration here. But he has given us something more. He recognized the relevance of man's religious experience to his psychological functioning. Between the benign religiosity of the once-born and the passion of the twice-born there extends the wide range of man's relation to God. In an age in which conflict has become an obsessive concern the benignity of the once-born may seem artificial, or at least superficial. But today the paradox of the twice-born strikes us with particular impact. One might question whether the once-born exists at all, or whether the demeanor of the once-born is not

---

[1] *Psychology: The Briefer Course* (New York: Harper, 1961).

after all a facade that cloaks the deeper conflicts and ambivalences of the depths.

The following excerpts are from James's *The Varieties of Religious Experience,* Lecture 7 (Garden City, N.Y.: Doubleday, 1902), pp. 155-176.

B. Selection: The Divided Self and the Process
of Its Unification

The last lecture was a painful one, dealing as it did with evil as a pervasive element of the world we live in. At the close of it we were brought into full view of the contrast between the two ways of looking at life which are characteristic respectively of what we called the healthy-minded, who need to be born only once, and of the sick souls, who must be twice-born in order to be happy. The result is two different conceptions of the universe of our experience. In the religion of the once-born the world is a sort of rectilinear or one-storied affair, whose accounts are kept in one denomination, whose parts have just the values which naturally they appear to have, and of which a simple algebraic sum of pluses and minuses will give the total worth. Happiness and religious peace consist in living on the plus side of the account. In the religion of the twice-born, on the other hand, the world is a double-storied mystery. Peace cannot be reached by the simple addition of pluses and elimination of minuses from life. Natural good is not simply insufficient in amount and transient; there lurks a falsity in its very being. Cancelled as it all is by death if not by earlier enemies, it gives no final balance, and can never be the thing intended for our lasting worship. It keeps us from our real good, rather; and renunciation and despair of it are our first step in the direction of the truth. There are two lives, the natural and the spiritual, and we must lose the one before we can participate in the other.

In their extreme forms, of pure naturalism and pure salvationism, the two types are violently contrasted; though here as in most other current classifications, the radical extremes are somewhat ideal abstractions, and the concrete human beings whom we oftenest meet are intermediate varieties and mixtures. Practically, however, you all recognize the difference: you understand, for example, the disdain of the Methodist convert for the mere sky-blue healthy-minded moralist; and you likewise enter into the aversion of the latter to what seems to him the diseased subjectivism of the Methodist, dying to live, as he calls it, and making of paradox and the inversion of natural appearances the essence of God's truth.

The psychological basis of the twice-born character seems to be a certain discordancy or heterogeneity in the native temperament of the subject, an incompletely unified moral and intellectual constitution.

"Homo duplex, homo duplex!" writes Alphonse Daudet. "The first time that I perceived that I was two was at the death of my brother Henri, when my father cried out so dramatically, 'He is dead, he is dead!' While my first self wept, my second self thought, 'How truly given was that cry, how fine it would be at the theatre.' I was then fourteen years old.

"This horrible duality has often given me matter for reflection. Oh, this terrible second me, always seated whilst the other is on foot, acting, living, suffering, bestirring itself. This second me that I have never been able to intoxicate, to make shed tears, or put to sleep. And how it sees into things, and how it mocks!"

Recent works on the psychology of character have had much to say upon this point. Some persons are born with an inner constitution which is harmonious and well balanced from the outset. Their impulses are consistent with one another, their will follows without trouble the guidance of their intellect, their passions are not excessive, and their lives are little haunted by regrets. Others are oppositely constituted and are so in degrees which may vary from something so slight as to result in a merely odd or whimsical inconsistency, to a discordancy of which the consequences may be inconvenient in the extreme. . . .

This amount of inconsistency will only count as amiable weakness; but a stronger degree of heterogeneity may make havoc of the subject's life. There are persons whose existence is little more than a series of zig-zags, as now one tendency and now another gets the upper hand. Their spirit wars with their flesh, they wish for incompatibles, wayward impulses interrupt their most deliberate plans, and their lives are one long drama of repentance and of effort to repair misdemeanors and mistakes.

Heterogeneous personality has been explained as the result of inheritance — the traits of character of incompatible and antagonistic ancestors are supposed to be preserved alongside of each other. This explanation may pass for what it is worth — it certainly needs corroboration. But whatever the cause of heterogeneous personality may be, we find the extreme examples of it in the psychopathic temperament, of which I spoke in my first lecture. All writers about that temperament make the inner heterogeneity prominent in their descriptions. Frequently, indeed, it is only this trait that leads us to ascribe that temperament to a man at all. A "dégénéré supérieur" is simply a man of sensibility in many directions, who finds more difficulty than is common in keeping his spiritual house in order and running his furrow straight, because his feelings and impulses are too keen and too discrepant mutually. In the haunting and insistent ideas, in the irrational impulses, the morbid scruples, dreads, and inhibitions which beset the psychopathic temperament when it is thoroughly pronounced, we have exquisite examples of heterogeneous personality. Bunyan had an obsession of the words, "Sell Christ for this, sell him for that, sell him, sell him!" which would run through his mind a hundred times together, until one day out of breath with retorting, "I will not, I will not," he impulsively said, "Let him go if he will," and this loss of the battle kept him in despair for over a year. The lives of the saints are full of such blasphemous obsessions, ascribed invariably to the direct agency of Satan. The phenomenon connects itself with the life of the subconscious self, so-called, of which we must ere long speak more directly.

Now in all of us, however constituted, but to a degree the greater in proportion as we are intense and sensitive and subject to diversified temptations, and to the greatest possible degree if we are decidedly psychopathic, does the normal evolution of character chiefly consist in the straightening out and unifying of the inner self. The higher and the lower feelings, the useful and the erring impulses, begin by being a comparative chaos within us — they must end by forming a stable system of functions in right subordination. Unhappiness is apt to characterize the period of order-making and struggle. If the individual be of tender conscience and religiously quickened, the unhappiness will take the form of moral remorse and compunction, of feeling inwardly vile and wrong, and of standing in false relations to the author of one's being and appointer of one's spiritual fate. This is the religious melancholy and "conviction of sin" that have played so large a part in the history of Protestant Christianity. The man's interior is a battleground for what he feels to be two deadly hostile selves, one actual, the other ideal. As Victor Hugo makes his Mahomet say: —

> *"Je suis le champ vil des sublimes combats:*
> *Tantôt l'homme d'en haut, et tantôt l'homme d'en bas;*
> *Et le mal dans ma bouche avec le bien alterne,*
> *Comme dans le désert le sable et la citerne."*

Wrong living, impotent aspirations; "What I would, that do I not; but what I hate, that do I," as Saint Paul says; self-loathing, self-despair; an unintelligible and intolerable burden to which one is mysteriously the heir.

Let me quote from some typical cases of discordant personality, with melancholy in the form of self-condemnation and sense of sin. Saint Augustine's case is a classic example. You all remember his half-pagan, half-Christian bringing up at Carthage, his emigration to Rome and Milan, his adoption of Manicheism and subsequent skepticism, and his restless search for truth and purity of life; and finally how, distracted by the struggle between the two souls in his breast and ashamed of his own weakness of will, when so many others whom he knew and knew of had thrown off the shackles of sensuality and dedicated themselves to chastity and the higher life, he heard a voice in the garden say, *"Sume, lege"* (take and read), and opening the Bible at random, saw the text, "not in chambering and wantonness," etc., which seemed directly sent to his address, and laid the inner storm to rest forever. Augustine's psychological genius has given an account of the trouble of having a divided self which has never been surpassed.

"The new will which I began to have was not yet strong enough to overcome that other will, strengthened by long indulgence. So these two wills, one old, one new, one carnal, the other spiritual, contended with each other and disturbed my soul. I understood by my own experience what I had read, 'flesh lusteth against spirit, and spirit against flesh.' It was myself indeed in both the wills, yet more myself in that which I approved in myself than in that which I disapproved in myself. Yet it was through myself that habit had attained so fierce a mastery over me, because I had willingly come whither I willed not. Still bound to earth, I refused, O God, to fight on thy side, as much afraid to be freed from all bonds, as I ought to have feared being trammeled by them.

"Thus the thoughts by which I meditated upon thee were like the efforts of one who would awake, but being over-powered with sleepiness is soon asleep again. Often does a man when heavy sleepiness is on his limbs defer to shake it off, and though not approving it, encourage it; even so I was sure it was better to surrender to thy love than to yield to my own lusts, yet, though the former course convinced me, the latter pleased and held me bound. These was naught in me to answer thy call, 'Awake, thou sleeper,' but only drawling, drowsy words, 'Presently; yes, presently; wait a little while.' But the 'presently' had no 'present,' and the 'little while' grew long. . . . For I was afraid thou wouldst hear me too soon, and heal me at once of my disease of lust, which I wished to satiate rather than to see extinguished. With what lashes of words did I not scourge my own soul. Yet it shrank back; it refused, though it had no excuse to offer. . . . I said within myself: 'Come, let it be done now,' and as I said it, I was on the point of the resolve. I all but did it, yet I did not do it. And I made another effort, and almost succeeded, yet

I did not reach it, and did not grasp it, hesitating to die to death, and live to life; and the evil to which I was so wonted held me more than the better life I had not tried." [2]

There could be no more perfect description of the divided will, when the higher wishes lack just that last acuteness, that touch of explosive intensity, of dynamogenic quality (to use the slang of the psychologists), that enables them to burst their shell, and make irruption efficaciously into life and quell the lower tendencies forever. In a later lecture we shall have much to say about this higher excitability.

I find another good description of the divided will in the auto-biography of Henry Alline, the Nova Scotian evangelist, of whose melancholy I read a brief account in my last lecture. The poor youth's sins were, as you will see, of the most harmless order, yet they interfered with what proved to be his truest vocation, so they gave him great distress.

"I was now very moral in my life, but found no rest of conscience. I now began to be esteemed in young company, who knew nothing of my mind all this while, and their esteem began to be a snare to my soul, for I soon began to be fond of carnal mirth, though I still flattered myself that if I did not get drunk, nor curse, nor swear, there would be no sin in frolicking and carnal mirth, and I thought God would indulge young people with some (what I called simple or civil) recreation. I still kept a round of duties, and would not suffer myself to run into any open vices, and so got along very well in time of health and prosperity, but when I was distressed or threatened by sickness, death, or heavy storms of thunder, my religion would not do, and I found there was something wanting, and would begin to repent my going so much to frolics, but when the distress was over, the devil and my own wicked heart, with the solicitations of my associates, and my fondness for young company, were such strong allurements, I would again give way, and thus I got to be very wild and rude, at the same time kept up my rounds of secret prayer

---
[2] *Confessions* 8. 5,7,11, abridged.

and reading; but God, not willing I should destroy myself, still followed me with his calls, and moved with such power upon my conscience, that I could not satisfy myself with my diversions, and in the midst of my mirth sometimes would have such a sense of my lost and undone condition, that I would wish myself from the company, and after it was over, when I went home, would make many promises that I would attend no more on these frolics, and would beg forgiveness for hours and hours; but when I came to have the temptation again, I would give way: no sooner would I hear the music and drink a glass of wine, but I would find my mind elevated and soon proceed to any sort of merriment or diversion, that I thought was not debauched or openly vicious; but when I returned from my carnal mirth I felt as guilty as ever, and could sometimes not close my eyes for some hours after I had gone to my bed. I was one of the most unhappy creatures on earth.

"Sometimes I would leave the company (often speaking to the fiddler to cease from playing, as if I was tired), and go out and walk about crying and praying, as if my very heart would break, and beseeching God that he would not cut me off, nor give me up to hardness of heart. Oh, what unhappy hours and nights I thus wore away! When I met sometimes with merry companions, and my heart was ready to sink, I would labor to put on as cheerful a countenance as possible, that they might not distrust anything, and sometimes would begin some discourse with young men or young women on purpose, or propose a merry song, lest the distress of my soul would be discovered, or mistrusted, when at the same time I would then rather have been in a wilderness in exile, than with them or any of their pleasures or enjoyments. Thus for many months when I was in company, I would act the hypocrite and feign a merry heart, but at the same time would endeavor as much as I could to shun their company, oh wretched and unhappy mortal that I was! Everything I did, and wherever I went, I was still in a storm, and yet I continued to be the chief contriver and ringleader of the frolics for many months after; though it was a toil and torment to attend them; but the devil and my own wicked heart drove me about like a slave, telling me that I must do this and do that, and bear this and bear that, and turn here and turn there, to keep my credit up, and retain the esteem of my associates: and all this while I continued as strict as possible in my duties, and left no stone unturned to pacify my conscience, watching even against my thoughts, and praying continually wherever I went: for I did not think there was any sin in my conduct, when I was among carnal company, because I did not take any satisfaction there, but only followed it, I thought, for sufficient reasons.

"But still, all that I did or could do, conscience would roar night and day."

Saint Augustine and Alline both emerged into the smooth waters of inner unity and peace, and I shall next ask you to consider more closely some of the peculiarities of the process of unification, when it occurs. It may come gradually, or it may occur abruptly; it may come through altered feelings, or through altered powers of action; or it may come through new intellectual insights, or through experiences which we shall later have to designate as "mystical." However it come, it brings a characteristic sort of relief; and never such extreme relief as when it is cast into the religious mould. Happiness! Happiness! Religion is only one of the ways in which men gain that gift. Easily, permanently and successfully, it often transforms the most intolerable misery into the profoundest and most enduring happiness.

But to find religion is only one out of many ways of reaching unity; and the process of remedying inner incompleteness and reducing inner discord is a general psychological process, which may take place with any sort of mental material, and need not necessarily assume the religious form. In judging of the religious types of regeneration which we are about to study, it is important to recognize that they are only one species of a genus that contains other types as well. For example, the new birth may be away from religion into incredulity; or it may be from moral scrupulosity into freedom and license; or it may be produced by the irruption into the individual's life of some new stimulus or passion, such as love, ambition, cupidity, revenge, or patriotic devotion. In all these instances we have precisely the same psychological form of event, — a firmness, stability, and equilibrium succeeding a period of storm and stress and inconsistency. In these non-religious cases the new man may also be born either gradually or suddenly.

Let me turn now to the kind of case, the religious case, namely, that immediately concerns us. Here is one of the simplest possible type, an account of the conversion to the systematic religion of healthy-mindedness of a man who must already have been naturally of the healthy-minded type. It shows how, when the fruit is ripe, a touch will make it fall.

Mr. Horace Fletcher, in his little book called *Menticulture,* relates that a friend with whom he was talking of the self-control attained by the Japanese through their practice of the Buddhist discipline said:—

" 'You must first get rid of anger and worry.' 'But,' said I, 'is that possible?' 'Yes,' replied he; 'it is possible to the Japanese, and ought to be possible to us.'

"On my way back I could think of nothing else but the words 'get rid, get rid'; and the idea must have continued to possess me during my sleeping hours, for the first conscious-ness in the morning brought back the same thought, with the revelation of a discovery, which framed itself into the reason-ing, 'If it is possible to get rid of anger and worry, why is it necessary to have them at all?' I felt the strength of the argument, and at once accepted the reasoning. The baby had discovered that it could walk. It would scorn to creep any longer.

"From the instant I realized that these cancer spots of worry and anger were removable, they left me. With the discovery of their weakness they were exorcised. From that time life has had an entirely different aspect.

"Although from that moment the possibility and desirability of freedom from the depressing passions has been a reality to me, it took me some months to feel absolute security in my new position; but, as the usual occasions for worry and anger have presented themselves over and over again, and I have been unable to feel them in the slightest degree, I no longer dread or guard against them, and I am amazed at my increased energy and vigor of mind; at my strength to meet situations of all kinds, and at my disposition to love and appreciate everything.

"I have had occasion to travel more than ten thousand miles by rail since that morning. The same Pullman porter, conductor, hotel-waiter, peddler, book-agent, cabman, and others who were formerly a source of annoyance and irritation have been met, but I am not conscious of a single incivility. All at once the whole world has turned good to me. I have become, as it were, sensitive only to the rays of good.

"I could recount many experiences which prove a brand-new condition of mind, but one will be sufficient. Without the slightest feeling of annoyance or impatience, I have seen a train that I had planned to take with a good deal of interested and pleasurable anticipation move out of the station without me, because my baggage did not arrive. The porter from the hotel came running and panting into the station just as the train pulled out of sight. When he saw me, he looked as if he feared a scolding, and began to tell of being blocked in a crowded street and unable to get out. When he had finished, I said to him: 'It doesn't matter at all, you couldn't help it, so we will try again to-morrow. Here is your fee, I am sorry you had all this trouble in earning it.' The look of surprise that came over his face was so filled with pleasure that I was repaid on the spot for the delay in my departure. Next day he would not accept a cent for the service, and he and I are friends for life.

"During the first weeks of my experience I was on guard only against worry and anger; but, in the meantime, having noticed the absence of the other depressing and dwarfing passions, I began to trace a relationship, until I was convinced that they are all growths from the two roots I have specified. I have felt the freedom now for so long a time that I am sure of my relation toward it; and I could no more harbor any of the thieving and depressing influences that once I nursed as a heritage of humanity than a fop would voluntarily wallow in a filthy gutter.

"There is no doubt in my mind that pure Christianity and pure Buddhism, and the mental sciences and all religions, fundamentally teach what has been a discovery to me; but none of them have presented it in the light of a simple and easy process of elimination. At one time I wondered if the elimination would not yield to indifference and sloth. In my experience, the contrary is the result. I feel such an increased desire to do something useful that it seems as if I were a boy again and the energy for play had returned. I could fight as readily as (and better than) ever, if there were occasion for it. It does not make one a coward. It can't, since fear is one of the things eliminated. I notice the absence of timidity in the presence of any audience. When a boy, I was standing under a tree which was struck by lightning, and received a shock from the effects of which I never knew exemption until I had dissolved partnership with worry. Since then, lightning and thunder have been encountered under conditions which would formerly have caused great depression and discomfort, without [my] experiencing a trace of either. Surprise is also greatly modified, and one is less liable to become startled by unexpected sights or noises.

"As far as I am individually concerned, I am not bothering myself at present as to what the results of this emancipated condition may be. I have no doubt that the perfect health aimed at by Christian Science may be one of the possibilities, for I note a marked improvement in the way my stomach does its duty in assimilating the food I give it to handle, and I am sure it works better to the sound of a song than under the friction of a frown. Neither am I wasting any of this precious time formulating an idea of a future existence or a future heaven. The heaven that I have within myself is as attractive as any that has been promised or that I can imagine; and I am willing to let the growth lead where it will, as long as the anger and their brood have no part in misguiding it."

The older medicine used to speak of two ways, *lysis* and *crisis,* one gradual, the other abrupt, in which one might recover from a bodily disease. In the spiritual realm there are also two ways, one gradual, the other sudden, in which inner unification may occur. Tolstoy and Bunyan may again serve us as examples, examples, as it happens, of the gradual way, though it must be confessed at the outset that it is hard to follow these windings of the hearts of others, and one feels that their words do not reveal their total secret.

However this be, Tolstoy, pursuing his unending questioning, seemed to come to one insight after another. First he perceived that his conviction that life was meaningless took only this finite life into account. He was looking for the value of one finite term in that of another, and the whole result could only be one of those indeterminate equations in mathematics which end with $0 = 0$. Yet this is as far as the reasoning intellect by itself can go, unless irrational sentiment or faith brings in the infinite. Believe in the infinite as common people do, and life grows possible again.

"Since mankind has existed, wherever life has been, there also has been the faith that gave the possibility of living. Faith is the sense of life, that sense by virtue of which man does not destroy himself, but continues to live on. It is the force whereby we live. If man did not believe that he must live for something, he would not live at all. The idea of an infinite God, of the divinity of the soul, of the union of men's actions with God—these are ideas elaborated in the infinite secret depths of human thought. They are ideas without which there would be no life, without which I myself," said Tolstoy, "would not exist. I began to see that I had no right to rely on my individual reasoning and neglect these answers given by faith, for they are the only answers to the question."

Yet how believe as the common people believe, steeped as they are in grossest superstition? It is impossible — but yet their life! their life! It is normal. It is happy! It is an answer to the question! Little by little, Tolstoy came to the settled conviction — he says it took him two years to arrive there — that his trouble had not been with life in general, not with the common life of common men, but with the life of the upper, intellectual, artistic classes, the life which he had personally always led, the cerebral life, the life of conventionality, artificiality, and personal ambition. He had been living wrongly and must change. To work for animal needs, to abjure lies and vanities, to relieve common wants, to be simple, to believe in God, therein lay happiness again.

"I remember," he says, "one day in early spring, I was alone in the forest, lending my ear to its mysterious noises. I listened, and my thought went back to what for these three years it always was busy with — the quest of God. But the idea of him, I said, how did I ever come by the idea?

"And again there arose in me, with this thought, glad aspirations towards life. Everything in me awoke and received a meaning. . . . Why do I look farther? a voice within me asked. He is there: he, without whom one cannot live. To acknowledge God and to live are one and the same thing. God is what life is. Well, then! Live, seek God, and there will be no life without him. . . .

"After this, things cleared up within me and about me better than ever, and the light has never wholly died away. I was saved from suicide. Just how or when the change took place I cannot tell. But as insensibly and gradually as the force of life had been annulled within me, and I had reached my moral death-bed, just as gradually and imperceptibly did the energy of life come back. And what was strange was that this energy that came back was nothing new. It was my ancient juvenile force of faith, the belief that the sole purpose of my life was to be *better*. I gave up the life of the conventional world, recognizing it to be no life, but a parody on life, which its superfluities simply keep us from comprehending" — and Tolstoy thereupon embraced the life of the peasants, and has felt right and happy, or at least relatively so, ever since.

As I interpret his melancholy, then, it was not merely an accidental vitiation of his humors, though it was doubtless also that.

It was logically called for by the clash between his inner character and his outer activities and aims. Although a literary artist, Tolstoy was one of those primitive oaks of men to whom the superfluities and insincerities, the cupidities, complications, and cruelties of our polite civilization are profoundly unsatisfying, and for whom the eternal veracities lie with more natural and animal things. His crisis was the getting of his soul in order, the discovery of its genuine habitat and vocation, the escape from falsehoods into what for him were ways of truth. It was a case of heterogeneous personality tardily and slowly finding its unity and level. And though not many of us can imitate Tolstoy, not having enough, perhaps, of the aboriginal human marrow in our bones, most of us may at least feel as if it might be better for us if we could.

Bunyan's recovery seems to have been even slower. For years together he was alternately haunted with texts of scripture, now up and now down, but at last with an ever growing relief in his salvation through the blood of Christ.

"My peace would be in and out twenty times a day; comfort now and trouble presently; peace now and before I could go a furlong as full of guilt and fear as ever heart could hold." When a good text comes home to him, "this," he writes, "gave me good encouragement for the space of two or three hours"; or "this was a good day to me, I hope I shall not forget it"; or "the glory of these words was then so weighty on me that I was ready to swoon as I sat; yet, not with grief and trouble, but with solid joy and peace"; or "this made a strange seizure on my spirit; it brought light with it, and commanded a silence in my heart of all those tumultuous thoughts that before did use, like masterless hell-hounds, to roar and bellow and make a hideous noise within me. It showed me that Jesus Christ had not quite forsaken and cast off my soul."

Such periods accumulate until he can write: "And now remained only the hinder part of the tempest, for the thunder was gone beyond me, only some drops would still remain, that now and then would fall upon me"; — and at last: "Now did my chains fall off my legs indeed; I was loosed from my afflictions and irons; my temptations also fled away; so that from that time, those dreadful scriptures of God left off to trouble me; now went I also home rejoicing, for the grace and love of God. . . . Now could I see myself in heaven and earth at once; in heaven by my Christ, by my Head, by my righteousness and life, though on earth by my body or person. . . . Christ was a precious Christ to my soul that night; I could scarce lie in my bed for joy and peace and triumph through Christ."

Bunyan became a minister of the gospel, and in spite of his neurotic constitution, and of the twelve years he lay in prison for his non-conformity, his life was turned to active use. He was a peacemaker and doer of good, and the immortal allegory which he wrote has brought the very spirit of religious patience home to English hearts.

But neither Bunyan nor Tolstoy could become what we have called healthy-minded. They had drunk too deeply of the cup of bitterness ever to forget its taste, and their redemption is into a universe two stories deep. Each of them realized a good which broke the effective edge of his sadness; yet the sadness was preserved as a minor ingredient in the heart of the faith by which it was overcome. The fact of interest for us is that as a matter of fact they could and did find *something* welling up in the inner reaches of their consciousness, by which such extreme sadness could be overcome. Tolstoy does well to talk of it as *that by which men live;* for that is exactly what it is, a stimulus, an excitement, a faith, a force that re-infuses the positive willingness to live, even in full presence of the evil perceptions that erewhile made life seem unbearable. For Tolstoy's perceptions of evil appear within their sphere to have remained unmodified. His later works show him implacable to the whole system of official values: the ignobility of fashionable life; the infamies of empire; the spuriousness of the church, the vain conceit of the professions; the meannesses and cruelties that go with great success; and every other pompous crime and lying institution of this world. To all patience with such things his experience has been for him a permanent ministry of death.

Bunyan also leaves this world to the enemy.

"I must first pass a sentence of death," he says, "upon everything that can properly be called a thing of this life, even to reckon myself, my wife, my children, my health, my enjoyments, and all, as dead to me, and myself as dead to them; to trust in God through Christ, as touching the world to come; and as touching this world, to count the grave my house, to make my bed in darkness, and to say to corruption, Thou art my father, and to the worm, Thou art my mother and sister. . . . The parting with my wife and my poor children hath often been to me as the pulling of my flesh from my bones, especially my poor blind child who lay nearer my heart than all I had besides. Poor child, thought I, what sorrow are thou like to have for thy portion in this world! Thou must be beaten, must beg, suffer hunger, cold, nakedness, and a thousand calamities, though I cannot now endure that the wind should blow upon thee. But yet I must venture you all with God, though it goeth to the quick to leave you."

The "hue of resolution" is there, but the full flood of ecstatic liberation seems never to have poured over poor John Bunyan's soul.

These examples may suffice to acquaint us in a general way with the phenomenon technically called "conversion."

C. Commentary and Analysis

We can acknowledge that the disposition of the twice-born, in one degree or other, is the common lot of man in our day. In the age of anxiety, our awareness of the fragmented nature of our existence is acute. The torment is not altogether new. Paul engraved it indelibly on the Christian consciousness when he wrote: "It is not the good my will prefers, but the evil my will disapproves, that I find myself doing." [3] With this Pauline theme ringing in our ears, we can listen to James when he says:

> It [natural good] keeps us from our real good, rather; and renunciation and despair of it are our first step in the direction of the truth. There are two lives, the natural and the spiritual, and we must lose the one before we can participate in the other.

If this be the religious burden of the twice-born, we want to inaugurate our inquiry by determining its relevance in psychological terms. The question that must be put is, what aspects of this internal division are relevant for an understanding of the human psyche? Or better still, in what terms can this conflict be formulated so that we can begin to move beyond the experience to the level of psychological understanding? It is James the psychologist who gives us an answer. "The psychological basis of the twice-born character seems to be a certain discordancy or heterogeneity in the native temperament of the subject, an incompletely unified moral and intellectual constitution. And further, this heterogeneity is connected with the life of the 'subconscious self.'"

It is immediately apparent that this is an inadequate answer. But even so it gives us a start. James's formulation has little more than historical interest, as it stands. But there is in it the implicit delineation of a problematic. On the one hand he suggests that the experienced conflict is paralleled by and reflects an inner discordancy, a heterogeneity in the very core of man. It is a conflict within the self, or between the subconscious self and what James might call the spiritual self. The phenomenon of conflict bespeaks an inner disorganization, a fragmentation within the human psyche, an internal ambivalence, the paradox of the self turned against the self. On the other hand, he implies not only that the religious experience is relevant to this phenomenon, but that it is related to the resolution of this inner discord. Like the discord itself, the intuition James offers us here is not new. It is as old as, if not older than, Christianity, and carries a perfectly acceptable Pauline stamp.

---

[3] Rom 7:19.

The traditional Christian elaboration of these insights has cast the problem in somewhat different terms. Paul recognized both the inner division in the human psyche and the healing power of faith and religious conviction. The frame of reference of the biblical recognition was both experiential and historical. The experience was no less vivid to Paul than it is to us. But the problematic posed in reflection on it extended no further than the salvific action of faith in Christ and the relation between this experience of conflict-and-resolution and salvation history.

In subsequent Christian tradition, the experience remained the same, but the terms of the problematic shifted somewhat. The problematic became theological first, and finally ontological. The product of this evolution was the treatise on grace of the scholastic manual. The issues that had to be faced within the confines of this problematic were the nature of divine action, its relation to divine existence, the ontological structure of grace and its relation to divine action, the ontological structure of man as a potency fit to receive this salvific action. There was also concern for the effects of grace, but the focus of attention was almost exclusively on the ontological structure and juridical consequences of the effects of grace. At its most sublime, this tradition offered a profound elaboration of the trinitarian dimension of the life of grace — the most meaningful and most revolutionary as well as the most theologically challenging aspect of revelation. All this was unquestionably a staggering accomplishment. But the approach that James is adopting suggests quite a different orientation toward man's religious experience.

James also takes the experience, presumably the same experience, as his point of departure. But he poses a different question. His question is not directed to the theological aspects, nor to the ontology of the religious experience. In fact, it seems quite plain that these considerations were far from his mind. His question was directed to man himself. His question was directed to an understanding of what happens within man as a result of this specifically religious experience. From a more theologically sophisticated position, we can recast the question. Granted the theological reconstruction that establishes the conditions of possibility and the juridico-salvific consequences, what does grace do within the soul that it touches?

I would like to suggest that this is a legitimate problematic that demands the serious consideration of Christian thinkers in the modern era. Not that the terms of the consideration or the relevant data need be cast in James's format. Indeed there is every reason to believe that the problem reaches further even than the far-seeing William James might have conceived.

James does attempt a sort of preliminary answer to the question. There are several things worth noting about the answer. First of all, he is dealing with an experience. This is fair enough, but it must be immediately observed that experience alone is far from an adequate basis for a consideration of the psychological relevance of man's religious involvement. There is much that transcends experience, much that does not translate itself into the terms of experience. What transpires at the level of conscious awareness does not exhaust the virtualities of divine action on the psyche in any given instance. In fact, it seems quite reasonable to presume that the effects are more unconscious than otherwise. Further, it must be kept in mind that the effects of grace simply cannot be identified on the basis of experience alone. Ultimately the grounds on which the action of grace must be identified must be theological. The theology of grace provides a frame of reference within which the phenomenology and psychology of grace can be worked out.

We may further note that James does not have the problematic of grace in mind at all. His message is couched in terms of the psychological implications of the experience of religious conversion. This is admittedly perhaps the most narrow concept of religious experience to analyze, but it serves James's purpose. He is working within a frame of reference dictated by this unique experience, and his objective is to understand something of how such an experience changes the inner psychic structure of the individual. He is not concerned with the demands of a theology of grace. One might almost say that, as far as James the psychologist was concerned, the inquiry into religious experience would have been just as valid and as interesting if there were no such thing as grace and no such being as the God who acts. From the traditional Christian perspective, of course, these are the elements that make all the difference. So, too, do they make all the difference within the problematic of the psychology of grace.

Despite this important difference, we should not forget that the question that James has raised is perfectly valid within the context of the Christian doctrine of grace. God's loving intervention in the lives of men presumably makes a difference. The question that we wish to pose is, what is that difference? This question has not been answered before. The difference has traditionally been spelled out in terms of theological concerns. The difference that has been brought into focus is the difference in man's relation or relatedness to God. But we are looking for a different difference. We want to know what changes are brought about in man, specifically within his psychic structure.

The answer that James proposes is that religious experience produces a psychological process which issues in unification of the self. The effect of religious experience is somehow to unify the discord, to resolve the division within the self, to integrate the heterogeneity of the twice-born. This is not so much an answer as a program for future investigation. As such, it lays out certain guidelines for the investigation which we would do well to pursue. In one sense, the remainder of our inquiry will be a following out of these guidelines.

James's answer indicates that the effects of religious experience are to be located in the self. It is no simple matter to specify what we mean by the self. We can get some inkling from James, when he speaks about the "spiritual me."

By the "spiritual me," so far as it belongs to the empirical self, I mean no one of my passing states of consciousness. I mean rather the entire collection of my states of consciousness, my psychic faculties and dispositions taken concretely. This collection can at any moment become an object to my thought at that moment and awaken emotions like those awakened by any of the other portions of the Me. When we *think of ourselves as thinkers,* all the other ingredients of our Me seem relatively external possessions. Even within the spiritual *Me* some ingredients seem more external than others. Our

capacities for sensation, for example, are less intimate possessions, so to speak, than our emotions and desires; our
intellectual processes are less intimate than our volitional decisions. The more *active-feeling* states of consciousness are
thus the more central portions of the spiritual Me. The very
core and nucleus of our self, as we know it, the very sanctuary
of our life, is the sense of activity which certain inner states
possess. This sense of activity is often held to be a direct
revelation of the living substance of our Soul. Whether this be
so or not is an ulterior question. I wish now only to lay down
the peculiar internality of whatever states possess this quality
of seeming to be active. It is as if they *went out to meet* all the
other elements of our experience.[4]

It seems to me that the essential elements in this analysis of the
self are the notions of centrality and activity. There is, of course,
much more to be said about the concept of the self than this, but
it is clear that, in James's conception of the self, it is the self that
lies at the very heart of personality. It is also clear that the self
is characterized or identified in terms of its activity. We will have
occasion to return to this insight as our inquiry progresses.

Part of the problematic which we are developing here involves
the clarification of a concept of the nature of man which is at once
consonant with the demands of a theological anthropology and
with the requirements of a scientific psychology. A theological
anthropology bases its image of man upon the data of revelation
and strives to formulate that image in a manner consistent with
the terms of that revelation. The approach of scientific psychology
to the concept of human nature is through the empirical data of
observation and experience. It is our contention that these two
approaches meet in the concrete existential human being. It should
be possible therefore to fashion an image of man which would
offer a sort of common ground, consistent with, and acceptable to,
both approaches. An essential part of this common ground image
is the notion of the self as the central, interior core of the human
person, as a dynamic, striving, evolving, fundamentally active force

---

[4] *Psychology: The Briefer Course*, p. 48.

which is the essential psychological component of the human personality.

James's answer carries within it two very important contributions to our inquiry. He locates the effects of grace in the "self" and he specifies these effects in terms of unification. The sense of these designations and their relation to the action of grace must be qualified in transferring them from the strictly phenomenological and psychological context in which James formulated them to the broader context we are trying to shape here. But we are not looking for conclusive formulations; if we were to find them there would be little sense in pushing on with our investigation. What we are given is more in the order of hints, clues, heuristic formulations directing our attention to certain aspects of the picture. Our attention in this matter is focussed on the inner core of the personality and upon its activity. Shifting from James's intuition into the impact of religious experience on the soul's psychological structure, to a consideration of the impact of grace upon the psyche, we are led to consider that the results of the action of grace are to be found within that part of the psychological structure which James called the self, and which later psychologists have come to know as the ego.

The specific effects in psychological terms have been denominated only as "unification." It is clear from James's elaboration of the term that unification has a psychological sense and that it exercises a corrective influence on the discordant elements of the human personality. He speaks of it as a general psychological process that involves "remedying inner incompleteness and reducing inner discord." It is essential to our inquiry to understand the significance of such unification in psychological terms. It is opposed to the anxiety, division, and emotional turmoil so characteristic of the twice-born. Without pursuing the matter any further at this point, we have a sufficient directive to point our consideration to the relevant psychological areas. The division and heterogeneity of the twice-born involves the unconscious, the instinctual, the emotional and conflictual aspects of psychological functioning. It is further suggested that the effects of grace are to be identified by the extent to which these elements are organized and integrated into a harmoniously functioning personality. Plainly a wide range of fascinating issues is raised by this suggestion.

James makes some further noteworthy points about unification. Although it is a more or less general process, its characteristics are subject to considerable variation. This warns us that the process is liable to be a reflection of the personality within which it is taking place. Consequently, we can expect wide variations from individual to individual. This is certainly no startling conclusion since the Christian experience of grace bears eloquent testimony to the broad range of its effects and the infinite variety of the ways in which such effects are realized. The further point is emphasized that the unification that accompanies religious experience is not unique to this experience. Inner unification can be achieved in a number of ways and religion is only one of these ways. The point is well taken, since it reminds us that the effects of grace may mirror the effects of other influences on psychic mechanisms. The action of grace can not be identified as such within our experience, but the effects of grace may be experienceable. When it comes to formulating the psychological dynamics corresponding to the action of grace, we may indeed find that the formulation parallels what might be involved in some other non-religious, grace-disconnected activity or process. This should be no surprise, so long as one keeps in mind that in this problematic we are concerned with specifically psychological effects which do not necessarily carry in themselves the stamp of their relatedness to grace.

Questions for Discussion

1. What reasons does the author advance for beginning his inquiry with a passage from William James?
2. How does James characterize the religion of the "twice-born"?
3. In what situation does heterogeneous personality show itself in the following: The citation from Alphonse Daudet? From John Bunyan? From Augustine? From Henry Alline?
4. What are some of the various ways unification is achieved?

5. What did religious unification involve in the case of Horace Fletcher? Of Tolstoy? Of Bunyan?

6. How does James explain his statement that "neither Bunyan nor Tolstoy could have become . . . healthy-minded"?

7. What is the value of James's formulation? What is the focus of James's question? Explain.

8. Is James's question concerned with grace? Why is it a valid question for our consideration here? What does James see as the solution to the problem of the divided self? Is this really an answer?

9. What essential elements can be singled out from James's analysis of the self as "spiritual me"? Explain.

10. How does James contribute to the present inquiry? What does the author note about James's concept of "self" and "unification"?

III
ERICH FROMM AND
LOVE OF GOD

A. Prenote

The life of grace is built upon and evolves from the love of God in some ultimate sense. From a theological perspective, the love of God serves as the pinnacle of development of the Christian's inner life. Some exploration into the notion of the love of God is thus necessary. I have selected this passage from Erich Fromm for a number of reasons, but primarily for the one central point he presents in a somewhat devious guise. The point is that the love of God is a reflection and an expression of the personal maturity of the individual.

The following excerpts are taken from Fromm's *The Art of Loving* (New York: Harper and Row, 1956), pp. 63-82.

B. Selection: The Love of God

It has been stated above that the basis for our need to love lies in the experience of separateness and the resulting need to overcome the anxiety of separateness by the experience of union. The religious form of love, that which is called the love of God, is, psychologically speaking, not different. It springs from the need to overcome separateness and to achieve union. In fact, the love of God has as many different qualities and aspects as the love of man has — and to a large extent we find the same differences.

In all theistic religions, whether they are polytheistic or monotheistic, God stands for the highest value, the most desirable good.
Hence, the specific meaning of God depends on what is the most
desirable good for a person The understanding of the concept of
God must, therefore, start with an analysis of the character structure of the person who worships God.

The development of the human race as far as we have any
knowledge of it can be characterized as the emergence of man
from nature, from mother, from the bonds of blood and soil. In the
beginning of human history man, though thrown out of the original
unity with nature, still clings to these primary bonds. He finds his
security by going back, or holding on to these primary bonds. He
still feels identified with the world of animals and trees, and tries
to find unity by remaining one with the natural world. Many primitive religions bear witness to this stage of development. An animal
is transformed into a totem; one wears animal masks in the most
solemn religious acts, or in war; one worships an animal as God.
At a later stage of development, when human skill has developed
to the point of artisan and artistic skill, when man is not dependent
anymore exclusively on the gifts of nature — the fruit he finds and
the animal he kills — man transforms the product of his own hand
into a god. This is the stage of the worship of idols made of clay,
silver or gold. Man projects his own powers and skills into the
things he makes, and thus in an alienated fashion worships his
prowess, his possessions. At a still later stage man gives his gods
the form of human beings. It seems that this can happen only when
he has become still more aware of himself, and when he has discovered man as the highest and most dignified "thing" in the world.
In this phase of anthropomorphic god worship we find a development in two dimensions. The one refers to the female or male
nature of the gods, the other to the degree of maturity which man
has achieved, and which determines the nature of his gods and the
nature of his love of them.

Let us first speak of the development from mother-centered
to father-centered religions. According to the great and decisive
discoveries of Bachofen and Morgan in the middle of the nineteenth
century, and in spite of the rejection their findings have found in

most academic circles, there can be little doubt that there was a matriarchal phase of religion preceding the patriarchal one, at least in many cultures. In the matriarchal phase, the highest being is the mother. She is the goddess, she is also the authority in family and society. In order to understand the essence of matriarchal religion, we have only to remember what has been said about the essence of motherly love. Mother's love is unconditional, it is all-protective, all-enveloping; because it is unconditional it can also not be controlled or acquired. Its presence gives the loved person a sense of bliss; its absence produces a sense of lostness and utter despair. Since mother loves her children because they are her children, and not because they are "good," obedient, or fulfill her wishes and commands, mother's love is based on equality. All men are equal, because they all are children of a mother, because they all are children of Mother Earth.

The next stage of human evolution, the only one of which we have thorough knowledge and do not need to rely on inferences and reconstruction, is the patriarchal phase. In this phase the mother is dethroned from her supreme position, and the father becomes the Supreme Being, in religion as well as in society. The nature of fatherly love is that he makes demands, establishes principles and laws, and that his love for the son depends on the obedience of the latter to these demands. He likes best the son who is most like him, who is most obedient and who is best fitted to become his successor, as the inheritor of his possessions. (The development of patriarchal society goes together with the development of private property.) As a consequence, patriarchal society is hierarchical; the equality of the brothers gives way to competition and mutual strife. Whether we think of the Indian, Egyptian or Greek cultures, or of the Jewish-Christian, or Islamic religions, we are in the middle of a patriarchal world, with its male gods, over whom one chief god reigns, or where all gods have been eliminated with the exception of the One, *the* God. However, since the wish for mother's love cannot be eradicated from the hearts of man, it is not surprising that the figure of the loving mother could never be fully driven out from the pantheon. In the Jewish religion, the mother aspects of God are reintroduced especially in the various currents of mysticism. In the Catholic religion, Mother is symbolized by the Church, and by the Virgin. Even in Protestantism, the figure of Mother has not been entirely eradicated, although she remains hidden. Luther established as his main principle that nothing that man *does* can procure God's love. God's love is grace; the religious attitude is to have faith in this grace, and to make oneself small and helpless; no good works can influence God — or make God love us, as Catholic doctrines postulated. We can recognize here that the Catholic doctrine of good works is part of the patriarchal picture; I can procure father's love by obedience and by fulfilling his demands. The Lutheran doctrine, on the other hand, in spite of its manifest patriarchal character carries within it a hidden matriarchal element. Mother's love cannot be acquired; it is there, or it is not there; all I can do is to have faith (as the Psalmist says, "Thou hadst let me have faith into my mother's breasts") [1] and to transform myself into the helpless, powerless child. But it is the peculiarity of Luther's faith that the figure of the mother has been eliminated from the manifest picture, and replaced by that of the father; instead of the certainty of being loved by mother, intense doubt, hoping against hope for unconditional love by *father,* has become the paramount feature.

I had to discuss this difference between the matriarchal and the patriarchal elements in religion in order to show that the character of the love of God depends on the respective weight of the matriarchal and the patriarchal aspects of religion. The patriarchal aspect makes me love God like a father; I assume he is just and strict, that he punishes and rewards; and eventually that he will elect me as his favorite son; as God elected Abraham-Israel, as Isaac elected Jacob, as God elects his favorite nation. In the matriarchal aspect of religion, I love God as an all-embracing mother. I have faith in her love, that no matter whether I am poor and powerless, no matter whether I have sinned, she will love me, she will not prefer any other of her children to me; whatever happens to me, she will rescue me, will save me, will forgive me. Needless to say, my love for God and God's love for me cannot be separated. If God is a father, he loves me like a son and I love him like a father. If God is mother, her and my love are determined by this fact.

---

[1] Ps 22:9.

This difference between the motherly and the fatherly aspects of the love of God is, however, only one factor in determining the nature of this love; the other factor is the degree of maturity reached by the individual, hence in his concept of God and in his love for God.

Since the evolution of the human race shifted from a mother-centered to a father-centered structure of society, as well as of religion, we can trace the development of a maturing love mainly in the development of patriarchal religion.[2] In the beginning of this development we find a despotic, jealous God, who considers man, whom he created, as his property, and is entitled to do with him whatever he pleases. This is the phase of religion in which God drives man out of paradise, lest he eat from the tree of knowledge and thus could become God himself; this is the phase in which God decides to destroy the human race by the flood, because none of them pleases him, with the exception of the favorite son, Noah; this is the phase in which God demands from Abraham that he kill his only, his beloved son, Isaac, to prove his love for God by the act of ultimate obedience. But simultaneously a new phase begins; God makes a covenant with Noah, in which he promises never to destroy the human race again, a covenant by which he is bound himself. Not only is he bound by his promises, he is also bound by his own principle, that of justice, and on this basis God must yield to Abraham's demand to spare Sodom if there are at least ten just men. But the development goes further than transforming God from the figure of a despotic tribal chief into a loving father, into a father who himself is bound by the principles which he has postulated; it goes in the direction of transforming God from the figure of a father into a symbol of his principles, those of justice, truth and love. God *is* truth, God *is* justice. In this development God ceases to be a person, a man, a father; he becomes the symbol of the principle of unity behind the manifoldness of phenomena, of the vision of the flower which will grow from the spiritual seed

---

[2] This holds true especially for the monotheistic religions of the West. In Indian religions the mother figures retained a good deal of influence, for instance in the Goddess Kali; in Buddhism and Taoism the concept of a god — or a goddess — was without essential significance, if not altogether eliminated.

within man. God cannot have a name. A name always denotes a thing, or a person, something finite. How can God have a name, if he is not a person, not a thing?

The most striking incident of this change lies in the biblical story of God's revelation to Moses. When Moses tells him that the Hebrews will not believe that God has sent him, unless he can tell them God's name (How could idol worshipers comprehend a nameless God, since the very essence of an idol is to have a name?), God makes a concession. He tells Moses that his name is "I am becoming that which I am becoming." "I-am-becoming is my name." The "I-am-becoming" means that God is not finite, not a person, not a "being." The most adequate translation of the sentence would be: tell them that "my name is nameless." The prohibition to make any image of God, to pronounce his name in vain, eventually to pronounce his name at all, aims at the same goal, that of freeing man from the idea that God is a father, that he is a person. In the subsequent theological development, the idea is carried further in the principle that one must not even give God any positive attribute. To say of God that he is wise, strong, good implies again that he is a person; the most I can do is to say what God is *not,* to state negative attributes, to postulate that he is *not* limited, not unkind, not unjust. The more I know what God is *not,* the more knowledge I have of God.[3]

Following the maturing idea of monotheism in its further consequences can lead only to one conclusion: not to mention God's name at all, not to speak *about* God. Then God becomes what he potentially is in monotheistic theology, the nameless One, an inexpressible stammer, referring to the unity underlying the phenomenal universe, the ground of all existence; God becomes truth, love, justice. God is I, inasmuch as I am human.

Quite evidently this evolution from the anthropomorphic to the pure monotheistic principle makes all the difference to the nature of the love of God. The God of Abraham can be loved, or feared, as a father, sometimes his forgiveness, sometimes his anger being the dominant aspect. Inasmuch as God is the father, I am the child. I have not emerged fully from the autistic wish for omniscience

---

[3] Cf. Maimonides' concept of the negative attributes in *The Guide for the Perplexed.*

and omnipotence. I have not yet acquired the objectivity to realize my limitations as a human being, my ignorance, my helplessness. I still claim, like a child, that there must be a father who rescues me, who watches me, who punishes me, a father who likes me when I am obedient, who is flattered by my praise and angry because of my disobedience. Quite obviously, the majority of people have, in their personal development, not overcome this infantile stage, and hence the belief in God to most people is the belief in a helping father — a childish illusion. In spite of the fact that this concept of religion has been overcome by some of the great teachers of the human race, and by a minority of men, it is still the dominant form of religion.

Inasmuch as this is so, the criticism of the idea of God, as it was expressed by Freud, is quite correct. The error, however, was in the fact that he ignored the other aspect of monotheistic religion, and its true kernel, the logic of which leads exactly to the negation of this concept of God. The truly religious person, if he follows the essence of the monotheistic idea, does not pray for anything, does not expect anything from God; he does not love God as a child loves his father or his mother; he has acquired the humility of sensing his limitations, to the degree of knowing that he knows nothing about God. God becomes to him a symbol in which man, at an earlier stage of his evolution, has expressed the totality of that which man is striving for, the realm of the spiritual world, of love, truth and justice. He has faith in the principles which "God" represents; he thinks truth, lives love and justice, and considers all of his life only valuable inasmuch as it gives him the chance to arrive at an ever fuller unfolding of his human powers — as the only reality that matters, as the only object of "ultimate concern"; and, eventually, he does not speak about God — nor even mention his name. To love God, if he were going to use this word, would mean, then, to long for the attainment of the full capacity to love, for the realization of that which "God" stands for in oneself.

From this point of view, the logical consequence of monotheistic thought is the negation of all "theo-logy," of all "knowledge about God." Yet, there remains a difference between such a radical non-theological view and a non-theistic system, as we find it, for instance, in early Buddhism or in Taoism.

In all theistic systems, even a non-theological, mystical one, there is the assumption of the reality of the spiritual realm, as one transcending man, giving meaning and validity to man's spiritual powers and his striving for salvation and inner birth. In a non-theistic system, there exists no spiritual realm outside of man or transcending him. The realm of love, reason and justice exists as a reality only because, and inasmuch as, man has been able to develop these powers in himself throughout the process of his evolution. In this view there is no meaning to life, except the meaning man himself gives to it; man is utterly alone except inasmuch as he helps another.

Having spoken of the love of God, I want to make it clear that I myself do not think in terms of a theistic concept, and that to me the concept of God is only a historically conditioned one, in which man has expressed his experience of his higher powers, his longing for truth and for unity at a given historical period. But I believe also that the consequences of strict monotheism and a non-theistic ultimate concern with the spiritual reality are two views which, though different, need not fight each other.

At this point, however, another dimension of the problem of the love of God arises, which must be discussed in order to fathom the complexity of the problem. I refer to a fundamental difference in the religious attitude between the East (China and India) and the West; this difference can be expressed in terms of logical concepts. Since Aristotle, the Western world has followed the logical principles of Aristotelian philosophy. This logic is based on the law of identity which states that A is A, the law of contradiction (A is not non-A) and the law of the excluded middle (A cannot be A *and* non-A, neither A *nor* non-A). Aristotle explains his position very clearly in the following sentence: "It is impossible for the same thing at the same time to belong and not to belong to the same thing and in the same respect; and whatever other distinctions we might add to meet dialectical objections, let them be added. This, then, is the most certain of all principles. . . ." [4]

This axiom of Aristotelian logic has so deeply imbued our habits of thought that it is felt to be "natural" and self-evident, while on the other hand the statement that X is A *and* not A seems to be

---

[4] Aristotle, *Metaphysics,* Book Gamma, 1005b. 20. Quoted from the translation by R. Hope (New York: Columbia University Press, 1952).

nonsensical. (Of course, the statement refers to the subject X at a given time, not to X now and X later, or one aspect of X as against another aspect.)

In opposition to Aristotelian logic is what one might call *paradoxical logic,* which assumes that A and non-A do not exclude each other as predicates of X. Paradoxical logic was predominant in Chinese and Indian thinking, in the philosophy of Heraclitus, and then again, under the name of dialectics, it became the philosophy of Hegel, and of Marx. The general principle of paradoxical logic has been clearly described by Lao-tse. *"Words that are strictly true seem to be paradoxical."* [5] And by Chuang-tzu: "That which is one is one. That which is not-one, is also one." These formulations of paradoxical logic are positive: *it is and it is not.* Another formulation is negative: *it is neither this nor that.* The former expression of thought we find in Taoistic thought, in Heraclitus and again in Hegelian dialectics; the latter formulation is frequent in Indian philosophy.

Although it would transcend the scope of this book to give a more detailed description of the difference between Aristotelian and paradoxical logic, I shall mention a few illustrations in order to make the principle more understandable. Paradoxical logic in Western thought has its earliest philosophical expression in Heraclitus' philosophy. He assumes the conflict between opposites is the basis of all existence. "They do not understand," he says, "that the all-One, conflicting in itself, is identical with itself: *conflicting harmony* as in the bow and in the lyre." [6] Or still more clearly: "We go into the same river, and yet not in the same; *it is we and it is not we.*" [7] Or "One and the same manifests itself in things as living and dead, waking and sleeping, young and old." [8]

Paradoxical logic has a significant bearing on the concept of God. Inasmuch as God represents the ultimate reality, and inasmuch as the human mind perceives reality in contradictions, no positive statement can be made of God. In the Vedantas the idea

[5] Max Mueller, ed., *The Sacred Books of the East,* Vol. 39, Lao-tse's *The Tâo Teh King* (London: Oxford University Press, 1927), p. 120.
[6] W. Capelle, *Die Vorsokratiker* (Stuttgart: Alfred Kroener Verlag, 1953), p. 134.
[7] Capelle, p. 132.
[8] Capelle, p. 133.

of an omniscient and omnipotent God is considered the ultimate form of ignorance.[9] We see here the connection with the nameless-ness of the Tao, the nameless name of the God who reveals himself to Moses, of the "absolute Nothing" of Meister Eckhart. Man can only know the negation, never the position of ultimate reality. "Meanwhile man cannot know what God is, even though he be ever so well aware of what God is not. . . . Thus contented with nothing, the mind clamors for the highest good of all." [10] For Meister Eckhart, "The Divine One is a negation of negations, and a denial of denials. . . . Every creature contains a negation: one denies that it is the other." [11] It is only a further consequence that God becomes for Meister Eckhart "The absolute Nothing," just as the ultimate reality is the "En Sof," the Endless One, for the Kabalah.

I have discussed the difference between Aristotelian and para-doxical logic in order to prepare the ground for an important difference in the concept of the love of God. The teachers of para-doxical logic say that man can perceive reality only in contradic-tions, and can never perceive in *thought* the ultimate reality-unity, the One itself. This led to the consequence that one did not seek as the ultimate aim to find the answer in *thought*. Thought can only lead us to the knowledge that it cannot give us the ultimate answer The world of thought remains caught in the paradox. The only way in which the world can be grasped ultimately lies, not in thought, but in the act, in the experience of oneness. Thus para-doxical logic leads to the conclusion that the love of God is neither the knowledge of God in thought, nor the thought of one's love of God, but the act of experiencing the oneness with God.

This leads to the emphasis on the right way of living. All of life, every little and every important action, is devoted to the knowledge of God, but a knowledge not in right thought, but in right action. This can be clearly seen in Oriental religions. In Brahmanism as well as in Buddhism and Taoism, the ultimate aim of religion is not the right belief, but the right action. We find the

---

[9] Cf. Zimmer, *Philosophies of India* (New York: Pantheon, 1951), p. 424.
[10] *Meister Eckhart,* trans. by R. B. Blakney (New York: Harper, 1941), p. 114.
[11] *Ibid.,* p. 247. Cf. also the negative theology of Maimonides.

same emphasis in the Jewish religion. There was hardly ever a schism over belief in the Jewish tradition (the one great exception, the difference between Pharisees and Sadducees, was essentially one of two opposite social classes). The emphasis of the Jewish religion was (especially from the beginning of our era on) on the right way of living, the Halacha (this word actually having the same meaning as the Tao).

In modern history, the same principle is expressed in the thought of Spinoza, Marx and Freud. In Spinoza's philosophy the emphasis is shifted from the right belief to the right conduct of life. Marx stated the same principle when he said, "The philosophers have interpreted the world in different ways — the task is to transform it." Freud's paradoxical logic leads him to the process of psycho-analytic therapy, the ever deepening experience of oneself.

From the standpoint of paradoxical logic the emphasis is not on thought, but on the act. This attitude had several other consequences. First of all, it led to the *tolerance* which we find in Indian and Chinese religious development. If the right thought is not the ultimate truth, and not the way to salvation, there is no reason to fight others, whose thinking has arrived at different formulations. This tolerance is beautifully expressed in the story of several men who were asked to describe an elephant in the dark. One, touching his trunk, said "this animal is like a water pipe"; another, touching his ear, said "this animal is like a fan"; a third, touching his legs, described the animal as a pillar.

Secondly, the paradoxical standpoint led to the emphasis on *transforming man,* rather than to the development of *dogma* on the one hand, and *science* on the other. From the Indian, Chinese and mystical standpoints, the religious task of man is not to think right, but to act right, and/or to become one with the One in the act of concentrated meditation.

The opposite is true for the main stream of Western thought. Since one expected to find the ultimate truth in the right thought, major emphasis was on thought, although right action was held to be important too. In religious development this led to the formulation of dogmas, endless arguments about dogmatic formulations, and intolerance of the "non-believer" or heretic. It further-

more led to the emphasis on "believing in God" as the main aim
of a religious attitude. This, of course, did not mean that there
was not also the concept that one ought to live right. But nevertheless, the person who believed in God — even if he did not *live*
God — felt himself to be superior to the one who lived God, but
did not "believe" in him.

The emphasis on thought has also another and historically a
very important consequence. The idea that one could find the truth
in thought led not only to dogma, but also to science. In scientific
thought, the correct thought is all that matters, both from the aspect
of intellectual honesty, as well as from the aspect of the application
of scientific thought to practice — that is, to technique.

In short, paradoxical thought led to tolerance and an effort
toward self-transformation. The Aristotelian standpoint led to
dogma and science, to the Catholic Church, and to the discovery
of atomic energy.

The consequences of this difference between the two standpoints
for the problem of the love of God have already been explained
implicitly, and need only to be summarized briefly.

In the dominant Western religious system, the love of God is
essentially the same as the belief in God, in God's existence, God's
justice, God's love. The love of God is essentially a thought experience. In the Eastern religions and in mysticism, the love of God
is an intense feeling experience of oneness, inseparably linked with
the expression of this love in every act of living. The most radical
formulation has been given to this goal by Meister Eckhart: "If
therefore I am changed into God and he makes me one with himself, then, by the living God, there is no distinction between us. . . .
Some people imagine that they are going to see God, that
they are going to see God as if he were standing yonder, and they
here, but it is not to be so. God and I: we are one. By knowing
God I take him to myself. By loving God, I penetrate him." [12]

We can return now to an important parallel between the love
for one's parents and the love for God. The child starts out by
being attached to his mother as "the ground of all being." He feels
helpless and needs the all-enveloping love of mother. He then

---

[12] *Ibid.,* pp. 181-182.

turns to father as the new center of his affections, father being a guiding principle for thought and action; in this stage he is motivated by the need to acquire father's praise, and to avoid his displeasure. In the stage of full maturity he has freed himself from the person of mother and of father as protecting and commanding powers; he has established the motherly and fatherly principles in himself. He has become his own father and mother; he *is* father and mother. In the history of the human race we see — and can anticipate — the same development: from the beginning of the love for God as the helpless attachment to a mother Goddess, through the obedient attachment to a fatherly God, to a mature stage where God ceases to be an outside power, where man has incorporated the principles of love and justice into himself, where he has become one with God, and eventually, to a point where he speaks of God only in a poetic, symbolic sense.

From these considerations it follows that the love for God cannot be separated from the love for one's parents. If a person does not emerge from incestuous attachment to mother, clan, nation, if he retains the childish dependence on a punishing and rewarding father, or any other authority, he cannot develop a more mature love for God; then his religion is that of the earlier phase of religion, in which God was experienced as an all-protective mother or a punishing-rewarding father.

In contemporary religion we find all the phases, from the earliest and most primitive development to the highest, still present. The word "God" denotes the tribal chief as well as the "absolute Nothing." In the same way, each individual retains in himself, in his unconscious, as Freud has shown, all the stages from the helpless infant on. The question is to what point he has grown. One thing is certain: the nature of his love for God corresponds to the nature of his love for man, and furthermore, the real quality of his love for God and man often is unconscious — covered up and rationalized by a more mature *thought* of what his love is. Love for man, furthermore, while directly embedded in his relations to his family, is in the last analysis determined by the structure of the society in which he lives. If the social structure is one of submission to authority — overt authority or the anonymous authority of the market and public opinion — his concept of God must be infantile and far from the mature concept, the seeds of which are to be found in the history of monotheistic religion.

C. Commentary and Analysis

The need to love, in Fromm's view, is born of the experience of separateness and the resulting need to overcome the anxiety of separateness by the experience of union. This is an acceptable statement in its context, but it neither fully expresses nor explains the driving impulse that we call the love of God, nor any other real love. Love is traditionally expressed in terms of union. If we investigate the human psyche we will unquestionably find a need to love. If we feel that this need accounts for the phenomenon of love, we need look no further. But mere description is itself inadequate if we are to gain understanding. The reality of love is more profound and altogether more positive than this limited view either suggests or connotes. One conclusion that we may derive from this description of love, however, is that the character of love is intimately related to and expressive of the psychological structure of the loving individual.

Fromm relates some of the broad outlines of the evolutionary development of man's self-consciousness in his relations to God. Whether the outlines are historically accurate or not is irrelevant. The significant thing is that they serve as the vehicle for the elaboration of some perceptive insights. In whatever guise one wishes to cast man's religious disposition, it is apparent that the quality of worship is related to man's inner needs. The evolution of worship parallels the inner psychic maturation of the human race. The identification of the divine with animals, idols, and with anthropomorphic deities parallels an inner development within man himself, a maturation of man's inner realization of his own capacities and dignity. The evolution in Fromm's view is cognitional and emotional. It might be best to describe the process as a psychological development without trying to spell out what was involved. The presumptions in such an effort are by no means secure.

At the anthropomorphic level of development, matriarchal and patriarchal forms of religious worship predominated. Fromm accepts the view that the matriarchal form developed into, and was replaced by, the patriarchal. This can be contested, but it fits well with the assumption that love of God as loving, protecting, and saving mother is somehow more primitive and infantile than the love of God as an all-powerful, just, rewarding, and punishing father. This view regards the evolution from patriarchal to monotheistic worship, which is exemplified by the Yahwistic revelation to Moses, as a transition from child-like love of the father to a depersonalized regard for God as a symbol of the truth of the principles of love and justice. These principles exist in man and to this extent the monotheistic development represents the ultimate development of religious expression. Here man has projected and deified that within himself which represents the noblest, most mature aspect of his own psychic existence.

The implications of this view of the history of religion are far-reaching. There is the assumption that any love of God that preserves elements from prior evolutionary forms represents a form of regression. Prior forms of worship are presumed to represent products of immature stages of development and the recurrence of such forms in a later period therefore represents an immaturity of psychological development. Fromm admits that a mature religious attitude can be theistic or nontheistic. His own preference is for the latter stance since he does not admit the existence of any spiritual realm outside of or transcending man. A personalized attitude toward the deity represents for Fromm both an illusion and a response to infantile needs.

Much of Fromm's reconstruction is debatable, of course, but the doubtful presumptions do not invalidate his primary intuition which underlies the whole enterprise. "The nature of the love of God is partially determined by the degree of maturity reached by the individual, hence in his concept of God and in his love for God." This seems to me to be a perfectly valid realization. I would also argue that there is a direct and intimate connection between the action of grace upon the soul and the psychological maturity from which the human act of love of God flows.

One must be clear as to the implications of such a proposition.

Fromm unfortunately confuses the issues by applying what is a most perceptive psychological insight to an anthropological and historical schema. Clearly the primitive stages of religious evolution in human history are something quite different from the psychological immaturity of an individual. The inference that the love of God as a father is an immature form of the love of God might be reasonable in Fromm's nontheistic frame of reference. But within the framework of a revealed theology, in which the concept of God as father is integral, this inference becomes highly questionable. However it remains profoundly true that the love of God in the human psyche expresses deep-seated psychological dispositions. In this respect the love of God is no different than any other form of love. A man's capacity to love God is measured by his capacity to love his fellowman, and his love for his fellowman is in some sense a function of his love of God.

The distinctions Fromm makes regarding Western and Eastern religious systems are interesting, although they might seem caricatures rather than characterizations. Western religion since the time of Christ has undergone a theological evolution in which the ideas of the place of faith and the cognitive dimensions of man's relation to God have undergone extensive development. However, it is not accurate to say that love has come to equal thought, and that the love of God has come to be identified with belief in God and in his love. The distinction between belief in God, knowledge of God, and love of God remains valid even though Christian theology has continued to insist that man cannot love God unless he believes in him. There is no need to dichotomize the experience of loving God in the Western tradition. Mysticism is an integral part of authentic Christian relatedness to God. Mystical experience on the most sublime emotional plane is a repeated theme in mystical literature. The love of God is a profound and complex human experience which somehow involves and expresses the whole of a man's psychic existence. Psychologists tend to associate the capacity for love with emotional maturity, along the lines suggested by Freud's "lieben und arbeiten."[13] This is the significance of the psycho-

---

[13] Freud was once asked what he thought were the essential qualities of a mature person. He answered, "Lieben und arbeiten." The mature person could be identified by his capacity for love and work.

analytic notion of genitality with its associated notions of industry, generativity, and intimacy. If we accept the notion that the love of God is sustained and generated on the one hand through the action of grace and that it is expressive and reflective of personal maturity on the other, it seems to me that the inner force of the argument directs one to the conclusion that the proper effect of grace in psychological perspective is potentiation of maturing forces within the personality.

The problematic we are attempting to establish is not concerned with the theology of grace, but with the psychological correlates that remain so far relatively undeveloped. The potential relation between the action of grace and psychological maturity raises a number of issues. Does psychological immaturity in some sense limit the individual's capacity to respond to grace? To what extent can psychological maturity be identified with the effects of grace, even in a limited psychological perspective? If grace does work its effects through inner dynamisms of the functioning personality, how can these effects be specified in a psychologically meaningful way? The question is raised as to whether prior maturity can be regarded in some sense and to some degree as a propaedeutic to the receptivity to grace. These are questions relevant to the problematic of the psychology of grace, and they remain, to a considerable degree, unanswered. They have also an immediate and pressing relevance to pastoral, ascetical, educational and spiritual concerns.

It is Fromm the psychologist who speaks, when he says: "One thing is certain: The nature of his love for God corresponds to the nature of his love for man, and furthermore, the real quality of his love for God and man is often unconscious — covered up and rationalized by a more mature *thought* of what his love is." The essential issue, then, that every human being must face in his re-latedness to God is the real quality of his love. This problem is as vital for the consecrated religious as for the rebellious agnostic. In trying to understand grace, too, we must remember that the real quality of the life of grace is often unconscious — covered up and rationalized by the thought of what grace and its action is.

Questions for Discussion

1. What is the primary reason for the author's including Fromm in this study?
2. Why, according to Fromm, must understanding of God begin with analysis of the worshiping person?
3. What in Fromm's view is the difference between "mother-centered" and "father-centered" religions?
4. What transformation of the figure of God takes place in Jewish religion and theology, according to Fromm?
5. What does Fromm see as the logical consequence of monotheistic thought?
6. How does Fromm think the opposition between Aristotelian logic and "paradoxical" logic affects Eastern and Western religious attitudes?
7. Fromm's view of the love of God is incomplete, yet emphasizes an important aspect of love. Explain.
8. What are the limitations and what is the usefulness of Fromm's explanation of the genesis of forms of worship?
9. What difficulties does the author find with Fromm's view of the evolution of Western religion?
10. What is the proper effect of grace, psychologically speaking? How do we arrive at this conclusion?

IV

GORDON ALLPORT AND
PERSONALITY AS SYSTEM

A. Prenote

The problematic of a psychology of grace is ultimately psychological. Given a theology of grace, further understanding and formulation must be in psychological terms. We will be unable to advance to such understanding and formulation unless the groundwork is laid. It is important to have both a sound theology of grace and sound psychology. The application of the separate and distinctive approaches of theology and psychology to the problem of grace is possible to the extent that it is possible to agree upon an image of man's nature that is both psychologically acceptable and theologically relevant.

Perhaps no other contemporary American psychologist has done more than Gordon Allport to further the understanding of the structure of human personality. Allport presents here a summary of his ideas on the nature of human personality as an "open system." There is little need to comment on this lucid distillation of his thought. But I will indicate in the commentary some of the implications of Allport's open view of human nature for the problematic of grace.

The following excerpt is taken from Allport's *Pattern and Growth in Personality* (New York: Holt, Rinehart and Winston, 1961), pp. 567-572.

B. Selection: Personality as System

The best hope for discovering coherence would seem to lie in approaching personality as a total functioning structure, i.e., as a *system*. To be sure, it is an incomplete system, manifesting varying degrees of order and disorder. It has structure but also unstructure, function but also malfunction. As [Gardner] Murphy says, "all normal people have many loose ends." And yet personality is well-enough knit to qualify as a system — which is defined merely as *a complex of elements in mutual interaction*.

Now systems may be classified as *closed* or *open*. A closed system is defined as one that admits no matter from outside itself and therefore "runs down" (is subject to entropy according to the second law of thermodynamics). Although some outside energies, such as change in temperature and wind, may play upon a closed system, it has no restorative properties and no transactions with its environment, and so, like a decaying barn, sinks into "thermodynamic equilibrium." No theory of personality holds to this view. Closed systems belong, if anywhere, to physics. All living systems belong to the class of open systems.

Open systems, we may say, are marked by four criteria: (1) There are intake and output of both matter and energy. (2) There are the achievement and maintenance of steady (homeostatic) states so that the intrusion of outer energy will not seriously disrupt internal form and order. (3) There is generally an increase of order over time, owing to an increase in the complexity and differentiation of parts. (4) Finally, at least at the human level, there is extensive transactional commerce with the environment.

Although all theories view personality as an open system, they do not agree on the emphasis to be placed on each of the criteria, nor on how many of the criteria to admit.

1. *Material and energy interchange.* Stimulus-response theory in its purest form concentrates on this criterion to the virtual exclusion of all others. It says, in effect, that a stimulus enters and a response is emitted. In between these poles there is, of course, machinery for summation, storage, and delay. But we need study only the two major poles in order to depict the functioning of personality. Some forms of methodological positivism would go one step further, and

say that we can dispense with the concept of personality altogether if we focus attention on our measurements of stimulus input and of behavioral output.

2. *Homeostasis*. As we saw in earlier chapters, many prominent theories of motivation and of learning rest on the assumption that personality is a process of satisfying needs, reducing tension, and therefore of maintaining homeostatic equilibrium. Thus the whole course of man's development may be regarded as simply an extension of the principle involved in temperature regulation, balance of blood volume or sugar content, within the physical body. Personality is an endeavor to balance inner and outer pressures in order to achieve a state of rest or equilibrium. All need-theories and quasi-mechanical explanations of learning acknowledge this criterion

Most current theories of personality take full account of these first two requirements of an open system. They allow for interchange of matter and energy, and for the tendency of organisms to maintain an orderly arrangement of elements in a steady state. Thus they emphasize stability rather than growth, "uncertainty reduction" (information theory) rather than creativity. In short, they emphasize *being* rather than *becoming*. These theories are biologistic in the sense that they ascribe to personality only the two features of an open system that are clearly present in all living organisms.

There are, however, two additional criteria, not stressed by positivist conceptions of the human person.

3. *Increased order over time*. Some theories correctly emphasize the tendency of human personality to go beyond steady states and to elaborate their internal order, even at the cost of disequilibrium. Theories of changing energies and of functional autonomy do so. These conceptions allow for a continual increase of men's purposes in life and for their morphogenic effect upon the system as a whole. Although homeostasis is a useful conception for short-run "target orientation," it is totally inadequate to account for the integrating tonus involved in "goal orientation."

Many of the theories that we have considered in this chapter and in previous ones put weight on this criterion. Woodworth's principle of behavior primacy, as opposed to need primacy, does so. So, too, Goldstein's doctrine of self-actualization and Jung's individuation.

One thinks of Maslow's growth motives, as opposed to deficit motives. Ego-psychology, with its allowance for autonomous and conflict-free motivation, belongs here. White's emphasis on competence, Lecky's self-consistency, Erikson's search for identity, Adler's style of life, McDougall's sentiment of self-regard — all are oriented to this criterion. Although these formulations differ among themselves, they all find the "go" of personality in some dynamic thrust that exceeds the pale function of homeostatic balance. They recognize increasing order over time, and view change within personality as a recentering, but not as abatement, of tension. Needless to add, existential thought moves in this same direction.

4. *Transaction with the environment.* The first three criteria view personality as a self-contained system — as it surely is. All writers acknowledge, of course, that the input and output of energies make for a certain interaction with the environment, but for the most part they focus upon the "inside" system.

Other writers point out that the personality system, more than any other living system, is wide open to the surrounding world. Countless objects are matters of interest and challenge. No other creature besides man attempts to mold the world, and even outer space, to his heart's content.

So vast is the outreach of the human person that some theories refuse to separate personality at all from its context. We saw how even a temporary "sensory deprivation," isolating a person from the environment, will cause serious disturbances of personality. Some cultures, the Buddhist, for example, regard the individual, society, and nature as forming a single tripod of existence, a single system. Why has Western thought, Murphy asks, drawn a razor-sharp distinction between the person and all else? Perhaps the Judeo-Christian religion is a primary factor, enhanced by the growing role of the individual in the industrial revolution. Whatever the reason, some writers insist that personality is an *interpersonal system;* it exists *only* in its social interactions with other people.

Our view stops short of this point, for if we are not wary we shall find ourselves studying only the social and cultural systems which include the person. There is also emphatically a neuropsychic system "within the skin" that is the object of our study. It is the personality system proper. We can hold to this position without in the least denying that one important mark of this system is its continuous intercourse with, and dependence upon, larger systems of interaction. For all his elaborate transactions with the world, the individual remains a separate unit. It is well to consider the personality system as the special assignment of psychology, and the social and cultural systems, within which the individual is located, as the special assignment of sociology and anthropology.

To view personality as a living system has the great merit of calling our attention to the patterning of detailed facts from whatever source they are drawn. Thus biological knowledge and genetics can be fitted in; so, too, nomothetic principles of growth; all valid portions of the quasi-mechanical laws of learning; the range of individual differences; homeostasis; principles of ego-defense; expressive behavior — everything that is validly established by positivist psychology. But since *system* is our focus of interest we must weave together with these data all our additional knowledge of individuality. Such knowledge comes from studies of propriate functions, of self-image, from configural understanding, from existential analysis, and from many other sources.

Within the framework of "system" one approach helps to correct the other. If positivism leans toward fragmentation and impersonality this bias can be tempered by emphasis on personal dispositions and unity. All that is valid in either approach must be fitted in. What is good in existentialism belongs to our study of system, although we cannot agree with its rash rejection of all methods other than phenomenology.

And so it goes. It is not fruitful to argue for one approach to personality at the expense of all others. Personality is many-sided, and needs many avenues of approach. It will not be difficult to reconcile them if we regard all data, from whatever source, as adding to our knowledge of a single organic system.

And we suspect that it is here the reconciliation of psychology and philosophy can occur. *System* is a concept congenial to most philosophy, for orderliness in nature has ever been the datum of philosophy. As psychology increasingly tells us how the personality system is patterned, we may call upon philosophy and theology to relate the findings as well as they can to cosmic order. . . .

We do not deny the proposition that psychology seeks general laws, but we have drawn special attention to those laws and principles that tell how uniqueness comes about. It is also our argument that each single life is lawful, for it reveals its own orderly and necessary process of growth. Lawfulness does not depend upon frequency or upon uniformity, but upon inner necessity.

Personality for us is a pattern that exists "out there." We boldly ask what a person is like in his essential nature (not merely how he affects other people, or how he behaves in different situations). Of course, his behavior is variable, but always within the limits and ranges set by the structure itself.

The analysis of personality should proceed at significant levels; the elements we seek must be genuine *parts* of personality, not remote abstractions. The elements should not be too microscopic, for personality exists only at a high degree of complexity. Personal dispositions viewed as subsystems within the total organic system are the most significant units. Among these dispositions, propriate interests and values are the most important. It is in the functionally autonomous motives of maturity that the mainsprings of adult personality are found.

Psychology, as we have seen, possesses many methods and many maps. This richness is remarkable in a science so young. It is inevitable that there should be discord. Whenever we have criticized a theory or a technique it has seldom been on the grounds of validity, but rather on the grounds that some one limited point of view is falsely pretending to cover the whole of the subject.

The personality system is a complex product of biological endowment, cultural shaping, cognitive style, and spiritual groping. Only if viewed in this way can all the diverse methods of inquiry be brought to a focus. Their separate contributions can best be blended if we regard personality as a system — incomplete but bent on growth and on becoming more than it is. Any other assumption falls short of the measure of man. . . .

C. Commentary and Analysis

The criteria Allport uses to distinguish the open system from the closed system are environmental transaction and the increase of

order over time. This implies a view of personality as somehow
transcending environment. It is the nature of a personality system
to act as well as react. Human personality is not a static structural
reality. It is a functioning system, always dynamically in process. It
is an evolving reality. It is at this point that Allport becomes most
authentically the disciple of James, for, as we saw above, it was
James who articulated the dynamic perspective of the self half a
century ago.

The distribution of energy is both dynamic and autonomous, and
is at the same time transactional. Action and transaction are always
knitted together in an integrally functioning system. But both
aspects of the functioning personality have to be kept in view. In
varying degrees one or the other dominates an individual's pattern
of behavior, but it is unusually difficult to draw the line. Modern
studies of human behavior have established the principle that
behavior is situational. Action and reaction are conditioned by the
complex interaction of influences which come to bear in the concrete situation. This insight has opened new avenues to the understanding of behavior. We have learned that the structure of family
relationships is significantly related to the development of the growing child's personality and functioning. We have become increasingly sensitive to factors of socialization and acculturation that mold
the child's responsiveness to the demand and expectations of the
community. We have learned that human adaptation and adjustment cannot be explained by intrapsychic variables alone. They are
related also to currents of interpersonal and sociological influence
which strongly affect their organization and functioning.

The transactional view of behavior makes the psychologist's life
considerably more complex since it draws in broad areas of interaction in which cause and effect relations are easily obscured. But
this very openness of man, his insertion into such a transactional
network as a functioning system, mirrors the complexity of life itself
and makes the understanding of man's psychic life all the more real.
The fullness of understanding demands that the full reality of transactional influences be taken into account. It has been a traditional
teaching of Christian theology that grace is a reality intimately related to the functioning of the human psyche. The Christian psy-

chologist cannot ignore this. But the difficulty has been to make this realization psychologically relevant.

The notion of personality as an open system is an essential first step in conceptualizing the psychological relevance of grace, for the closed system banishes grace. But the open system permits us to think of man as functioning on multiple levels in relation to a multiplicity of extrinsic influences. Once ontological grounds for the possibility of an intrinsic action of grace have been established, there is no reason to reject the notion of grace as a transcendental influence working in complementary fashion to the other elements of a heterogeneous transactional system.

The open system is characterized by the increase of internal order over time. Personality is thus an integral system with an intrinsic principle of unity. This system is constantly in a state of dynamic flux involving the capacity for maximizing internal order. The integrity of the organization is neither static nor complete. Moreover, the progress through time to increasing order is not derived from an extrinsic ordering agency, nor from the transactional involvement of the personality. On the contrary, the organizing principle is intrinsic to the evolving structure.

William James saw the impact of religious experience in terms of the inner unification of the self. Allport speaks here of the increase of order. Linking these separate insights with the effects of grace, we can suggest that it is somehow through an ordering, unifying, integrating agency within the personality that the structural correlates of the action of grace can be formulated. Allport suggests to us the connection with ego-psychology. The active, dynamic, organizing, integrating agency within the personality is the ego itself — that portion of inner psychic structure that lies at the core of my experience of myself as person and personality. The implication dawns then that the ego and the action of grace are in some sense linked together.

Allport briefly touches on another theme that calls for comment. He remarks: "Among these dispositions, propriate interests and values are the most important. It is in the functionally autonomous motives of maturity that the mainsprings of adult personality are found." This theme we can only touch on since the understanding of the origin and function of values in the organization and direction of human behavior is a major problem area in itself. We do, however, suggest some lines of connection. Values serve in some fashion as internal norms of judgment and behavior. The value system conversely belongs properly to the more or less conscious and autonomous ego-system. The development of a value system depends in part upon the quality of the ego's interaction with reality. As a principle of interpretation this would seem to apply, not only to the perceptual-cognitive level of interaction, but also to higher conceptual levels. The quality of this interaction is, therefore, susceptible to the influence of highly complex factors including identifications, education and the manifold of cultural forces. Within and through the receptivity and transaction in relation to these multiple forces, the ego shapes a system of values that serve as a functional framework of reference for the patterning of subsequent behavior.

I draw attention to this aspect of ego-functioning since it seems to me to represent a possible focus for analyzing the effects of grace. There are of course problems in such a consideration. It would be difficult to reach a consensus as to what values are, particularly in psychological terms. It would also be difficult to reach a consensus as to their relationships with the functioning personality. I will content myself with suggesting here that the concept of value-system serves as a useful one for drawing together many aspects of personality function and relating them to the action of grace.

The formation of values is a function of the ego acting as an open system involved in continual transaction with the environment. From a religious point of view, this transaction involves concrete influences which mold the individual's value orientation by all the many devices of formation — educational, instructional, directional, devotional, and so on. The complex of influences generated within the family unit itself is primary in terms of conscious attitudes and unconscious identifications with parental figures. These influences, however, remain without meaning unless the ego assimilates and integrates them into a functioning system of values. Value formation, therefore, demands ego-activity which is both transactional and fundamentally autonomous.

We would propose, as a criterion for the adequacy or maturity of a given individual value-system, its reality orientation. The same criterion serves us in evaluating the functioning of the ego itself. But the reality in question is useless as a criterion unless it includes the whole reality within which the ego is involved. Here it would seem that the reality of the spiritual order as defined by the tradition of Christian theology and experience becomes relevant. The reality of grace, as the dynamic influence and act of the saving God in the current of human affairs and history, is also relevant. It is precisely through spiritual values, then, that the person is adapted to the spiritual order of reality. We may suggest that the influence of grace, mediated through the intrinsic and autonomous activity of the ego, culminates in a specific effect or effects which are intimately involved in the formation of reality-ordered and spiritually relevant values. There is a presumption in this argument that the entire spectrum of realistically oriented and congruent values are consistent and potentially integrable with the hierarchical order of spiritual values.

Questions for Discussion

1. What is the significance of Allport's work?
2. How does Allport define a "system"? How does he define a "closed system"? An "open system"?
3. Discuss the two criteria of open systems stressed by positivist theorists of personality.
4. Discuss the two that are not stressed by positivist theorists.
5. What is the relation of personality as living system to the various approaches to knowledge of personality?
6. What personality elements does Allport regard as most significant for the analysis of personality?
7. Briefly characterize the transactional view of human behavior.
8. Why does the transactional view complicate the psychologist's life?
9. How does the author link the effects of grace with the separate insights of James and Allport?
10. What does the author propose as a norm for judging individual value-systems? How does this norm apply to religious values?

V
JOSEPH NUTTIN AND THE
NEED FOR EXISTENTIAL SUPPORT

A. Prenote

The argument is beginning to take shape, however tentatively. We have offered the suggestion that the openness of human personality is an openness to the whole of reality. The wholeness of reality encompasses all orders of existence from the grossly material to the sublimely spiritual. Correlative to this is the implication that one cannot evaluate the functioning of the human personality until one has considered it in relation to all orders of the real.

Human spiritual development, psychologically regarded, involves a relatedness to the spiritual order, just as human psychological development stems from a relatedness to the real order of objects and persons. The terms in which such relatedness is formulated are not important. What is important rather is that the reality and the relatedness be recognized for what they are. Canon Joseph Nuttin, in this selection, recapitulates some of the issues we have already discussed and advances the argument along several lines.

Nuttin endorses the concept of man as a vital center which opens out onto the whole of reality. The congruence of this with the notion of dynamic activity, vitality and openness of the personality is obvious. Consequently, we can further delineate the developing image of man with Nuttin's assistance.

The following excerpts are taken from Nuttin's *Psychoanalysis and Personality* (New York: Sheed and Ward, 1962), pp. 246-252.

B. Selection: The Need for "Existential" Support and Universal Integration

Man is . . . a vital center maintaining the "internal environment" of his life and organism by means of regulative mechanisms and adaptations in his behaviour; that form of psychic life which consciously finds itself amongst creatures like itself and desires to unfold as a "person" amongst them; a being who in his interaction with the world assimilates biochemical agents and develops "significant" situations; *furthermore, he opens out upon the whole of reality, in which he feels himself to "exist."* Man is a being who knows himself to be situated in *that which is*. In other words, man lives his own life in the world, in such a way that he is neither exhausted nor absorbed by that which *affects* him. This undeniable cardinal fact must be realized — that man is a being who asks himself questions *about his very existence*. Contact with the "world" causes biochemical reactions in him; this is a fact, examined in all its detail by natural science; but this same contact with the "world" rouses the problems of existence in him — this is another fact, which we see no reason for science — in this case, psychology — to remain silent about.

It is because, and insofar as, he is not completely absorbed in his social and biological environment, insofar as he truly *is* and truly lives his existence, that, as we shall show, man experiences the need to maintain his existence and develop himself in existence, and the further need to "illuminate" his existence. This need for development in the consciousness of existence takes diverse forms. For some, it means developing complicated philosophical ideas — in the affirmation of immortality or in theories of the purest materialism. But all, by trying to realize what they are, or what they imagine themselves to be — i.e., by growing fully conscious of their own existence — will be obeying the *need to be more completely themselves*. *Non omnis moriar* is one expression of this need for self-preservation and self-development; but a philosopher who considers that his personality will disappear forever into matter is being no less obedient to the need to realize the meaning of existence, i.e., to be more completely oneself by understanding as a *conscious* being what one is.

It is more pertinent here, however, to examine the expressions of this need in its more ordinary manifestations in the ordinary, everyday man. In the first place, we discover this need of self-preservation and self-development extending beyond the limits of biological and social "fact," in certain universal *religious tendencies* of mankind; a need sometimes expressed in the saying that man wants to "save his soul." Now, from the psychological point of view, "saving one's soul" means primarily maintaining oneself in existence as a personality integrated with the absolute.

It is true that in our civilization *this religious form* of the desire for self-preservation and self-development according to an absolute order of values has been transformed for many people into aspirations of a more or less philosophical kind. But the man who sees his life as a link in the chain of evolution or the development of matter is trying, no less than the person who aims to save his soul, to maintain himself and develop through the same kind of integration into an absolute order.

Again, at a certain moment in the individual's existence or in the development of human culture, this general need for self-preservation and self-development can appear in a much more pronounced fashion at the psycho-social level than at the absolute level, so that it will be difficult to recognize the need in its absolute form. A man of thirty, for example, experiences this need much more intensely in its social form than as a desire to make sure of his eternal salvation. The opposite can be true of the man who retires from social life. Thus Liebman, in his famous *Peace of Mind,* was able to say that modern man is concerned about success in the same way as the man of the middle ages was preoccupied with his eternal salvation.[1] It would be a mistake to imagine that the social need is a temporary or artificial one, but it is true that the philosophical ideas which man develops about human existence in general can change *the forms* in which the corresponding dynamism *appears.*

In this particular field of philosophy, and of intellectual life in general, the same need is again apparent in the natural tendency,

---

[1] Joshua Liebman, *Peace of Mind* (New York: Simon and Schuster, 1946). See also Werner Wolff, *Values in Personality Research* (New York: Grune and Stratton, 1950): "The cause of neurosis . . . is man's experience of having lost his connection with the universe."

profoundly rooted in man, to believe in the immortality of his soul, or in some sort of persistence of life after death — in the form, for instance, of survival through his descendants or his work. This tendency is also obviously bound up with the fact that through knowledge man *transcends* what is *actually* given and experienced.

It is not our intention here to analyze in detail all these manifestations of the need for preservation and self-development. There are characteristic forms of this need in Chinese and Egyptian civilization. It appears in the joy of the grandfather who holds on to life by growing attached to his grandson; it can be found in the zeal of the master who educates his disciples to prolong the life of his own ideas and discoveries.

Many and manifold are the concrete manifestations of the need, felt universally by man, to preserve and develop himself on the specifically human level to which he has been raised by his transcendent spirit. The force which drives man to exploit the earth and incessantly enlarge his fields of knowledge and technique comes partly at least from the need he feels to develop the intellectual aspect of his personality. It is not only the scientific research-worker, the engineer, the technician, who experiences this need; the adolescent can exhibit it in a pronounced degree. In the same way, the man who adopts as his supreme law of conduct fidelity to himself, to his own past and his own principles, and remains consistently himself, is manifesting a form of the need to maintain and develop the moral personality.

Here again we find the need for internal consistency which we have discussed before. This need is even stronger at the level of spiritual and moral personality than it is at the level of social life. To remain one's self, to be true to one's self, is an aspect of the need to be one's self and to preserve one's own personality. Concretely, remaining true to one's self often means remaining true to a scale of values which one has adopted and to which one freely adheres. In this sense, "self-consistency" is an element of freedom and self-determination.[2]

We have also already spoken of another manifestation of the

---

[2] See also on the subject of fidelity the work of M. Nédoncelle, *God's Encounter with Man* (New York: Sheed and Ward, 1964).

same need, that of self-determination in the sense of having a say in one's own behaviour and even in one's destiny. Man feels the need to shoulder a certain amount of responsibility.[3] A complaint commonly heard from people who have undergone psychotherapy is that they had no responsibilities to assume or choices to make in the course of therapy. We can say that in general man feels the need for spiritual freedom and for the exercise of that freedom.

It must be remembered that at this spiritual level the ways by which man tends to maintain and develop his personality are not physiologically conditioned, as is the case for his biological develop-ment. At the spiritual level man tends to maintain and develop him-self in a certain direction according to his own plan for his personal life or according to the ideals set before him by society; hence the great variety of forms in which this need can appear in different people and in different civilizations. The concrete form of the need depends upon either a cognitive element or a theory of life.

On this spiritual and transcendent level of our human existence the need for *contact* manifests itself in specific forms. Before any biological or bodily interaction, and even before communion of any other kind with his fellow-men, man needs a more universal sort of communication and support and integration; he needs *to be able to know and feel himself integrated into an absolute order of exis-tence.* Perhaps never before in human history has there been such intense experience of *absolute* despair and loneliness, such a feeling of utter dereliction, such lack of all transcendental contact, as there is today.

In a time like ours, when the various attachments to past and future, to the earth and the family — when the thousand and one things to which existence attaches itself, and which give existence its meaning and value — have been dissolved, man feels utterly "uprooted." The need to find some absolute meaning in life, i.e., the need to become integrated with existence, makes itself felt more and more imperiously. But this need has gone on being frustrated: man has continued to see before him nothing but the horror and emptiness of his isolation and the absurdity of his existence. It is a

---

[3] Cf. P. Matussek, *Metaphysische Probleme der Medizin* (Berlin: Springer, 2nd ed., 1950).

situation which brings out more clearly than ever the *reality* of man's "spiritual" needs — and it is amazing to find so many contemporary psychologies incapable of seeing this and giving all their attention to mere "tissue needs" instead.

Here one is faced with a concrete manifestation of a fundamental need of human existence itself: a need for contact with the whole order of reality, the only kind of contact which can give meaning to life. It is this frustrated need which gives rise, at this moment of the world's history, to the metaphysical misery and despair apparent not only in the philosophy and literature of existentialism but as the background to a great deal of the insecurity and psychic troubles of today.

We mention these cultural facts simply to give tangible reality to the need in question. The *positive* forms of higher needs are usually less tangible than the states of derangement caused by their frustration, and it is through these negative manifestations that there becomes evident a form of need which can easily pass unperceived in the man whose conception of the world makes up a harmonious whole.

Several recent authors have emphasized the importance of these needs in the study and treatment of psychic disturbance. For example, we could cite the more or less philosophically oriented current in psychotherapy in the German-speaking countries (*Existenzanalyse* and *Medizinische Anthropologie*). Certain Jungian theories are now also recognized by some American authors. Fromm writes that man without faith, without love, and without truth is the prey of confusion and anxiety, and that psychic disturbance often results from an inability to accept and develop moral and spiritual responsibilities.[4] Wolff has also expressed the idea that the origin of neuroses must be sought in the direct experience of a loss of contact with the universe.[5] We do not think it would be accurate to emphasize these spiritual factors exclusively, as certain authors tend to do as a reaction against Freudian psychoanalysis; spiritual, social, and biological forms of need are intimately bound

---

[4] E. Fromm, *Psychoanalysis and Religion* (New Haven: Yale University Press, 1950).
[5] W. Wolff, *Values in Personality Research*.

together, and it is difficult to untangle their combined influence in the origin of the disturbance.

To mention a few more positive manifestations of the need for contact at the spiritual level of our existence: religion — a phenomenon so universal that, though it can be *replaced* by other forms of transcendent contact, it can rarely be *extinguished* — provides one of the most striking manifestations of the need for a kind of interaction and contact which goes beyond physical and social facts. It can be expressed in the *feminine* form of a "request" for support from the absolute, or in a more masculine kind of desire to be *at peace* with one's conscience or with God. Not to be at peace with one's conscience or with God means, in fact, to experience the rupture of a transcendent order of absolute values.[6]

In the *intellectual and philosophical* domains, as we have said, there is the need *to give a meaning to existence,* i.e., the need to know oneself integrated meaningfully into an absolute order of existence. This is the vital force behind our spiritual existence itself, forcing us out of our absolute isolation. Just as the organism is stifled and asphyxiated when it is isolated from its biological sphere, so a spiritual being becomes absurd to itself when it does not open out and enter into significant contact with the whole of reality.

The power of this spiritual impulse appears most clearly, we have said, when it remains *unsatisfied.* Besides certain currents in contemporary culture to which we have already alluded, psychopathology too directs our attention towards this human need. A great number of people who on the surface seem very sure of themselves are subject to neurotic disturbances whose roots must be looked for in their failure to integrate themselves into a wider

---

[6] In some people the need to be at peace with God or their own conscience may also be the manifestation of a desire for a stainless egoistic perfection. Such people do not want to be debtors to anybody; they want to manage their own affairs to perfection. They transpose to the absolute level of their relationship with God the mentality of a petty accountant. They want to "win" what God has promised to give them. Thus they try not to get beaten, to affirm themselves, or protect themselves. This attitude of mind toward God and religion has been described most suggestively by Mauriac in his novel *Woman of the Pharisees* (New York: Doubleday, 1959). This reveals once again the way several tendencies are *involved* in one single human activity. We shall have to return to this point, *ex professo,* in a later paragraph.

reality, i.e., their failure to give a meaning to life. The Social Security Board of the United States of America recently expressed concern at the increasing number of neurotics in that country. On the other hand, the immense enthusiasm recently aroused there in the hearts and souls of millions of readers by Liebman's book, *Peace of Mind,* reveals something of *what is* missing in these "restless" people, and *what* lies at the root of their distress. To these millions of readers, all seeking interior peace, Liebman says that it is their "insecurity and forlornness," from lack of any metaphysical basis to their lives, which makes it impossible for them to surmount their existential misery unless they have faith in the "worth-whileness" and therefore the *meaning* of life. The only thing that can reestablish the disturbed equilibrium is "the confidence that God will *not cast us aside* but will *use each of us as a piece of priceless mosaic in the design of his universe.*" The echo aroused by these words in the souls of millions of readers gives the psychologist some idea of the "reality" of the need for universal contact and integration, the need to know and feel oneself as a precious stone in the universal mosaic of the absolute divine plan. The moment this need is frustrated, it begins to raise its voice above all the noise of *business relations* and *sex appeal,* creating in the human soul a cry and an emptiness that no external agitation can fill.[7]

In all these forms of aspiration we see the needs for self-development and contact which we have already discovered on the psycho-physiological and psycho-social levels of human existence. Here specific forms of these needs arise because human existence is conscious of itself and conscious of being involved in a whole order of reality, and we see the dynamism of the spiritual ego which in its *knowledge* and its *aspirations* transcends its spatial and temporal limitations. This spiritual ego too experiences the tendency to *develop its existence* and *feel itself in contact* with its spiritual environment. . . .

---

[7] See also Fulton J. Sheen, *Peace of Soul* (New York: McGraw-Hill, 1949).

C. Commentary and Analysis

Two primary characteristics of the personality are need for self-preservation and need for self-development. However basic these needs may be, they do not take shape in a vacuum, but in terms of a frame of reference. If the psychologist interprets such basic needs in terms of mere physical preservation and development, he truncates the reality of personality. Self-preservation has many meanings. Within the religious context which concerns us here it represents a desire for authentic existence according to an absolute set of values. The man who accepts the validity of revelation, and who recognizes the inner necessity of the conclusions of a theological interpretation of that revelation, has no alternative but to seek to discern the pattern of relations between himself and this order of reality.

There is in the human personality a basic need for self-determination and responsibility. With this observation, Nuttin raises the fundamental issue of freedom. Christian theology is agreed upon two essential points: first, that man is free, and second, that the action of grace does not violate that freedom. From a psychological point of view, it is inconsistent to believe that a personality system that is open, autonomous, active, and self-ordering could also not be self-determining. For scientific psychology, as well as for philosophy, this is a complex issue. The only point I would like to make here is that freedom is not a conclusion or a construct, but a datum of experience. Within a strict framework of causal analysis as set up within a positive-physical model of causality, the concept of freedom is quite ambiguous, and difficult if not impossible to fit into the analysis. But in the framework of a transactional analysis, or within the framework of analysis which accepts the principle of overdetermination of behavior, the psychological understanding of freedom is by no means impossible. If one accepts the concept of the ego as possessing autonomous and independent energies, there is no violation of causality or scientific understanding in the concept of freedom. Self-determination is precisely the essential dimension of any activity of the personality which gives that activity its special quality as an ego-function.

All of this is involved in what we might denominate "giving

meaning to existence." It is not easy to say what the significance of this "meaning" is. There are many ways to formulate it. I should like to think that it is partially synonymous with Erikson's now famous phrase, the "sense of identity." [8] In any event, there is in it a presumption that the person has existence. This may appear obvious, but its significance is by no means obvious. Personal existence transcends the mere physical existence that man shares with other physical bodies. It is existence as a person, existence as a free, autonomous, vital, active center of awareness and dynamic process. As such, personal existence is a self-determining process; it is an evolving process even as it is dynamic. There is no question here of undercutting the substantiality of the person, since the dynamic process involved in personal existence is not ontological, but psychological. Personal existence, then, is a psychological achievement, the result of a process of development that is unending and always dynamic.

The need for meaning is basic to this process of development. The ego grows and sustains itself on meaning. The sense of identity is a function of the degree to which the ego can discover or define that meaning proper and intrinsic to itself. As Erikson has said so well, the inner self-reflective meaning is correlative to, and supported by, the meaning projected toward others and reflected by them in the course of social interaction. The significant point is that man finds meaning at the level on which he exists. The meaning that ultimately satisfies him is in some sense correlative to the spiritual and personal quality of that existence.

It is not hard to see that grace is involved in this dimension of the maturation of the ego. It is a vital force that touches man precisely at the level of his existence in which his most profound meaning lies. The details and the implications of the religious context of human existence and personal significance are the points of contact at which the disparate interests and methods of psychology and theology approach each other. But the meaning of the life of grace is explicable only in theological terms. The psychologist is limited to phenomenological presentations of the need aspects of

---

[8] E. Erikson, *Childhood and Society* (New York: Norton, 1950).

the dynamic of meaning and to the integration of such a propulsive element into a total picture of psychic functioning.

It seems good to observe at this point that the whole issue of inner personal meaning hinges on the continuing efforts of ego to define itself. The agency of this dynamic process is the ego itself, which Allport suggested acts autonomously and transactionally. But the defining element, the meaningful activity, is that of the ego. If I attempt a synthesis of notions and call this action self-determination, I use the word with a conscious advertence to its double meaning. The act of self-determination is that act which both reflects the nature of ego as autonomous and determines the inner meaningfulness of personal existence. From this point of view, personal meaning and freedom have common roots. The connotations of this communality will be considered later.

Questions for Discussion

1. What concept of man does Nuttin endorse?
2. What is the cardinal fact about man, according to Nuttin?
3. What is the psychological meaning of the human religious tendency sometimes expressed as wanting to "save one's soul"?
4. Indicate some of the forms in which the human tendency to self-preservation shows itself.
5. In what ways is this tendency manifested on the spiritual and moral level of personality?
6. What does Nuttin say about the need for contact on the spiritual level? Indicate some positive manifestations of this need.
7. What does self-preservation mean in a religious context?
8. How is freedom known? Can ego-psychology accept the concept of freedom?
9. What is the psychological import of personal existence? How does "meaning" fit in here?
10. Where do personal meaning and freedom find common roots?

VI
GORDON ALLPORT AND
THE RELIGIOUS SENTIMENT

A. Prenote

It is to Gordon Allport more than anyone else in contemporary psychology that we owe the insistence on the openness of human personality. But it is imperative in accepting the notion that we ask the question: To what is personality as system open? This is important not only to Allport's own thinking, but it is also imperative to an understanding of the total psychology of human personality.

It is especially significant, in view of our concern with the concrete aspects of man's psychic relatedness to God, that Allport should isolate the religious sentiment as a significant part of his analysis of becoming. Some of the points he makes concerning the religious sentiment are even more significant. It is plain that in conceptualizing his notions of the organization of the personality system in terms of "becoming," he is insisting on the evolutional dimension of the human personality. Personality is therefore neither static nor merely structural, but rather dynamic and functional. Personal becoming is process and continued synthesis.

The following excerpts are taken from Allport's *Becoming* (New Haven: Yale University Press, 1960), pp. 93-98.

B. Selection: The Religious Sentiment

If we ask what psychology has contributed to our understanding of the religious nature of man, the answer is "Less than we might wish." We can explain and to some extent justify this backwardness by pleading the inherent difficulties in working out a scientific psychology of the more complex stages of growth. The religious sentiment, we are now in a position to understand, has attachments to the most elusive facets of becoming, including propriate striving, generic conscience, and intentionality.

We may, to be sure, point to three modest lines of scientific advance in the present century. 1. In his examination of the varieties of religious experience, William James provided us with an excellent typology which, in spite of its looseness, is difficult to improve upon. 2. Modern methods of questionnaires and polling give us reliable, if superficial, data on the extent of religious beliefs and opinions. 3. Depth psychology has made us aware of the role of unconscious processes, particularly of those that impede normal integrative growth. One of the chief merits of depth psychology is its wholesome warning against projecting one's own sentiments into scientific discussions. The danger of projection is, of course, especially acute in discussions of religion where ambiguities of meaning are so prevalent.

If, however, our outline of the process of becoming has validity, certain consequences for the psychological understanding of religion follow. First of all, our analysis warns us against the trivial view that holds adult religion to be merely a repetition of the experiences of the child. Although a child may sometimes extend the image of his earthly father to a divine Father, it is a nonsequitur to say that all religious adults do the same. True, some adults may never outgrow their tendency to cling to a partisan deity who, like an overindulgent father, responds always to special pleading. Yet the healthy person in possession of normal intelligence, insight, and emotional maturity knows that he cannot solve life's problem by wishful thinking or cure his own partialness by fictionizing. To cure his partialness he must find something more convincing than partialness itself. Hence the developed personality will not fabricate his religion out of some emotional fragment but will seek a theory of Being in which all fragments are meaningfully ordered.

The developed religious sentiment, therefore, cannot be known in terms of its many empirical origins. It is not a mere matter of dependency or of reliving the family or cultural configuration; nor is it simply a prophylaxis against fear; nor is it an exclusively rational system of belief. Any single formula by itself is too partial. The developed religious sentiment is the synthesis of these and many other factors, all of which form a comprehensive attitude whose function it is to relate the individual meaningfully to the whole of Being.

To feel oneself meaningfully linked to the whole of Being is not possible before puberty. This fact helps to explain the one-sided emphasis we encounter in many psychological discussions of religion. Becoming has been much more thoroughly studied for the years preceding puberty than for adolescent and adult years. It is, therefore, understandable that the factors influencing the religion of childhood should loom large in our present view: familism, dependence, authority, wishful thinking, and magical practice.

Since, however, the process of becoming continues throughout life, we rightly expect to find the fully developed sentiment only in the adult reaches of personality. The adult mind, provided that it is still growing, stretches its rational capacities as far as it can with the logic of induction, deduction, and a weighing of probabilities. While the intellect continues to exert itself, the individual finds that he needs to build aspiring defenses against the intellect's almost certain failure. He learns that to surmount the difficulties of a truculent world he needs also faith and love. Thus religion, engaging as it does reason, faith, and love, becomes for him morally true. Most religious people claim that it is also metaphysically true because they feel that outer revelation and mystical experience have brought them supernatural assurance. Thus the warrant for certitude comes from the total orientation that the person attains in his quest for a comprehensive belief-system capable of relating him to existence as a whole.

Psychologically speaking, we should point to the close analogy that exists between a religious orientation and all other high-level schemata that influence the course of becoming. Every man, whether he is religiously inclined or not, has his own ultimate presuppositions. He finds he cannot live his life without them, and for him they are true. Such presuppositions, whether they be called ideologies, philosophies, notions, or merely hunches about life, exert creative pressure upon all conduct that is subsidiary to them (which is to say, upon nearly *all* of a man's conduct).

The error of the psychoanalytic theory of religion — to state the error in its own terminology — lies in locating religious belief exclusively in the defensive functions of the ego rather than in the core and center and substance of the developing ego itself. While religion certainly fortifies the individual against the inroads of anxiety, doubt, and despair, it also provides the forward intention that enables him at each stage of his becoming to relate himself meaningfully to the totality of Being.

From this line of reasoning we might expect most adults to be religious people, as in fact they are. Yet there is endless diversity among them in the degree to which religion plays a part in their lives, and in the forms and relative maturity of their religious out-look.[1] It could not be otherwise, for religious becoming is influenced by our temperament and training, and is subject to arrest as well as growth. Some of the arresting forces leave the individual with an infantile form of religious belief, self-serving and super-stitious. Neurotic insecurities may demand an immediate and compulsive ritual of reassurance. Sometimes the extreme rigidity of training in the home or church presents only a partial criterion for testing truth, with the result that the child may either grow fiercely partisan and intolerant or else at a later age react against his training and embrace a negative attitude of unbelief. There are many conditions that make for arrested development.

All phases of becoming are subject to arrest. Psychopathy may be regarded as an arrest in self-extension, so that no sense of moral obligation evolves. Exhibitionism and other perversions are arrests in genital development; narcissism an arrest in the growth of the self-image. Infantilism in religion results in an arrest due to the immediate needs for comfort and security or self-esteem. Unbelief, while it may be the product of mature reflection, may also be a reaction against parental or tribal authority, or may be due to a one-sided intellectual development that rules out other areas of

---

[1] Cf. G. W. Allport, *The Individual and His Religion* (New York: Macmillan, 1950).

normal curiosity.[2] We find many personalities who deal zealously and effectively with all phases of becoming except the final task of relating themselves meaningfully to creation. For some reason their curiosity stops at this point.

Others, however, devote themselves wholly to this task. Their religious aspiration is their cardinal characteristic. For them the religious form of propriate striving alone seems worth while. It provides them with a synthesis of all that lies within experience and all that lies beyond. It monitors the growing edge of personality. Such individuals exercise their capacity for self-objectification, viewing with detachment their reason and their unreason, seeing the limitations of both. They hold in perspective both their self-image and ideal self-image, thus providing themselves with a criterion for conscience. They discriminate between their propriate striving and their opportunistic adjustments, thus distinguishing matters of importance from mere matters of fact. They weigh probabilities in the theological realm, and ultimately affirm a view of life that seems to leave the least possible remainder. Intricate as the process is, it seems to be the way in which mature personalities adopt and validate the religious premise of their course of becoming.

As a science, psychology can neither prove nor disprove religion's claims to truth. It can, however, help explain why these claims are so many and so diverse. They represent the final meanings achieved by unique personalities in diverse lands and times. Organized religious sects reflect comparable sets of meanings within which the unique meanings achieved by individuals may cluster for purposes of communication and common worship.

Psychology can also illuminate the field of religion by following the course of becoming to its ultimate frontiers of growth. It can study man as a representative of his species, as a creature of many opportunistic adjustments, and as a product of tribal molding. But it can study him as well as a self-assertive, self-critical, and self-improving individual whose passion for integrity and for a meaningful relation to the whole of Being is his most distinctive capacity. By devoting itself to the entire course of becoming — leaving out

---

[2] Cf. H. C. Rümke, *The Psychology of Unbelief* (New York: Sheed and Ward, 1962).

no shred of evidence and no level of development — psychology can add progressively to man's self-knowledge. And as man increases in self-knowledge he will be better able to bind himself wholesomely and wisely to the process of creation.

The final truths of religion are unknown, but a psychology that impedes understanding of the religious potentialities of man scarcely deserves to be called a logos of the human psyche at all. . . .

C. Commentary and Analysis

Our primary concern in analyzing Allport's contribution is to see the relevance of the religious sentiment to the organization and functioning of the human personality. To begin with, the religious sentiment is properly characteristic of the maturely functioning personality. This concept is not generally shared by modern psychologists, and stands in particular opposition to the classic psychoanalytic position. Whether one assumes the position that the religious sentiment is a manifestation of infantilism or of maturity is not really psychologically significant. The issue for the psychologist is one of explanation. If, as with Freud, the explanation of religion as regressive fits in with other nonscientific assumptions regarding religious practices and beliefs, the psychologist is likely to support this view. If, as with Allport and as seems equally reasonable and defensible, the religious sentiment seems consonant with and proper to the mature ego, then a different position will be assumed. Both positions are psychologically defensible, and to some extent valid. Much depends on where one starts and what one looks at. If one looks at a patient population redolent with immaturities and infantility, one will find religious infantility. If one looks at a group of normally functioning and relatively mature subjects, one is much more likely to find mature religious attitudes and behavior. Most of the disagreement in this area can be eliminated by recognition that the discussants are talking about different things.

Allport makes it very clear that he is dealing with religion as a mature expression of the personality. The religious sentiment is not possible before puberty and is fully developed only in adult life. It is evident that the religious sentiment develops; that it evolves over time just as other dimensions of "becoming" evolve. If we accept the basically religious or theistic position, the problematic takes shape in terms of the stages of evolution of the religious sentiment. Given the fact of revelation and the actuality of the supernatural order, we are left to define psychologically the stages and the mechanisms by which the human response to the divine intervention shapes itself.

Some of Allport's hints can be of service. He is quick to reject a reductionist explanation. "Any single formula is too partial." The religious response is decidedly complex even from a purely psychological vantage point, but its terms can no more be specified in purely psychological terms than can the complex currents of history. If such psychologism is misleading and therefore dangerous, then reductionism within a psychological approach is still more misleading. Human potentialities exhaust the capacity of the theorist to formulate adequate hypotheses, but the inquiring mind demands understanding. Understanding demands that a critical sense respect the complexities and profundities of its object. Those who analyze some truncated version of religious experience do a disservice to scientific understanding. The understanding of man's religious orientation must respect both the intricacy of human personality and the conditions of theologically meaningful behavior. One must begin, therefore, with a conception of the psychological organism which reflects the best and the worst of human behavior. These prerequisites can be severely demanding. However sophisticated our present-day efforts to understand the human psyche, there is still much to be learned. Much that our psychological experience has taught us has yet to be elaborated scientifically. We are limited to tentative formulations and questionable theories. With this necessary caution, we are on good ground when, as Allport suggests, we regard the religious sentiment as closely analogous to other high level schemata which influence the course of personality development and function.

Allport joins James and Nuttin in locating the religious function in the core of the ego. It is influenced by both temperament and training, and is modeled progressively by the residues of experience. It undergoes, as does the ego itself, a detectible pattern of growth. It is subject to the vicissitudes of arrest and retardation as well. Consequently, the religious sentiment is subject to psychological study. One can study the development in isolation from the religious context and be methodologically legitimate. One must recognize the truncation however. The development has meaning only within a religious context and can be understood only in a partial manner if divorced from that context. The psychologist is dependent on the theologian to determine the conditions and terms of the religious setting.

It can be said in this general context that the religious sentiment and grace are related as effect and cause. In psychological perspective, however, the manner of such causality must be worked out and integrated into an explanatory formulation along with a host of other and diverse causes. The system, as we are aware, is open, and no single cause or set of causes can exhaust the intelligibility of an open system. Because behavior is to this extent overdetermined, our understanding, if it is to escape partiality, must respect this overdetermination. One pressing problem is to bring the actuality of grace into focus in such a way that its action is psychologically intelligible. To recapitulate: We have come to the conclusion that grace is operating in and through the ego itself, but we have not yet touched on the function of grace within the ego, nor have we shed any light on the mechanisms by which such functions are implemented. These are tasks that lie ahead and which will demand the best efforts of psychological understanding and theological sensitivity.

Questions for Discussion

1. What various values of Allport's treatment are pointed out in the author's prenote?
2. What are the three lines of twentieth-century scientific advance in the study of religious experience that Allport points out here?

3. What difficulty does Allport find in the view that adult religious experience is merely repetition of childhood experience?
4. What remarks does Allport make on puberty and adulthood in his discussion of the religious sentiment?
5. Where does classical psychoanalytic theory err in its treatment of religious belief?
6. How does Allport characterize the mature personality in its approach to religion?
7. What is the chief objective of the author's analysis here?
8. How does Allport differ, in his view of the religious sentiment, from, for example, Freud?
9. Indicate some of the cautions we must observe in approaching religious experience.
10. How are grace and the religious sentiment related? What special problems face the psychologist here?

VII
ISIDOR CHEIN AND
THE IMAGE OF MAN

A. Prenote

The nature of our inquiry into the life of man under grace is essentially psychological because it is formulated in psychological terms and pertains to psychological structures and functions. However, this psychological inquiry is carried on in a theological context because the phenomena involved do not permit direct psychological definition. It is impossible to point to some segment of behavior or experience and attribute it to the influence of grace. Our psychological inquiry, then, must provide itself with an image which is congruent with theological understanding, yet cast in psychologically meaningful terms.

We can find help in our effort to locate such a common image in the following excerpts from a long article by Isidor Chein, first published in *The Journal of Social Issues* 18:4 (1962), pp. 1-35.

B. Selection: The Image of Man

1. Introduction [1]

Sigmund Koch [2] has remarked that ". . . psychology has been far more concerned with being a science than with courageous and

---

[1] An abridged version of this paper was presented as the presidential address to the Society for the Psychological Study of Social Issues at the seventieth annual convention of the American Psychological Association on September 3, 1962. This material will be published in an expanded version by Basic Books, Inc., with a more complete and rigorous treatment of fundamental concepts and an elaboration of the bearing of these concepts on aspects of psychology not dealt with herein.

[2] S. Koch, "Psychological Science Versus the Science-humanism Antimony: Intimations of a Significant Science of Man," *American Psychologist* 16 (1961), pp. 629-639.

self-determining confrontation of its historical subject matter."
Koch is embarrassed by how little scientific psychology has contributed to the humanities when he is convinced that ". . . psychology . . . *must* be . . . that area in which the problems of the
sciences, as traditionally conceived, and the humanities intersect."
He traces the difficulty to the fact that "psychology (and social
science) has constructed a language which renders virtually impossible" its living up to its promise.

The trouble with this account is that psychological language is
not an arbitrary construction but a reflection of the way psychology
has confronted its subject matter. If the language is defective, then
this is because the subject matter is being violated. The proper
source of discontent is that psychology has failed to live up to its
promise to itself, not that it has failed to live up to its promise to
the humanities. It has correctly identified, but, in the interests of
a simple-minded conception of the nature of science,[3] it has pro-
ceeded to ignore its subject matter. A striking case in point is the
position taken by Miller, Galanter and Pribram [4] that, now that

---

[3] Koch charges that "the philosophy of science still talked about in psychological literature is approximately twenty years out of date" (p. 631).

[4] G. A. Miller, E. Galanter, and K. H. Pribram, *Plans and Structure of
Behavior* (New York: Holt, 1960). Thus, "Once a teleological mechanism
could be built out of metal and glass, psychologists recognized that it was
scientifically respectable to admit they had known it all along" (p. 43).
Similarly, in commenting on a quotation from Clark Hull, they write that
"Passages such as this suggest that nothing less than the construction of a
teleological machine would convince an experimental psychologist that
there is not something occult implied by the terms 'goal,' 'purpose,' 'expectation,' 'entelechy' " (p. 45). Note that the point at issue here is quite
different from another point discussed by Miller, Galanter and Pribram in
the same general context and involved in their quotation from Hull and
their discussion of the Turing principle — *viz.,* whether the ability to simu-
late a psychological process in a machine is a necessary and sufficient test
of the *completeness* of one's comprehension of the psychological process.
Two readers of an earlier version of this paper, not having read the book,
felt that the tone of these quotations suggests that the authors were
satirizing the experimentalists. If any other readers get the same feeling, I
can only urge that they go back to the original. I hasten to add that, but
for such passages, the book, to my mind, stands head and shoulders above
most contemporary contributions to psychological theory. That theorists
of such stature should fall victim to the kind of scientific claptrap I have
just quoted is a measure of the pseudo-scientific indoctrination of contemporary psychologists.

machines (computers) have been built that behave purposively, *purpose* has become a legitimate scientific concept. Apart from the question as to whether they properly construe the nature of purpose, the crucial present issue is whether faithfulness in the observation of one's subject matter can be validated by any extrinsic considerations. Does one decide upon the nature of behavior on the basis of one's observations of it or on the basis of what one observes a machine to do?

Yes, the issue runs deeper than the service of psychology to the humanities. It concerns the nature of psychology itself and, at the heart of this issue, I find the issue of the *image of man*. Specifically, I suggest, we must choose between two images. The first is that of man as an *active, responsible agent,* not simply a *helpless, powerless reagent.* Man, in this image, is a being who actively does something with regard to some of the things that happen to him; a being who, for instance, tries to increase the likelihood that some things will happen and to decrease the likelihood that others will happen; a being who tries to generate circumstances that are compatible with the execution of his intentions; a being who will try to inject harmony where he finds disharmony or who will sometimes seek to generate disharmony; a being who seeks to shape his environment rather than passively permit himself to be shaped by the latter;—a being, in short, who insists on injecting himself into the causal process of the world around him. If man is said to respond to his environment, the word *response* is to be taken in the sense that it has in active dialogue rather than in the sense of an automatic consequence.

The contrasting and, among psychologists whose careers are devoted to the advancement of the science, the prevailing image of man is that of an impotent reactor, with its responses completely determined by two distinct and separate, albeit interacting, sets of factors: (1) the forces impinging on it and (2) its constitution (including in the latter term, for present purposes, momentary physiological states). *Response* is at all times and at every moment an automatic consequence of the interaction of body and environment. Man, as such, plays no role in determining the outcome of the interplay between constitution and environment. He is implicitly viewed as a robot — a complicatedly constructed and programmed robot, perhaps, but a robot nevertheless.

Note well that the issue is not simply whether behavior is purposive. One may conceive of man as driven by powerful instinctual drives which impel him to seek particular ends; if the environment permits, the ends will be attained and, if not, a definite something else will happen. This model, commonly thought of as a purposive one, leaves man a passive victim of the interplay between constitution and environment no less than do the non-purposive S-R models. Man, as such, has nothing to do with the outcome. He does nothing; things happen to him.

To my mind, we can only hold the second image by violating our cardinal obligation as scientists — to maintain faith with our subject matter, to report scrupulously that which we observe, and to observe fully without willful bias.

The opening sentence of *Ethical Standards of Psychologists* is that "The psychologist is committed to a belief in the dignity and worth of the individual human being." But what kind of dignity can we attribute to a robot? What is there in an impotent reactor that is of such intrinsic value as to require an unconditional commitment by psychologists to a belief in its worth? Can the requirement of such a belief be deduced from the images of man presented in our textbooks or represented in the pages of our scientific journals? Or, contrarily, does it derive from our extra-scientific indoctrination in the spirit of such statements as "And God said: We will make man, in our image and after our likeness"? [5] A Talmudic commentary [6] on the biblical narrative of the creation remarks on a unique aspect of the creation of man. Unlike all others, man was created in the singular — and from the contrast, the rabbis deduce that each man must justify himself in his own life; no man may derive merit from having different ancestry than another. Moreover, the rabbis caution, God is not to be mistaken for an ordinary artisan who "may stamp his seal upon one piece of gold, and upon another. All the impressions are identical. But the Creator of the universe stamped millions of pieces of clay in

---

[5] Gen 1:26. I am aware that the rendition, "We will make," is not a familiar one, but it is a literal translation of the Hebrew text.

[6] *Mishneh, Sanhedrin,* Chap. 4.

his image and no two human beings are alike. For this reason, each person is entitled to say, 'For my sake was the world created,' " and, the rabbis go on to infer, "He who destroys a single life is considered as if he had destroyed the whole world, while he who saves a single life is considered as having saved the whole world." This is the kind of poetic association that is evoked by statements of a commitment by psychologists to a belief in the dignity and worth of the individual human being. Small wonder that some self-appointed high-priests of science found themselves embarrassed by their connection with the American Psychological Association and were led to organize a new society under whose auspices they can pursue the path of what they consider the requirements of science, without fear of contamination. The real wonder is that the rest of us, perhaps unworthy of being called *psychonomists* rather than psychologists, have not been equally embarrassed by the manifest inconsistency of our code of ethics with the image of man incorporated in the prevailing scientific models. It seems to me that we must decide whether the premised commitment in the code is consistent with our defined subject matter.

If there is any antinomy here, it is not as Koch would have it between psychological science and the humanities, but between our professed concerns as psychologists and our dedication to scientific method. Happily, there is no real antinomy at all. The manifest contradiction stems from the falsity of the prevailing model, and not from any contradiction between our concerns and the requirements of science.

I am charging that psychologists maintain the image of man as a passive corporeal entity governed by a thermodynamic principle because of their philosophical precommitments and in flagrant disregard of contradictory information. To avoid misunderstanding, I want to put this charge in perspective before I present my argument. I know that most psychological research, my own included, is in itself indifferent to the metatheoretical issues I shall be discussing. A research finding stands regardless of the metatheoretical frame of reference to which it is referred. Any alternative metatheoretical position that can neither assimilate it nor explain it away is, on the face of the matter, a defective metatheory. I also know that the majority of psychological researchers and teachers give little thought in their workaday lives to philosophical issues and that, in fact, they have no commitment to any consistent view of these matters. Apart from the confusing oscillation between mutually inconsistent frames-of-reference,[7] there are, however, two major ways in which I think we go astray.

The first occurs when we try to integrate the various bits of accumulating psychological information into a more comprehensive coherent whole. A special case of this is that, since we do not derive our research problems out of a vacuum, we do have some more or less vague and tacit notion of how the bit of information we hope to contribute will fit into the totality. Hence, our individual research projects, in themselves indifferent to the metatheoretical issues, are presented in a language and conceptualized in terms that are consistent with our metatheoretical frames of reference. The individual research project thus carries within itself a tacit directive as to how it should be dealt with in a larger integration.

Consider, for instance, research on conditioning. The basic phenomena are interpretable in terms of perceived contextual relationships and relevant motivation. Typically, however, the concepts and phenomena are presented in terms that are more or less explicitly reminiscent of wired switchboards or hydraulic erosion. That is, conditioning, taken as the prototype of all learning, is presented in terms that presuppose a passive image of man. Even when motivation is introduced in the model, it is only to admit a factor that affects the openness of neural pathways. To be sure, the passive-being image implicit in conditioning theory either blandly disregards such simple facts as that the conditioned response is *different* from the unconditioned response or else introduces such complications into the theoretical model as to bring into serious question its greatest alleged virtue, the parsimonious explanation [8]

---

[7] Some psychologists, of course, take pride in not thinking fundamental issues through. In one extreme case, I can recall having a criticism answered by the startling observation, "That is *logic,* not *science,*" as though the scientist has no obligation to think straight.

[8] The issue of parsimony is relevant to my entire argument in a more fundamental sense. The principle states that explanatory constructs should not needlessly be multiplied; that is, it tells us to stay as close as we can to available data. But how is *needlessly* to be assessed? Does it require the bringing to bear of *all* relevant data or does it apply to limited sets of data?

that it offers. My immediate concern, however, is not with the deficiency of the model *per se* but with its effect on the tone and scope of psychological thinking in general.

The second major way in which we go astray is in the distribution of psychological research effort. There may be good reason for such a distribution apart from our metatheoretical frames of reference — for instance, our tendency to follow available research techniques rather than to pursue rationally derived problems. The question, however, is whether we are justified in a sense of contentment about that distribution and the course it is likely to take or whether we ought to be worried about it. In terms of the prevailing image of man, I think we may well rest content. In terms of the active image, I think we should be worried about our failure to generate imperatives in the upcoming generation of psychologists (to say nothing of our own doings) to confront problems which we ourselves avoid.

Let me try to illustrate the point. Whatever else I know about learning, I know that cognitions play an important role in my own learning processes. For me to take non-cognitive learning theories seriously, I must assume that there are, in all other creatures, learning processes that look just like my own but that are really quite different. That is, for what look like quite similar processes, I must assume that different principles of learning operate: one set of principles that apply to me and another set that applies to all other creatures. Simply on the grounds of parsimony, therefore, and Lloyd Morgan's canon notwithstanding, I must assert that the burden of proof rests on the anticognitive theorists — especially so when some of the latter have privately confessed to me that they, too, sometimes operate with cognitive maps.

Note that I have absolutely nothing against any psychologist setting out to determine whether there are dependable S-R relationships when cognitive, etc., processes are disregarded. The point, if any, at which my quarrel with him begins is when he starts pretending that what he has disregarded does not exist or is not a proper concern of the scientific enterprise and when he remains obtusely oblivious to the fact that — having *ignored* cognitive, etc. factors — he is in no position to say anything about the variation or lack of variation in these factors under the conditions of his observations and, hence, that he is equally in no position to judge whether and how the dependability of the relationships he discovers itself depends on the status of the variables he has ignored. The principle of parsimony was never intended as a license to achieve *simplicity* by ignoring the *un*parsimoniousness of nature. The *simplicity* demanded by the principle is of the *explanation,* not of the *explicandum.* Note my emphasis on *needlessly* in my statement of the principle and the phrase "except by necessity" in Occam's original statement.

It follows, then, that, while my charge of flagrant disregard of relevant fact may have bearing on the work and thought of individual psychologists, it is with the totality of our scientific enterprise that I am concerned.

Now, to my argument. I will first ask whether the passive or the active image fits, and in doing so I will examine the issue of freedom *vs.* necessity, deal with the meaning of freedom, and examine the nature of motivation. Second, I will try to show that the contemporary emphasis on the body, which goes hand-in-glove with the passive view, is misplaced. Third, I will argue that a prevailing contemporary model of motivation which also supports the passive image, the tension-reduction concept, is false.

2. Man or Robot?

The fact is that no man can act in terms of the image of himself as a totally impotent being. On any attempt to do so, determinism degenerates into fatalism. We cannot dispose of the issue with a, "What will be, will be." The latter may well be the case; but, if this is so it is only, in part, *because* of what man will do (including, if this happens, *because* he adopts a fatalistic attitude and does nothing), not *despite* what he will do. Now, the class man includes the psychologist who adopts the image of man as an impotent being; and this psychologist, like everyone else, cannot live by this image. He may try to apply it to everyone else, but he cannot apply it to himself as a basis of action. He thus professes a faith in an order of law that applies to everyone else, but, implicitly at least, he reserves to himself a special order of law. He knows that he can intervene in events, but he claims that no one else can — and this in the name of science!

He does not even attempt to redeem himself with the saving grace of accepting the *active role* as a *manifest* property of behavior and then attempt to show that this role is an illusion, to say nothing of the acceptance of responsibility for determining the conditions of the illusion. The premise of the *active role* on which he acts is reserved for himself; for everyone else, and for that matter in his abstract speculation about himself, he sets up a model of behavior which simply denies or ignores the facts of observation. He may take the position that, if he can account for the facts of behavior without reference to the issue of freedom, he has discharged his responsibility as a scientist. But, if the behavior for which he accounts has been arbitrarily defined to exclude a salient apparent aspect of behavior, then the only one who can take such an account seriously is one who places his philosophy above his responsibility to his subject matter. . . .

I am saying that a molar activity unit has consequences as a *molar* unit which are not the same as the consequences of the molecular units that it includes. This contrasts with the view which, if it permits reference to molar units at all, does so only for descriptive purposes — using the molar expression as a shorthand expression for an enumeration of molecular components or as a confession of ignorance of the molecular components — and which assumes that causality can only exist on a molecular level. It is also implicit in my view that *molar* and *molecular* are relative terms, the molecular with regard to one molar unit becoming molar with regard to the molecular units that it includes.

Perhaps the point at issue may be made a bit clearer by referring again to Miller, Galanter and Pribram's conclusion that the concept of *purpose* is now scientifically respectable since the construction of machines that behave purposively. You may recall that, in my earlier allusion to this conclusion, I implied that there is some question as to whether these authors properly construe the nature of purpose. The crux of the issue is contained in their confident expectation (*op. cit.,* p. 16) that what they call a *plan* will turn out to be formally identical with a computer *program.*

Let us consider the kind of machine that is alleged to behave purposively. Such a machine is so designed that at every moment its activity is governed by the opening and closing of circuits which are built into it, and the sequence of openings and closings is controlled by the input. What is uniquely special to such a machine (in contrast to other humanly constructed machines) is that the input itself depends, in part, on the consequences of the immediately preceding action. The feature of feedback, however, does not change the fact that every action is completely determined by the succession of events in the constitution of the machine and the succession of events in its environment. The machine does not engage in a nested hierarchy of activities, such that some higher level of the hierarchy, if carried to completion, temporally includes all lower levels within itself and such that the higher level helps to determine what happens at the lower levels. That is, the machine engages in no molar activities *vis à vis* the environment which, as such, play a role in the selection of their molecular components. The sequence of events is completely determined molecularly. Hence, once the machine is set into operation, there is nothing in it or in its relation to the environment that is in any sense analogous to a *plan* — *plan* being defined by the authors as "any hierarchical process in the organism that can control the order in which a sequence of operations is to be performed" (p. 16). Note that Miller *et al.* assign a controlling function to the hierarchical process, as such, and that they use the term *hierarchical* to refer to the simultaneous organization of behavior at several levels of complexity, from the all-inclusive molar unit to molar subunits down to the molecular units (*cf.* p. 15). In other words, by their own conceptualization, their allegedly purposive machine does *not* have any plan. If there is any plan in the functioning of the computer, the plan is associated with the programmer who must anticipate every possible contingency if the molecular processes of the machine are to continue as the programmer intends; and, if an unanticipated contingency arises, the machine stops functioning. The machine, at best, even if it is programmed to program, functions *according to* plan — the programmer's plan — it has no plan of its own; it functions according to plan in the same sense that any well-designed machine functions according to its user's plan.

Why not assume that the behaving organism also functions in such a quasi-purposive manner — that is, in a succession of molecular actions *in accordance with* a plan externally imposed upon it by some rational or, for that matter, non-rational process? The answer to this question is that such an assumption is in flagrant contradiction of observation — not, mind you, in contradiction of presupposition, hypothesis, or theory, but in contradiction of observation. Behavior *is* hierarchically organized, and the higher hierarchical levels have observable consequences; and if anyone asserts the contrary, the burden of proof rests squarely on his shoulders. What is more, when it comes to such matters as linguistic behavior, Miller, Galanter and Pribram cite proof that such behavior can only — in principle! — be comprehended in terms of such hierarchically organized processes.

Let me now make one final point in my effort to clarify the relatively unfamiliar notion of a motive viewed as a behavior. I hope it will be clear that motivation, as I conceive of it, implicitly involves perception, learning, memory, inference, meaning, and all other psychological processes. The notion of one behavior motivating another would be, in my terms, nonsensical if it were not presupposed that the actor, on some basis, accepts the premise that the latter behavior advances the former. By the same token, motivation is to me the master integrative concept in psychology. I can, for instance, describe the conceptual properties of cognition without reference to motivation, but I cannot do the reverse. I can, for that matter, *describe* any behavior without reference to its motivation or to any of the other conditions that determine it; but I cannot conceive of a complete listing of the conditions of behavior without reference to its motivation.

To recapitulate: I have located some of the determinants of behavior in the concurrent behaviors of the organism and have indicated that these determinants cannot be subsumed under the heading of constitutional conditions, nor under the heading of environmental conditions. It follows that the organism (and this is as true of the animal as of the human) is an active agent in the universe. It is not merely a passive medium for the interplay of constitution and environment; its own activities affect that interplay.

But, you ask, aren't its first activities and hence, sequentially, all of its activities themselves determined? I say, of course — I have already told you that I am a determinist — but once the commitment to activity has been generated, something new has been added to subsequent activity — a motive. Insofar as this happens, it doesn't matter at all with regard to the point at issue whether the motive has been determined by constitution, environment, or their interaction, or whether it was planted there at the whim of a sorcerer, or a divine creator, or whether the creator designed the totality of his creation so that this must inevitably happen to this particular creature. Once a motive is there, it is there — and, through it, the organism has become a partner in the causal process. The search for objects and object-relations that can eliminate the drive is neither constitution nor environment, but an active concern of the individual.

Now, let me return to the issue of *freedom*. Whether we assert *freedom* or *necessity* depends on the frame of reference. Insofar as the frame includes all of the determinants of an event, the event must happen — but it is only a tautology to add that if the frame does not include all of the determinants, then the event is not completely determined within that frame.

If, then, the behavior of an animal is not completely determined within a frame that includes only environment-facts and, separately, body-facts, the animal is left with some degrees of freedom. What else has anyone ever meant by freedom than that the individual's motivation plays some role in determining his behavior?

Let me also note that the generation of a motive may be in part determined by an already existing motive. Thus, I am holding my pen because I am writing, but I am writing because I am delivering a message; and I am delivering the message because . . . — well, maybe I had better not go into that.

I think that such a hierarchy, or *nest,* of motives is not beyond a rat — so that, even in the case of a rat, not all of its motives are wholly constitutionally-environmentally determined. Man can, of course, carry out such hierarchical processes to a degree that presumably cannot be matched by a rat. He can, for instance, enter into activities with extremely long-range goals. Thus, even relatively young humans have been known to undertake programs of study that last for four or more years. This commitment can motivate them to undertake the shorter range behaviors of doing passing work in certain courses that would otherwise not arouse a shadow of an interest, and the latter undertaking may in turn motivate them to read and report on certain books that they would otherwise rather not be caught dead with, and the latter commitment may in its turn motivate them to do a lot of other reading that will make the book intelligible and facilitate the writing of a report, and, lo, somewhere at the bottom of the hierarchy, there may come the motivation to take pen in hand.

I have obviously oversimplified the nested hierarchical structure of motivation involved in getting through college, have paid no attention to the relevance of the college situation to other and more embracing long-range motives, and have not mentioned the emergence of motivations in the college context that *per se* have nothing to do with the furtherance of the behavior of getting the coveted sheepskin. My point is, however, that when we get to deal with motives that are rooted in motives, we have come a long way indeed from actions like reflexes which are fully determined by the interplay of constitution and environment.

There is also another point that can be drawn from the college-study situation. There undoubtedly are motives that can rather quickly be traced to the discomforts of drive states; thus, the motivation to get substances that can allay hunger and, hence, the motivation to behave in ways that will facilitate getting these substances. In the college-study case, however, if we attempt to retrace the derivational path that motivates the most circumscribed behavior mentioned — i.e., the student's taking his pen in hand — we are led further and further away from immediate drive states.

I have elsewhere [9] developed some concepts which are germane. I have already, without naming it, discussed one of these concepts, the *derivation of motives* — i.e., the fact that carrying out a behavior may require some subsidiary behavior which in turn may require a behavior subsidiary to it. I want now to recall two other concepts, that of the *perpetuation of motives* and that of the *imbrication of motives*.

By the *perpetuation of motives* I mean that, because of the recurrence of distressing bodily states and because of difficulties in carrying out the relieving behaviors, the *conditions* of performing the latter become continuing concerns of the individual. The individual thus continues to act with regard to the distresses engendered by drives even while the latter do not exist. Similarly, in the case of many derived behaviors: difficulties in carrying out these behaviors make for continuing concern with the *conditions* of satisfying them so that the individual continues to act with regard

---

[9] "Personality and Typology," *J. Soc. Psychol.* 18: 89-109 (1943); "The Awareness of Self and the Structure of the Ego," *Psychol. Rev.* 51 (1944), pp. 304-314.

to the execution of certain behaviors even while there is no immediate requirement of them. Thus, a person may be concerned with getting food even while he is not hungry; and he may be concerned with achieving recognition even while he has no immediate need for recognition. That is, hunger and recognition-seeking, and many other motives, become perpetuated activities of the individual; and they go on motivating other behaviors at times when they themselves do not *have to be* satisfied.

Note that a perpetuated motive is not to be confused with an intermittently recurring behavior. That perpetuated motives are indeed *continuing* concerns is evidenced by their effect on other behaviors and by the vigilance of the individual with respect to circumstances that may have bearing on them, even while he seems to be engaged in irrelevant activities. I am not saying that a perpetuated motive may not seem to be interrupted, but that, if it stops being a central activity, it will be resumed without reinstigation and that, even while seemingly interrupted, the person stays sensitive to data that are relevant to its again becoming a central activity.

By the *imbrication of motives* I mean the interpenetration of motives that results from the fact that behaviors are not univocally related to the motives from which they are derived or to the behaviors that they motivate. That is, the same behavior may be derived from a variety of motives and, depending on circumstances, motivate a variety of different behaviors. A particular sex behavior, for instance, may be related to the palliation of sexual hungers, to the maintenance of self-esteem, to the debasing or the glorification or the fulfillment of the needs of the sexual object, to the achievement of economic security — to any, or to some, or simultaneously to all of these or to other motives. On the other hand, these motives (and others that, in themselves, never call for sex behavior) may require sexual restraint; and the perpetuated motive to indulge may itself, depending on the circumstances, call for non-indulgence at a particular time.

In brief, as in the case of sex, any motive may become complexly interrelated with other motives, and itself become profoundly modified from what it might otherwise be as it is drawn into such a complex network of relationships. A behavior may even become a motive of the behaviors that initially motivated it. Thus, because being admired may enhance a person's power and because power may evoke admiration, admiration-seeking and power-seeking may become reciprocally motivating — and both may motivate and be motivated by striving for achievement, efforts to attain some measure of autonomy, and so on and so forth. Some behaviors may have simultaneous bearing on so many others as to become dominant continuing concerns of the individual.

The net effect of motivational derivation, perpetuation, and imbrication is that stable, self-sustaining systems of motives develop. Such motivational systems, commonly referred to as *character* and *personality,* are a long way from the primitive distresses and pleasures associated with particular bodily states that may have started these developments. My earlier allusion to the fact that the back-tracking of the motivational derivations that give rise to particular behaviors often — let me now add, most often — lead further and further away from physiological drive states may now be understood in terms of the involvement of such motivational systems and long-range continuing behaviors.

The order of freedom thus envisioned is high indeed. Among the determinants of behavior that, in principle, cannot be dealt with in purely constitutional terms or in purely environmental terms, or in terms of the interplay of purely constitutional and purely environmental factors, are motives, and motives of motives, and a complex personality and character structure. Man not only plays an active role in the causal complex of the world about him, but he also plays an active role in shaping himself, both as a psychological being and, need I add in these days of psychosomatic medicine, as a biological organism.

The role of the psychologist in investigating man, so imaged, is to investigate the many degrees of freedom left over when we have discounted the purely environmental and the purely constitutional factors — that is, to discover and to order and to investigate the conditions and consequences of the third set of determinants. And, if in my exposition I have given the primary place to motivation, let me remind you that motivation as I have expounded it, implicitly involves perception, learning, memory, inference, meaning, and any other psychological process that you may care to designate. In other words, there is no implication in anything that I have said that psychologists should stop studying perception, or learning, or whatever else may be of interest to them. I am talking about the frame within which the outcomes of such studies are to be integrated and about philosophical presuppositions which favor or disfavor theorization and derivative research which make an honest and square look at human behavior possible. I am saying that we should not permit ourselves to be seduced, as so many of us have been, by those pretentious high-order conceptualizations of psychology that would deny to man the quality that is inalienably his, the quality of freedom — and, in the denial, make man, as a psychological agent, inaccessible. As the distinguished neurologist Kurt Goldstein remarked to one of my former students, "Aaron," he said, "if the patient doesn't agree with the book, throw the book away! The book was written about the patient, not the patient about the book." In the same vein, I say: If the scientific conceptualizations do not agree with man, throw the conceptualizations away; the science is about man, not man about science.

But I have advanced the image of man as an active and free agent in the context of a deterministic viewpoint. Is the notion of responsibility compatible with such a viewpoint? By *responsibility,* I am merely recognizing that the activities of man have consequences, and that major determinants of these activities are to be found in man as he has been shaped at the time he carries out these activities. I assume that the concept applies only to those activities into which he is not driven by forces beyond his control so that his motivation becomes irrelevant and I also assume that he is in a position to anticipate, if not the precise consequences that ensue, then at least the risks of some unfavorable consequences and the probabilities of favorable ones.

What of man's essential dignity and worth? What greater measure of dignity and worth can be accorded to him than to recognize, in the fact of his motives helping to generate motives, his role in his own creation? Let me again refer to the first chapter of Genesis. I have already mentioned one difference between the account of the creation of man and the remaining order of creation — *viz.,* that man was initially created in the singular. Let me now mention a few other striking differences. Every one of the acts of creation,

except for the creation of man, is introduced by a simple commandment. Thus: "And God said, let there be light." When it comes
to the creation of man, the text shifts from the imperative mood
to the simple future tense. "We will make man," is the statement
attributed to God. Moreover, every one of the acts of creation,
again excepting the creation of man, is accompanied by an affirmation that the commandment was implemented. Thus: "and there
was light," "and it was so," or, simply, "and God saw that it was
good." Now, the phrase, "and it was so," does occur in the context
of the work of the sixth day, but this affirmation comes — not with
the statement of the creation of man — but in a later context of
God's statement to man (by now, in the plural, including both
male and female) describing their dominion.

In brief, the creation of man is, remarkably, stated in the future
tense; and there is no affirmation that the creation has in fact been
completed. Add the implication of the initial statement of the
creation of man in the singular form — *viz.,* that no man may
justify his existence by appeal to his special ancestry, but must
account for himself. Finally, note the implications of the plural,
"We," in "We will make man." If the "we" is the *"we"* of majesty,
why the delay? Does it refer to the hosts of heaven? Why should
God suddenly need collaborators? What more sensible account is
there, then, but that the *we* is literally a plural form which takes
each individual human being into partnership with God in the act
of the completion of the creation of man? And what more magnif-
icent creation, short of the creation of the universe itself, can be
attributed to God than a self-creating being?[10]

Whether you take the bible text as divine revelation or as a
humanly inspired allegory which nevertheless expresses one of
mankind's greatest and most influential aspirations, the point of
my little bit of biblical exegesis has been to show that a central
theme of the coupling of the image of man with the image of God
is the role asssigned to man with respect to his own creation. In

---

[10] Although the development of the implication of the biblical text that man
is in partnership with God in his own creation, as here given, is perhaps a
novel one — the implication itself is not merely something that I am now,
in the twentieth century, reading into the text; it has been a recurrent
theme in the rabbinic literature, finding support in various ways through
interpretation of the text.

any case, however, you prefer to take the bible and whatever you may make of my exposition of its first chapter, the image, I suggest, is a true one, I further suggest that any psychological science that does not face up to the aspects of the image that I have tried to develop runs the risk of concerning itself with psychological trivia arbitrarily torn out of the context of their natural setting; and such a science can certainly justify no commitment of psychologists to a belief in the dignity and worth of the individual human being.

3. Personality: Integumented or Open?

I want now to turn to a second aspect of the image of man, and I hope you will forgive me if I again refer to the same biblical text. If one accepts that man was created in the image of God, then it follows that, in some sense, God exists in the form of the image of man. Now, if you look at a man, the most obvious thing that you see is his external physical habitus, and, on this basis, you infer that God, too, must have a head, eyes, ears, nose, mouth, neck, trunk, arms, legs, and so on — a God that is bound by the limits of his integument just as is man and, naturally, you endow him with the gender of the superior sex. No mature bible scholar can, of course, take seriously any such literally anthropomorphic image of God. But, if we reject the latter image, then does it not follow that, in focusing on his physical habitus, we have somehow misperceived the essential nature of man? That is, the image of man that is projected by the bible cannot be taken as referring to the physical man. If the emphasis on corporeality falsifies the image of God, it by the same token falsifies the image of man.

Again, I do not here refer to the bible for its authority, but to pose a problem. I take the bible, for the present purposes, as an influential document which offers an image of man that is in striking contrast with the image that prevails in contemporary scientific psychology. Contemporary psychologists, it seems to me, tend to be rather obsessed with the corporeality of man and to be constantly diverted from the human being to the human body. This is entirely consistent with their view of man as a robot. Conversely, the corporeal image of man makes it somewhat easier to view him as a robot. In any case, the emphasis on corporeality puts the image of man into a violently distorted perspective.

The emphasis on corporeality as the essential quality of man is, of course, evident in the naive — if persistent — effort to reduce psychological to bodily process. This is again a matter of philosophy dictating psychological theory. If one starts with the presupposition that only that which is physically palpable is real, then obviously one must either deny the reality of psychological events or reduce them to physical terms. Apart from the inherent absurdity of such a position which takes sensation as a criterion of physical reality and then takes the latter to deny the reality of sensation, those who share this reductionist aspiration carefully shut their eyes to the fact that there are manifestly no sensations (to say nothing of such matters as aspirations) in the body and that there is no unexplored space to find them in. To show that some brain damage will result in a loss of sight is no more to equate sight with the functioning of that part of the brain than a parallel operation on the eyes would equate sight with the eyes. Nor does what goes on in eyes, neural pathways, and brain location add up to vision. The simple logic of the matter is that these parts of the body, and events occurring in them, may be necessary correlates and conditions of vision, but conditions and correlates are not the same as that which they are conditions and correlates of. The reductionists are, of course, impervious to logic; what is more important is that they are callously indifferent and faithless to their professed subject matter.

Do not misunderstand me. I do not reject physiological psychology as a legitimate field of scientific inquiry. I deem it a fine thing that there are scientists who concern themselves with the body. I cannot, however, recall having ever come across anything to encourage the hope that we are likely to learn much about the bodily conditions and concomitants of psychological processes from people who habitually confuse an aching-*tooth* with a tooth-*ache,* enzymatic deficiencies with mental retardation, the conditions of events with the events that they condition — or, for that matter, from people who industriously speculate about the physiological conditions and concomitants of psychological events long before they are clear about the nature of the psychological events whose conditions and concomitants they are seeking. Nor do I know of a single instance in which a strictly physiological inquiry — that is, one framed with the objective of casting light on the physiological conditions of psychological processes, whether such an inquiry is speculative, empirical, or experimental — has contributed to an improved description or classification of the latter or to any discoveries or improved comprehension of interrelationships among them.

The naive reductionists do not, however, bother me. I do become bothered when I see more sophisticated and responsible psychologists falling into a similar trap. It bothers me, for instance, to see psychologists who ought to know better become blinded by a focus upon the body so that they fail to observe that essentiality to biological survival is not necessarily correlated with the significance of the reduction of a particular drive in the stream of behavior. How many of the textbook writers who list thirst and hunger among the most important of human motives recognize that they have taken as their criterion of importance a biological rather than a psychological desideratum? What proportion of human behavior, in the ordinary course of human events, is influenced by the body's dependence on the maintenance of a supply of water? Or, even within the restricted context of eating behavior, how much of such behavior is conditioned solely by states of nutritional deficiency?

There is a story, perhaps apochryphal, of Gregory Zilboorg asking a class, "What does the liver have to do with psychoneurosis?" To the reply, "Why, nothing, Dr. Zilboorg," it is said that he surveyed the class coldly and scathingly demanded, "Can someone without a liver have a psychoneurosis?" There is doubtless as wholesome a lesson for psychologists as for psychoanalytic trainees in the anecdote, and it is just as cogent if you substitute *perception* or *learning* for *psychoneurosis*. Does it follow, however, that psychologists ought to devote a major share of their teaching and research to the liver?

Let me confront the issue of corporeality in the image of man in the case of a psychologist who, in all other respects, comes as close to a valid image of man as any psychologist I know. That this psychologist should elect to stand by the corporeal aspect of the image is a measure of the power of our deeply ingrained habits of thinking along these lines. In a recent paper,[11] Gordon Allport presents the view that the person is an open system. He advances four criteria of such a system: first, that in an open system "there is intake and output of both matter and energy"; second, that "there is the achievement and maintenance of steady (homeostatic) states"; third, that "there is generally an increase in complexity and differentiation of parts"; and, fourth, that "at least at the human level, there is more than mere intake and output of matter and energy: there is extensive transactional commerce with the environment."

I call your attention to the fourth criterion. It is not a distinct criterion, but merely a somewhat broadened version of the first. In fact, as stated, it is not a criterion of open systems at all because it explicitly does not apply to all open systems. If we were simply to rewrite the first criterion to say that, "in an open system there is intake and output of both matter and energy which, in some instances and particularly so at the human level, involves extensive transactional commerce with its surround," we would have incorporated what Allport wants to say in his fourth criterion without having to advance a noncriterial criterion.

So, Allport has only three criteria. What of it? Well, I think it no error that, in his combing of definitions of open systems, Allport counts *four* criteria. It seems clear from his discussion of his fourth criterion that he actually does have a fourth criterion in mind that is different from what he stated as the fourth criterion, but that he shies away from putting the real fourth criterion into words because his rejection of it would also compel him to reject his view of the person as an open system. The real fourth criterion, I suggest, is that an open system has no definite, clear-cut boundary with respect to its surround.

This criterion, never explicitly faced as such, Allport rejects in favor of the view of "personality as something integumented, as residing within the skin." He refers to some theorists like Kurt Lewin, Martin Buber, and Gardner Murphy who challenge this view, "considering it too closed"; but, in the main, Allport attributes the rejection of the integumented personality concept to

---

[11] G. W. Allport, "The Open System in Personality Theory," *J. Abnorm. Soc. Psychol.* 61 (1960), pp. 301-310.

Eastern philosophy. "As Western theorists," he tells us, "most of us . . . hold the integumented view of the personality system. I myself do so."

Now, it should be apparent that, whatever the personalistic and individualistic emphases of the major strands of Western traditions and thought, Professor Allport is still begging the question with regard to the fourth criterion of an open system. What is at issue is not the personalistic and individualistic emphasis, but the question of whether such an emphasis, even if accepted, necessarily requires an integumented view of the personality.

It is my opinion that neither Professor Allport nor anyone else can locate within the bounds of the integument what he thinks is to be found there. He writes that "It is the duty of psychology, I think, to study the person-system, meaning thereby the attitudes, abilities, traits, trends, motives, and pathology of the individual — his cognitive styles, his sentiments, and individual moral nature and their interrelations." I submit that not one of these components of a person can be located in the interior of the integumented organism. I cannot conceive of an ability stripped of all reference to the objects to be manipulated when the ability is put to work. If to talk of an ability you must at least implicitly refer to objects not included within the bounds of the integument, then the concept of an ability has no meaning if it is restricted to something that is completely included within these bounds. If *writing* means setting down intelligible marks on paper, then the *ability to write* means that a person is capable of setting down intelligible marks on paper. But what is the meaning of *ability to write* when you eliminate the reference to paper? I can conceive of some *conditions* of an ability as being within the body, but not of the objective reference. I similarly cannot conceive of any procedure that will permit us to describe or to observe an ability, a cognitive style, a sentiment without simultaneously encompassing actor and object; a trait without repeated observation of transactions between person and environment; a hallucination or a delusion without checking on the true transorganismic situation; a moral nature with no external reference.

I have stated that the cardinal obligation of a scientist is to maintain faith with his subject matter, and I do not know of a single psychological datum that violates the rule that it involves a relationship between an actor and an object. But psychologists do go on pretending that the datum is still complete when it has been stripped of the object. They do this, not because of what they observe, but because of what they think they should be observing.

To repeat, Allport cannot escape the fact that what he includes in the person-system is transactional in character. Well then, why does he not face up to this fact? Because he is afraid that in conceiving the personality in transactional terms he will lose the person in a series of transient transactions. "There is," he affirms, "a persistent though changing person-system in time, clearly delimited by birth and death." This affirmation, I must agree, accords in the main with my own observation — except that I am not quite ready to agree that the newborn infant is already a person. Moreover, I must agree that the person-system engages in transient transactions that Allport wants to accommodate in his defective fourth criterion. Does this leave me in the paradoxical position of claiming that a *persisting* personality is a transactional system composed of *transient* transactions?

Note that Allport assumes that the only thing about a person which persists is the body. What he overlooks is the persisting system of derived, perpetuated, and imbricating motives and (something that I have discussed elsewhere) [12] the fact that at the heart of this system is the self, with its permanent and unchanging core—*viz.,* that the self is always at the center of the phenomenal space-time continuum. This system, when it finds itself in a particular situation, does engage in transactions that come to an end as new situations develop and then becomes involved in new transactions. As I write this paper, for instance, I can foresee that the writing will come to an end, that the time will probably come when I will be reading the paper, and that (although it may be difficult for you at this moment to share my foresight) the time will then come when I will have finished reading the paper. Such a series of transactions does not define my personality. The enduring motivational structure that characterizes me, however, does enter into

---

[12] "The Awareness of Self and the Structure of the Ego," *loc. cit.*

each of these transactions and this does not alter the fact that the enduring motivational system is itself transactional in character.

The enduring motivational structure, moreover, does seem to be intimately bound to the body. It moves around with the body, many of its conditions are demonstrably in the body, it is in many ways concerned with the body, and there is no critical observational evidence that it can survive the body. None of which serves to prove that it is identical with the body or that it is contained in the body. The turning of a wheel is not in the wheel nor in the surround of the wheel; it is a relationship between the wheel and its surround. In the same manner, I conceive of the personality as a complex system of relationships of the organism to its surround.

The essential human quality is, thus, one of commitment to a developing and continuing set of interdependent, interacting, and mutually modifying enterprises, the requirements of which influence day-to-day and moment-to-moment activities. I am not saying that such commitment is the only concern of the human being, that there may not be crises (crises associated with intensified drive states or intense emotion or with circumstances in which one or more of the component enterprises is gravely threatened) in which the overall commitment is temporarily overwhelmed. I am not saying that the human being may not also become involved in relatively isolated enterprises that escape the internal discipline of mutual modification characteristic of jointly undertaken enterprise. Nor am I saying that he may not so misperceive or misconstrue his situation as to take actions that are not consonant with his commitment. I am saying that the commitment I have described is what most distinguishes man from a mere biological organism, that to the extent that he has failed to develop such a commitment he is not yet human, and that to the extent that cortical injury or other stresses may permanently disrupt the commitment he becomes dehumanized. The other matters to which I have just referred (the overwhelming crises, the unintegrated enterprises, the misperceptions and misconstructions), I cannot take the time to discuss now — except to note that they are also part of my image of man, perhaps the part that makes him somewhat less than godlike.

4. Motivation: Entropy or Commitment?

There is still one more matter on my agenda. My talk of commitment and the general conceptions of motivation that I have advanced are a long way from the conception of motivation associated with the prevailing image of man among contemporary psychologists. I refer to the notion of motivation as tension reduction.[13] Being based on an analogy to thermodynamic systems, this is one of the key conceptualizations that helps to maintain the image of man as a robot. I know that this notion has been challenged from time to time [14] and that it is perhaps becoming more fashionable to do so.[15] Even so, I think that the tension reduction model is still the prevailing one; and, like so many aspects of the prevailing image of man, it is manifestly false.

It is not that Hullians, let us say, are not aware that consummatory responses — typically, highly stirred up states — and the crescendo of activities that often lead up to them can be intensely pleasurable. It is simply that, by the rules of scientific behavior that they have adopted, it is scientifically illegitimate to mention such a fact. That a rule can wipe out a fact is not surprising from people who make a virtue out of being more concerned with their observational operations than with the phenomena which these operations are designed to help them observe. At any rate, they would have us believe that since it does not exist insofar as science is concerned, pleasure does not signify that the activity is rewarding, but that the reward is the aftermath, the reduction of excitation or tension.

Contrast such a view with the following summary of observations by Freud. He wrote that the erogenous zones

---

[13] It is possible to define "tension" to mean simply that the actor is still separated from his goal. In this sense, a tension-reduction principle is tautologically implicit in any concept of motivation. I am not here using the term in this sense. The tension-reduction principle under discussion involves the notion that any excitation or stirred up state impels the organism into activity that will eliminate the excitation and restore quiescence.

[14] Cf., for instance, S. A. Diamond, "A Neglected Aspect of Motivation," *Sociometry* 2 (1939), pp. 77-85.

[15] Cp. R. W. White, "Motivation Reconsidered: The Concept of Competence," *Psychol. Rev.* 66 (1959), pp. 297-333.

are all used to provide a certain amount of pleasure by *being stimulated* in a way appropriate to them. This pleasure then leads to an increase in tension which in its turn is responsible for producing the necessary energy for the conclusion of the sexual act. The penultimate stage of that act is once again the appropriate *stimulation* of an erotogenic zone . . . by the appropriate object . . . and from the *pleasure yielded by this excitation* the motor energy is obtained . . . which brings about the discharge of the sexual substances. This last pleasure is the highest in intensity . . . it is wholly a pleasure of satisfaction and with it the tension of the libido is for the time being extinguished.

This distinction between the one kind of pleasure due to the *excitation* of erotogenic zones and the other kind due to the discharge of the sexual substances deserves . . . a difference in nomenclature. The former may be suitably described as "fore-pleasure" in contrast to the "end-pleasure". . . . (Italics added.)[16]

Alas, even if we are disposed to disregard Freud's overlooking of the pleasure of the orgasm *per se* (a highly stirred up state and properly described as "end pleasure" so that Freud's "end pleasure" would have to be described as "after pleasure") Freud's conceptualization is no better than that of other psychologists impressed by the entropy principle. He writes that,

I must insist that a feeling of tension necessarily involves unpleasure. What seems to me decisive is the fact that a feeling of this kind is accompanied by an impulsion to make a change in the psychological situation, that it operates in an urgent way which is wholly alien to the nature of the feeling of pleasure (*Ibid.,* p. 209).

Immediately, he notes a paradox:

If, however, the tension of sexual excitement is counted as

---

[16] S. Freud, "Three Essays on Sexuality," in *The Standard Edition of the Complete Psychological Works of Sigmund Freud,* Vol. 7 (London: Hogarth, 1953).

unpleasurable feeling, we are at once brought up against the fact that it is also undoubtedly felt as pleasurable. . . . How then are this unpleasurable tension and this feeling of pleasure to be reconciled? (*Ibid.,* p. 209).

One might think to resolve the paradox by assuming that the first kind necessarily gives rise to excitations in other parts of the body — thereby withdrawing the excitation from the parts first aroused and fulfilling the tension-reduction condition of pleasure — and so on until the final climax when all tension disappears. Not only is the assumption of a necessary progression demonstrably false, as is the further assumption that such pleasure necessarily, as Freud suggests, "soon passes over into the most obvious unpleasure if it cannot be met by a further accession of pleasure" (p. 210), but Freud himself notes that "In every case in which tension is produced by sexual processes it is accompanied by pleasure; even in the preparatory changes in the genitals a feeling of satisfaction of some kind is plainly to be observed" (*Ibid.,* p. 209). That is, Freud agrees that some states of excitation are *per se* pleasurable.

In the "Three Essays," Freud disclaims any intention to deal with the problem of the paradox other than to learn as much as possible from the sexual instance. In 1924, however, he added a footnote indicating that he had attempted to solve the problem in his paper on "The Economic Problem of Masochism." [17] The footnote gives no indication of repentance with regard to a former error, so that it seems fair to conclude that, subsequent to the latter publication, Freud still took seriously the views just quoted. Unfortunately, from the viewpoint of a consistent position, he does little more in the relevant section of the latter than to state the problem in what is for him its most critical form — *viz.,* that the pleasure and Nirvana principles, respectively serving the life and death instincts, have been stated in identical terms, *i.e.,* the reduction of excitation. Having stated the problem and noted that excitation may be pleasurable, he writes:

Pleasure and unpleasure, therefore, cannot be referred to in an increase or decrease of a quantity (which we describe as

---

[17] *Standard Edition,* Vol. 19 (London: Hogarth, 1961).

"tension due to stimulus"), although they obviously have a great deal to do with that factor. It appears that they depend, not on this quantitative factor, but on some characteristic of it which we can only describe as a qualitative one. If we were able to say what this qualitative characteristic is, we should be much further advanced in psychology. Perhaps it is the rhythm, the temporal sequence of changes, rises and falls in the quantity of stimulus. We do not know (p. 160).

In other words, Freud's effort to deal with satisfaction in terms of quantities of excitation has come to just about nought, to say nothing of utter confusion. Freud, however, has, at least, the virtue of remaining an honest observer; he remains in the state of confusion by refusing to permit his theories to dominate his observation.

Let me consider one other instance in which the tension-reduction principle looms large. Festinger,[18] explicitly accepting the meaning of *reward* as referring to the reduction of excitation and starting with the observation that, by the criterion of resistance to extinction, less adequate rewards may lead to more effective learning than more adequate ones, argues for the need to supplement the principle that organisms learn to repeat those activities that lead to reward with a second principle which is "rather of an opposite character."

The second principle, Festinger finds in his general theory of *cognitive dissonance.* As applied to the paradoxes of learning behavior, Festinger's principle may be stated as follows: If an organism "exerts a great deal of effort, or endures pain, in order to reach some ordinary objective, there is a strong tendency for him *to persuade himself* that the objective is especially valuable or especially desirable." (Italics added.) Or, more fundamentally: There is a need to reduce the dissonance between the cognition that one has voluntarily committed oneself to an activity which, "all other things being equal," one would avoid doing and the cognition that the reward that has been obtained is inadequate; and, "this dissonance can be reduced if the organism *can persuade*

---

18 L. Festinger, "The Psychological Effects of Insufficient Rewards," *Amer. Psychol.* 16 (1961), pp. 1-11.

himself that he really likes the behavior in which he is engaged or if *he enhances for himself* the value of what he has obtained as a result of his actions." (Italics again added.) Four objections can be raised to the adequacy of Festinger's formulation. In presenting these objections, I hope it will be clear that I am not here discussing the general theory of cognitive dissonance, nor other applications of dissonance theory to problems of motivation, but the particular application I have just described.

First, as Festinger himself notes, one means of reducing the dissonance, and the one which "is undoubtedly the one most frequently employed by organisms," is to refuse to perform the action again — so that the formulation leaves totally unclear why an organism should *ever* go to the trouble of persuading itself that the activity has been worthwhile. To say, as Festinger does, that he is considering "only those situations in which this means of reducing dissonance is not available to the organism. That is, . . . only situations in which the organism is somehow tricked or seduced into continuing to engage in the activity, in spite of the dissonance which is introduced," merely begs the question. For there exists no dissonance until the organism has discovered that it has been tricked or seduced, or at least that the returns are not as great as anticipated. At this point, the organism does in fact have the alternative of withdrawal — or, if it does not, then there is no dissonance since the continued participation is not voluntary. If it does elect to continue, therefore, is it not more plausible to assume that it is getting more satisfaction than the experimenter is willing to credit — perhaps from the seduction itself, perhaps from other sources — and may not this extra measure of satisfaction wrap the entire situation in a rosier glow than would otherwise have been experienced?

Second, it is questionable, in principle, whether the condition, "all other things being equal," can ever be satisfied if the organism voluntarily commits itself to activity that it would avoid in other contexts. Thus, the pain encountered in the context of voluntary participation in an experiment for the advancement of science cannot be compared to a similarly induced pain in an accidental encounter with a live wire; nor a pain experienced by a teen-ager with his girl friend as an observer with a similarly induced pain when only his mother is present as an observer. Perhaps Festinger would agree that the phrase, "all other things being equal," should be deleted from the statement of the principle, but then what would this change imply for the conditions of dissonance? If I set out to determine how much pain I can endure, is it dissonance that increases my degree of gratification with every increment of pain that I can stand?

In the third place, if — as in Festinger's experiments — there is no voluntary commitment whatever to that portion of the activity which involves the expenditure of extra effort or the endurance of unanticipated frustration or pain, or if the degree of pain, effort, or frustration turns out to be more than anticipated, then there is no reason for the first of the two "dissonant" cognitions. Why should a person not say to himself, "That damned experimenter (or salesman, or whatever): He sure concealed from me what I was letting myself in for (or buying, or whatever)"?

Finally, the principle is stated without limit. Thus, Festinger's rats should develop more and more affection toward the delay box, the longer they are delayed — an outcome which I must, to say the least, doubt. By the same reasoning, a hostess who can count on the politeness of her guests should serve only tough and rubbery steaks; the tougher the steak, the better — or so they will persuade themselves — it tastes. I am certain that Festinger does not mean to apply the theory without limit; but, if the theory does not contain within itself any principle that defines its limits of application, then it is no theory; for, in any new application, we have no theoretical way of anticipating whether the limit has been exceeded.

It is to be noted that Festinger shares the premise behind the principle which he declares to be insufficient—*viz.,* that stimulation, effort, pain, frustration, anything that impedes the discharge of tension or that results in the building up of tension should evoke avoidance reactions and displeasure; otherwise he would not need to account for the fact that activities which are less effective in reducing such excitations are sometimes advantaged in comparison with activities that are more effective in doing so. If my criticisms of Festinger's theory are sound, however, dissonance theory does not provide the corrective needed for the tension-reduction principle. I suggest to you that this application of Festinger's theory is so fundamentally unsound because, among other things, Festinger's initial premise, the tension-reduction principle, is false to start with.

My own views of these matters are relatively simple minded. They are based on crude observations. They are not as attractive as tightly constructed hypothetico-deductive theoretical systems. Their only virtue is that they seem to fit the facts of human and, to some extent, of animal behavior.

To begin with, I distinguish between *pleasure,* a turbulent, stirred-up, zestful enjoyment, and *pleasantness,* a relaxed, serene, calm, passive enjoyment.

Pleasure is associated with certain kinds of sensory stimulation. It also comes with the sense of advancement of one's enterprises; increases, probably in accordance with some principle of diminishing returns, when the advancement occurs in the face of difficulties (including pseudo-threatening conditions that one knows will be overcome); is proportionately greater, depending on the number and weight of the perpetuated motives that are directly entailed in the advancing behavior; and reaches maxima as component behaviors are successfully consummated, the relative heights of the successive maxima depending also on the degree of effort required for successful consummation and the direct bearing of the component behavior on the number and weight of the perpetuated motives entailed.

Pleasantness is associated with reduced effort or monotonous stimulation, especially as a sequel to a period of intensely pleasurable sensory stimulation which has run its full course or as an aftermath of the successful consummation of effortful behavior.

There are other modes of sensory stimulation which are associated with displeasure, discomfort or pain. So is the sense of non-advancement of one's enterprises, the displeasure mounting with the degree of expectation of failure, and perhaps reaching a maximum at the point at which failure is definite. The aftermath of the acceptance of failure may, however, be quite pleasant.

I have, in the preceding paragraphs, repeatedly omitted the phrase, "in the absence of contrary conditions" — *viz.,* the concurrence of conditions that produce opposite effects. Other qualifications are also needed, particularly that the pleasures and displeasures associated with one's enterprises tend to dominate the pleasures and displeasures associated with sensory stimulation. A person committed to losing weight may, for instance, find it gratifying to leave the dinner table hungry, and pain may be gratifying in the context of a test of endurance or in the context of expiation of guilt. Similarly, sexual congress with one's ideal mate may be quite unpleasurable if it occurs under conditions that threaten the maintenance of self-esteem or that enhance one's vulnerability to other kinds of threat. Carrying on with pleasurable activity beyond the point of satiation converts the pleasure into displeasure, sometimes because of a change in conditions of sensory stimulation, sometimes because of the mounting displeasure at the non-occurrence of a desired consummation, sometimes because of an increasing sense of urgency to attend to temporarily deferred other commitments. Similarly, pleasantness cannot be indefinitely prolonged; nor does it seem to be compatible with an expectation that it will never give way to pleasure.

The assurance of the conditions of future pleasure and of the avoidance of future displeasure may, and typically does, become a component of the total system of enterprises to which an individual is committed, but this is by no means necessarily the dominant component of the system. Let me, however, note some special aspects of this enterprise which flatly contradict the notion that the absence of excitation is a rewarding state. A person who loses his desire for food does not typically rest content in his blessed state, but finds this an occasion to seek medical or psychotherapeutic assistance; and I suspect that even a dyed-in-the-wool S-R operationalist would, *horribile dictu*, seriously contemplate going to a psychoanalyst if he finds himself without sexual libido or given to quick discharge of sexual tension by virtue of premature ejaculation. Most of us, I dare say, do not look forward with great enthusiasm to the day when we will be able to satisfy all of the nutritive needs of our bodies and to anticipate hunger by taking an appropriate pill. In matters of food, sex, and other recreational enterprises, human beings have devoted great ingenuity and planning to the development of means and devices to intensify desire and to prolong the period of gratification that precedes repletion.

V. Epilogue

I would thoroughly agree with any critic of these remarks about pleasure if he pointed out that they contain all too many discrete propositions and too many relatively vague terms. I would welcome a neater and more tightly wrapped package. To produce such a package is a scientific goal. But it is a sad commentary on the state of psychological science that almost anyone but the so-called scientific psychologist is willing to take cognizance of these matters. When a psychologist tells me that what I have said applies fairly well to his own case (and I suppose that I can anticipate a marked reduction in such confessions in the future), but that it is not proper for a scientist to say such things, that some matters are better ignored, that it is better for theory construction to adopt such postulates as the tension-reduction principle (regardless of the fact that common observation tells us that the principle is false), that self-contained theories lead to more research (without regard to the question of where such research can possibly lead) — then I can only say to such a fellow that (protestations of self-righteousness, quotations from innumerable philosophers, and accolades from the Psychonomic Society, all to the contrary notwithstanding) he is no scientist. He is the modern counterpart of the medieval scholastic counting angels on a pinhead, albeit he may be accumulating his numbers in the austere environs of a laboratory rather than generating them in the comfort of an armchair or while reclining on a hard cot in a stimulus-deprived monastic cell. He is a fellow who enjoys intellectual games. He is devoted to spinning out, exploring, and articulating his theories. He may even be, and I suppose typically is, devoted to his family and friends and to other psychologists who talk his language and share his biases. He, alas, has no parallel devotion to his subject matter; and a fellow who can treat his subject matter cavalierly is no scientist.

I have been pleading for an approach to man that respects our primary — naturalistic, if you will — observations of his behavior. I am not anti-theoretical and certainly not anti-metatheoretical. I happen to believe that metatheoretically (and soundly metatheoretically based theory, if anyone can come up with the latter) guided studies are most efficient means of advancing knowledge, but the theories should be consistent with our naturalistic observations or, if they are not consistent, start with some reason for believing that the naturalistic observations are in specific ways misleading — misleading, not improper. I am not even opposed to including postulates in the theory that are contradicted by observation, provided that the total postulate-set has been selected with, among other things, an eye to accounting for the manifest contradiction. I am not against middle- or even low-level theories, but I have no use for theories that achieve tightness and rigor, consistency with data, and high predictive accuracy by arbitrarily slicing the psychological subject matter so as to leave out relevant data. I agree that it is sound scientific strategy to work on low level theories before attempting to elaborate all-encompassing theories, but I see no scientific purpose that can be served by taking seriously low- or middle-level theories of which it can be foretold that they cannot possibly fit the totality — not even if they are productive of research, since such research can only either lead nowhere or, at best, turn out to be of some significance by virtue of accidental relevance to an alternative theory which does not suffer from the same limitation. I am not opposed to rigorous experimental research. Quite the contrary, but I see little scientific merit in experiments, no matter how rigorous, that have lost contact with the primary subject matter. I am all in favor of rigorous definitions, sound conceptualization, intersubjective validation, and well-founded, thoroughly tested conclusions; but I am opposed to mistaking these goals of science for its starting point.

I happen to share the belief that it is probably impossible to make observations in a completely open-minded — I am tempted to say, empty-minded — fashion. But, still, we sometimes do make unanticipated observations in the naturalistic setting, and sometimes these may even go contrary to our expectations, and we owe such unexpected observations respect. I have belabored the issue of the tension-reduction principle because it offers a dramatic illustration of how psychologists can ignore the manifest falsity of one of their favorite preconceptions. That it is a favorite preconception is evidenced by the wide variety of psychological theorists who pay obeisance to it. There are not many theoretical issues where you can find a Freud, a Hull, and a Festinger in one corner — and the wrong corner, at that.

It is in the desire to help psychology to do justice to itself by ridding itself of its false images that I have attempted to portray man as I see him. I know that, in the time available, I could not deal with all aspects of that image. Nor have I attempted to give due credit to my psychological predecessors (Freud, E. B. Holt, Pierre Janet, Kurt Lewin, Gardner Murphy, Tolman, Woodworth and many others) in whose thinking my own notions are rooted. Somewhere in the course of my intellectual history that preceded the writing of this paper, however, I realized that I was but re-capturing a rather ancient image, one that has somehow gotten lost in the midst of a great deal of pseudo-scientific claptrap. That is why I have taken the somewhat unusual course among psychologists of turning to the bible for my basic references on the image of man. . . .

C. Commentary and Analysis

There is a deep methodological issue which has serious implications for psychology as a science.[19] Historically, the science of psychology has moved in divergent directions. The original separation from philosophy was effected at the end of the nineteenth century by men like Wundt, Helmholtz, Brentano and others. Since then, psychology has moved in directions determined by the nature of the methods employed and the kinds of problems studied. Experimentalists have employed rigorous scientific method and have concentrated on simple, quantifiable problems. Clinicians, on the other hand, have tended to employ more descriptive and experiential methods and have concentrated on understanding the adaptation of the total living organism. The important point here is

---

[19] W. W. Meissner, "Intervening Constructs — Dimensions of Controversy," *Psychological Review* 67 (1960), pp. 51-72; "The Implications of Experience for Psychological Theory," *Philosophy and Phenomenological Research* (to be published).

that psychology need not restrict itself to a single methodology. The rigidity of the experimental-mathematical approaches is appealing, but there are many important problems that cannot be reduced to these terms. Consequently, one must take care, in speaking of an image of man, that the image of man be consistent with a given psychological approach and that the logical grounds on which the image is accepted be recognized. Thus, the robot image of man which Chein rejects is inadequate, but it need be rejected only if the psychological theorist extends it beyond the proper limits. Within its own proper area of relevance it is a useful and scientifically acceptable image.

A psychology of grace must formulate for itself an image of man that is as complete and integral as possible. This concept must encompass the physical, physiological, psychological and spiritual dimensions of man's concrete existence. We therefore cannot accept the image of man as passive, determined, closed or functioning in terms of the determinants of another level of organization. Allport's notion of personality as an open system should be recalled here. But mere openness is not enough. Openness can be passive, and man is not just passively open. The notion of activity is essential, as Chein points out. The development of a psychology of grace requires an internal principle of activity. Grace itself is a reality in the order of action. It is divine action and expresses itself in terms of the operations of the human agent. That activity works within man's psychic structure. It is not itself a structural reality, even in psychic terms, but it is a functional reality. In metaphysical terms it is equivalently the concurrent activity of God operating within the very activity (*operatio, actus secundus*) of the organism. Divine concurrent activity is intimately related not only to the very existence of the organism (*esse*) but also to its existential projection into activity (*agere*).

We have already observed that man's freedom is an element which we must include in the psychology of grace. It may be helpful to try to clarify this point. Grace is not a force, but an action. Specifically it is an action of love. Acts of love are freely given and freely received. The action of grace, then, is effective only within and through the free activity of the human subject. The great debate over the effects of grace which has echoed through the Christian tradition has been concerned with the relation between divine providence which is all-knowing and all-powerful and the fact of human freedom. The swirling currents of this debate have served to sharpen the issues, but one is left with divine providence on one side and human freedom on the other, and in between them, mystery. Whatever may be the exigencies of the ontological argument, I would like to suggest here that in psychological terms the argument is irrelevant, because first of all it preserves human freedom (which is psychologically relevant), and secondly because the effects of grace, however conceived, must respect that freedom. The nature of grace is such that it demands human freedom as one of the psychological conditions of its possibility. The corollary of this suggestion is that, not only is freedom required for the effects of grace, but the effects of grace are proportional to the degree of human freedom. Further, the potentiality for human freedom is proportional to the action of grace. Freedom is, therefore, a condition of the action of grace, and grace is, conversely, the condition for man's growth in freedom.

It is essential that the psychological image of man include self-determination as an essential element. To say that freedom is self-determination is not the same thing as saying that the individual's motivation plays a role in the determination of behavior. Self-determination and motivation are quite different things. One can make a very good case for the influence of motivation, conscious or unconscious, on self-determination. To this extent self-determination is subject to determination from many sources. Self-determination itself is, therefore, overdetermined. From the point of view of causality, self-determination is the insertion of the ego as a causal agent in the determination of behavior. The essential point which is underlined by the phrase "self-determination" is that such self-mobilization on the part of the ego is proper only to itself; or, alternatively, that the ego is the independent source of its own operation. The ego's activity is thus determined within the context of motivating factors which contribute to its overdetermination. But within the context of its own operation, it is undetermined by anything outside itself. Much of the argument over determinism and freedom is caught up in the confusion of these contexts. We shall have more to say later.

Chein strikes an important note when he poses the notion of man as a self-creating being. This recalls the notion of man as *imago Dei*, one of the basic themes of the Judaeo-Christian tradition. God creates *ad extra*, man creates *ad intra*. This idea is psychologically important, for in some sense man's psychological being is continually in the process of becoming (Allport). The evolution of personality takes place within the ego as a result of the ego's own activity. Self-realization is a goal of the synthetic activity of the ego. Every exercise of human freedom is an act of self-determination, and thus an act of self-realization, an act of becoming, an act of ego-synthesis, and contributes in its own measure to the evolution of personality.

It is primarily for these reasons that we have chosen to advance the idea that grace acts within the ego. Such a decision must be taken on both psychological and theological grounds. It is an important decision since it indicates the direction which our investigation of the psychology of grace is to take. It is important to note that Chein criticizes conceptions of man which underplay the significance of the ego and its activities. Moreover, the options he adopts as proper to the image of man are consonant with a psychology of the ego and its activities. Consequently he rejects reductionism and reductive explanations. But the work of constructing an image of man adequate to the full understanding of the functioning of the ego remains to be accomplished. What we would like to suggest is that an accurate conceptualization of the functions and structure of the ego will provide the best foundation for the understanding of man's openness to grace.

Questions for Discussion

1. In his prenote, the author summarizes again the purpose of the inquiry. What is this purpose? How does the selection fit in with this purpose?

2. What are the two images of man between which the psychologist must choose, according to Chein? Characterize both images. Which image does Chein reject and why?

3. What three objectives does Chein set himself at the end of the first part of his article?
4. How does he argue each of the three points, in parts 2, 3 and 4 of the article? How is the bible used in arguing points 1 and 2?
5. What four objections does Chein raise to the adequacy of Festinger's formulation of the theory of cognitive dissonance?
6. In his epilogue, how does Chein restate his objective and his reasons for it?
7. What is the methodological issue discussed by the author here? What is his conclusion?
8. Why is the "great debate" over the effects of grace not relevant to the psychological study of grace?
9. In what sense is self-determination subject to determination? Why is Chein's notion of man as a self-creating being psychologically important?
10. What idea does the author advance primarily on the ground of the ego's self-realizing character?

VIII
ALDEN FISHER ON
FREUD AND THE IMAGE OF MAN

A. Prenote

Our inquiry has led us to locate the action of grace within the ego and has suggested that the action of grace is intimately connected with human freedom. The present selection recapitulates from a somewhat different vantage point much of what has been said here. It takes us a step further by raising the issue of the meaningfulness of human action.

The excerpts below are taken from an article by Alden L. Fisher published in the *Proceedings of the American Catholic Philosophical Association* 35 (1961), pp. 45-77.

B. Selection: Freud and the Image of Man

The status of the empirical sciences of man and their relationship to philosophical anthropology poses a thorny question indeed, and one which has given rise to a whole spectrum of positions. They range from the view that science is the only source of objective knowledge about man to the opposite extreme that only philosophy provides access to such knowledge — a position in which science is either reduced to the role of fact finding or considered altogether erroneous.[1] Perhaps the view most widely held

---

[1] For a detailed review of these positions and some of the difficulties they entail, cf. George Klubertanz, S.J., "The Doctrine of St. Thomas and Modern Science," *Sapientia Aquinatis* (Rome: Officium Libri Catholici, 1955), pp. 89-104.

by philosophers and scientists alike is a middle position which, while conceding a certain validity to each, considers them to be radically distinct, independent, and *isolated* from each other.[2]

It seems obvious enough that genuine communication between philosophical anthropology and the sciences of man is ruled out in principle by the two extreme views and rendered difficult by the third.

This last view is based, I would suggest, on the conviction that the scientific investigation of man proceeds without philosophical presuppositions or implications, that science is completely neutral with respect to the ontological status of the object it studies, and that the "scientific method" itself is a neutral instrument of investigation which can be applied univocally to any object whatsoever. But this claim to philosophical neutrality, on the part of the sciences of man at least, is an untenable myth. For the explicit view of the object constituted by the conclusions of science is specified and determined by the method of investigation. And the method itself is a function of a pre-scientific and implicitly philosophical view of the status of the object, a view which is "secretly at work in the *choice* and *interpretation* of the facts." [3]

This latent ambiguity located at the center of all the sciences of man is particularly manifest in the mainstream of contemporary academic psychology. For it is evident that a large number of psychologists ". . . conceive of their discipline as a psychological physics, that is, they remain prisoners of the preconceived idea that reality, of whatever order, is composed of atomistic elements, the [mechanical] interactions of which must be observed according to the methods perfected by the natural sciences. But the idea that man is simply another object in [physical] nature along with

[2] Cf. De Waelhens, "Sciences humaines, horizon ontologique et recontre," *Existence et Signification* (Louvain: Nauwaelerts, 1958), pp. 233-261, for an interpretation of the origin and significance of this position. I am deeply indebted to this author in general and to this essay in particular for the analysis of the present problem and the solution proposed in this section. I must also acknowledge the strong influence on my thought here of Father Klubertanz, especially *art. cit.*, and Jean Ladrière, "La liberté de la recherche dans les sciences de la nature," *Liberté et vérité*, pp. 169-188 (Louvain: Publications universitaires de Louvain, 1954).
[3] De Waelhens, p. 234.

all the others, a thing to be observed like any other material being, is a philosophical idea, even though a bad one." [4]

This state of affairs is not without its adverse consequences for psychology, however, for it gives rise to a tension at the very heart, a tension which may be interpreted in part as a conflict between two apparently opposing goals: the effort, on the one hand, to model psychology after the pattern of the natural sciences both with respect to method and with regard to the object presupposed by the method, and, on the other, the effort to make psychology psychological, that is, relevant and meaningful for man as he actually exists in and lives his world.[5] This dilemma has its ultimate roots, I would suggest, in the irreducible character, the incorrigible irrepressibility of the psychologically real.

It is precisely this last fact which may provide the ground and beginning of a way out, for it points to the possibility that the conclusions of psychological research can themselves operate a certain corrective of the original conception.

But such transformations of the meaning of the results and consequently of the pre-conceived notions of the psychologist concerning the nature of his object and of the proper method of his discipline can only be fully realized within the framework of a "radically different point of departure." [6] Moreover it seems probable that progress in the sciences of man will be achieved just to the extent that such new perspectives are rendered explicit and fully explored.

The case of Freud and psychoanalysis is particularly instructive on this point. By training and inclination Freud was deeply imbued with the reigning Helmholzian medical philosophy of the middle

---

[4] De Waelhens, p. 235. The author is analyzing the case of sociology; our free translation is paraphrased for application to psychology. Any acquaintance with the history of modern psychology and the dominant stream of contemporary American psychological thinking is sufficient to verify the accuracy of this description (cf., for example, many of the essays in Melvin H. Marx, ed., *Psychological Theory* (New York: Macmillan, 1951); there are, of course, striking exceptions as well.

[5] Cf. W. W. Meissner, S.J., "Nonconstructural Aspects of Psychological Constructs," *Psychological Review,* 65:3 (1958), pp. 143-150, for evidence of this tension and its consequences even in the most rigorously behavioristic psychological systems.

[6] De Waelhens, p. 235.

and late nineteenth century. This school, of which Freud's teachers, Brücke and Meynert, were brilliant leaders, was massively reductionist and mechanistic in orientation.[7] When circumstances forced Freud to abandon the research laboratory for private practice he carried with him not only his training in method but also this scientific *Weltanschauung.* Time does not permit our tracing the fascinating history of Freud's intellectual search during this early period, a history, by the way, which we have come to know in any detail only in the last ten years.[8] Suffice it to indicate here that it is a time during which Freud made a succession of attempts to apply the methods and theories of his mentors to that confused wilderness of the mentally ill, only to have each new effort collapse in apparent failure. So reluctant was Freud to abandon his reductionist frame of reference that in 1895, long after the elements of his subsequent revolution were available to him, he still embarked with enthusiasm upon the writing of a "Project for Scientific Psychology," the opening pages of which contain the following manifesto:

> The intention of this project is to furnish us with a psychology which shall be a natural science: its aim, that is, is to represent psychical processes as quantitatively determined states of specifiable material particles and so to make them plain and void of contradictions.[9]

---

[7] For a general account of this school, cf. Ernst Jones, *The Life and Work of Sigmund Freud,* Vol. 1 (New York: Basic Books, 1953). Of the formation of what came to be known as the Helmholz School of Medicine Du Bois-Reymond wrote: "Brücke and I pledged a solemn oath to put into effect this truth: no other forces than the common physical-chemical ones are active within the organism. In those cases which cannot at the time be explained by these forces one has either to find the specific way or form of their action by means of the physical-mathematical method or to assume new forces equal in dignity to the chemical-physical forces inherent in matter, reducible to the force of attraction and repulsion" (Jones, pp. 40-41). Of Meynert, Jones writes: "For Meynert mind and brain were so closely connected that they could be spoken in the same breath, and sometimes interchangeably; the 'mechanics of the brain' was a favorite phrase of his . . . . his psychology was essentially founded on the 'association psychology' of Herbart and Fechner" (p. 375).

[8] Since the publication of Freud's notes and letters in Freud, *The Origins of Psycho-analysis* (London: Imago, 1954).

[9] Freud, *Origins,* p. 355.

Erikson calls this Freud's last act of "desperate obedience" to the "physicalistic-physiologic" method of his tradition.[10] One month after its completion Freud is disgusted with the entire paper and calls it a "kind of aberration."

But to break with this conceptual framework was a task of no small proportions. During the next five years Freud struggled with crises on three fronts, that of technique or method, that of the conceptualization of clinical experience, and that of the generality of his conclusions.[11] The resolution of these crises is documented in *The Interpretation of Dreams,* published five years later, and from it the authentic dimensions of the Freudian revolution begin to emerge.

In the area of technique Freud came to see that mental illness is not necessarily the result of neurological damage or degeneration but rather the outcome of the psychological, that is, meaningful history of the individual, that progress in understanding the nature of his patients' mental disturbance lay not in the direction of neurological research but in learning to read the *language of symptoms.*

This revolution in the character of psychological evidence and its method of observation implied necessarily a radical revision in the categories of conceptual generalization essential to the building of a psychological science. Here it must be admitted that Freud's success was partial, but from this point on Freud speaks only of psychic or mental processes and warns again and again against taking his mechanical models as the literal truth.[12]

The third crisis grew out of Freud's self-analysis (which we now know was not exactly a self-analysis) and yielded the significant but dangerous insight that the unconscious conflicts discovered as the source of his patients' illness were in principle shared by himself and all men.[13] This insight is significant because it provides

10 E. Erikson, "The First Psychoanalyst," in *Freud and the 20th Century,* B. Nelson, ed. (New York: Meridian, 1957), p. 89.

11 *Ibid.,* p. 87.

12 Jones, *op. cit.,* p. 398. Freud, *The Interpretation of Dreams,* Vols. 4 and 5, *The Standard Edition of the Complete Psychological Works of Sigmund Freud* (London: Hogarth Press, 1953); cf. Vol. 5, pp. 536–37.

13 The formulation of this insight into a systemic proposition is subject, of course, to the limitations and qualifications of any empirical generalization. It has been repeatedly verified by psychoanalysis, however, as well as by child psychology and anthropology. Cf. especially E. Erikson, *Childhood and Society* (New York: Norton, 1950).

the ground, in principle, for psychoanalysis to become a general psychology of human behavior. It is dangerous because it deals a serious blow to the proud image of man as fully rational by right and not by effort.

These dimensions will come up again; the point to be retained here is that the genuine significance of Freud's discoveries could only be appreciated within the framework of a radically different point of departure. That Freud was able to accomplish this to the extent which he did is the mark of his genius. That the full implications of this transformation were only partially seen and exploited by him is a mark of his humanity.

This brings us back to the question raised at the beginning of this section and poses for us the real problem: the relationship between the sciences of man and philosophical anthropology. For the sciences of man in general and psychoanalysis in particular are clearly not philosophy and philosophy evidently does not fit the pattern of an empirical science. Each claims, with real justice, a certain independence and autonomy.[14] But everything depends upon the character of this autonomy and the significance accorded to it. For if this autonomy is held to " . . . consist . . . in the complete and reciprocal ignorance [of the sciences of man and philosophy] the only result [can be] to render them mutually incomprehensible and to introduce into our culture a state of permanent crisis." [15]

Implicit in the foregoing discussion and emerging from it is another interpretation of this autonomy and consequently another view of the relationship between philosophical anthropology and the sciences of man. Time does not permit its complete exposition here nor even a fully argued defense.[16] But the broad outlines of this position must at least be traced in order to provide the essential framework for our subsequent discussion. In the final analysis this position is based upon and argues its validity on the ground of one

---

[14] Cf. Ladrière, *art. cit.,* for the justification and character of the autonomy proper to science and philosophy; and Klubertanz, *art. cit.*

[15] De Waelhens, "Sciences humaines," p. 238.

[16] For this the reader is referred to the article cited above by De Waelhens, his other writings, and those of Maurice Merleau-Ponty, Ladrière, and Klubertanz.

fundamental thesis, which we may call "the primacy of perception." This thesis maintains that the perceptual world of *lived experience* is the absolute starting point and ultimate validating reference for the empirical sciences as well as for philosophy.[17] In other terms, it contends that the immediate lived experience which I have of myself, others, and the world — in the language of Husserl, what is constitutive of the *Lebenswelt* — forms a common matrix out of which both philosophy and science develop and which constitutes for both, therefore, their common ground and common point of departure.[18]

But an all pervasive tendency of a certain scientific attitude has been the effort to divorce itself from this necessary origin, to construct another view of the world and substitute it for the immediate world of lived experience. This abstract and "more objective" conception is then held to represent the real world, the true reality, in relation to which the so-called subjective world of lived experience is granted only the status of appearance, in principle if not in fact derivable from the abstract world described by science.[19]

Whatever the results of this procedure for science in general, its consequences in the realm of the sciences of man have been disastrous. In the instance of psychology, instead of leading to the clarification of its proper object, the concrete reality of human behavior, this view, pushed to its logical consequences, succeeds in rendering the whole scientific enterprise devoid of meaning. For it is based on the pretension that the psychologist owes nothing in his *grasp* of the psychological fact to the natural experience of his own subjectivity. Yet without such experience as an indispensable

---

[17] De Waelhens, "Science, phénoménologie, ontologie," *Ex. et Sig.*, pp. 105-122.

[18] It is crucial to note that this "immediate lived experience" is not to be identified with the "common sense" world, already a highly interpreted one. On this point, cf. De Waelhens, "Science humaines," pp. 241-42.

[19] How such appearance arises from "objective" reality is now itself a problem, one relegated to a special part of "objective" psychology. The circularity here should be evident for it will always be by perception that scientific propositions are validated and not science which validates perception. This is in principle the same critique of science as that made by Whitehead in his analysis of the "fallacy of misplaced concreteness"; cf. *Science and the Modern World* (New York: Macmillan, 1925).

foundation it becomes impossible to know what it is of which psychological theory is the supposed explanation.

In short, the impossible circularity sketched above can be avoided only by admitting that "All scientific explanation must, of necessity, refer back, perhaps through a long series of intermediate steps, to the experienced world of immediate perception." [20] Lacking such a reference, science ceases to be an explanation *of* anything, and loses all real, that is, extra-logical significance.

This is in no way to suggest that psychology cannot make real discoveries nor, especially in the case of psychoanalysis, reveal a dimension of reality incapable of being readily known in any other way. But it is to insist that "scientific knowledge is necessarily an explanation *of* a moment of experience of the lived world," [21] in the case of psychology, of the experience that man has of himself as a being in the world. Thus the psychological facts discovered and their explanation "become significant only by their insertion in a perspective which goes beyond them," [22] in the framework, that is, of an implicit ontology.

Now it is evidently not the task of psychology to elucidate the ontological structure, the mode of being, of its object, which *de facto* it must presuppose. Within the perspective being sketched here, however, it is this same immediate lived experience which is the proper starting point of philosophy — in the case of philosophical anthropology, man's experience of himself, with others, existing in the world. It is precisely the task of the philosopher to reflect upon this given and render it explicit in its essential structure. Given a clarification of the mode of being of his object, the psychologist will proceed to do just what he does now, make observations *and interpret* them. But in exercising his science the psychologist (or psychoanalyst) will be implying a conception of man compatible with the actual meaning of his findings, and in the light of which they can be seen in their true significance.[23]

From this point of view it is clear that the relations of philosophical anthropology and the sciences of man are intimate indeed.

---

[20] De Waelhens, "Sciences humaines," p. 240.
[21] *Ibid.*, pp. 240-241.
[22] *Ibid.*, p. 239.
[23] *Ibid.*, p. 245.

Nevertheless, there is implied here "neither subordination nor simple coexistence." [24] While the philosopher will have the task of clarifying the ontological status of the object which the sciences of man in fact imply and presuppose, the findngs of these latter will be of immense value to the philosopher in his own proper task of elucidation. Moreover, and in the case of psychoanalysis, our primary concern here, the philosopher will have the obligation of giving an account of the mode of being actually revealed through psychoanalytic observation.[25] Thus, while maintaining their mutual autonomy, in this perspective, the relationship between these two disciplines would be one of close collaboration and mutual enrichment. . . .

Already though some of the broad lines of a properly philosophical view of the image of man appearing on the horizon of the psychoanalytic endeavor have begun to emerge, a philosophical view which psychoanalysis can be said in a sense both to presuppose and to confirm in its actual exercise.

In attempting to make more explicit some of the essential contours of this view, and by way of entering into more concrete dialogue with the substance of Freudian thought, it may be well to center attention around two fundamental hypotheses or guiding ideas of psychoanalysis and consider some of the implications which they appear to entail in this broader frame of reference. These two propositions are selected, first, because they have and do constitute for a wide range of thinkers the most difficult barriers to acceptance of psychoanalysis [26] and, second, because they

---

[24] *Ibid.,* p. 261.

[25] This will be strictly true just to the extent that the evidence presented in psychoanalysis reveals, as is often the case, a dimension of the existent as such and is not due simply to the constructural activity of the scientific mind. Such evidence, while not exclusively revealed by psychoanalysis, is nonetheless strikingly so, and in a wealth of detail. Here psychoanalysis can provide a corrective, to say the least, of certain philosophical orientations.

[26] These barriers are surpassed in difficulties raised perhaps only by the widespread notion that all psychoanalytic explanation implies explanation in reductively sexual terms. Whatever the historical grounds for this conception, it clearly does not represent Freud's final view nor that of contemporary psychoanalytic theory. Hence, it is properly a misconception and will not be discussed further here.

provide, I think, access to some of the richness and depth of Freudian thought, a richness which it is evidently impossible to distil and
exploit completely in a single paper. I am referring to the all embracing assumption of "strict psychic determinism" and to the
postulate of unconscious mental processes. In psychoanalytic
thought these two propositions are closely interdependent, since
the former seems verifiable only on the basis of the latter and the'
exploitation of the latter provides in many ways the strongest
confirmation of the former. It is my hope that our earlier reflections
will allow some light to be thrown on both of these crucial issues
so deeply embedded in psychoanalytic thought.

The principle of psychic determinism, or causality [27] as it is
sometimes called, postulates that "in the mind, as in physical
nature about us, nothing happens by chance, or in a random way.
Each psychic event is determined by the ones which preceded it."
Moreover, this principle is widely interpreted to imply a strict denial of human freedom. Once again everything depends upon the
way in which this principle is understood and the precise significance which should be attributed to it.

If this principle is taken to mean that mental processes and the
behavior consequent upon them are rigidly determined in the way
in which the interworkings of a complex machine and its consequent "output" are determined, then it must be rejected, in spite of
the fact that this seems to be the interpretation of many psychoanalytic theorists and occasionally of Freud himself. It must be
rejected in the first place, I would suggest, not because it is un-
acceptable to the uncritical image we have of ourselves nor to
certain philosophical or theological views of man established on
other grounds, but because it is unintelligible in itself, on the one
hand, and incompatible with the genuine significance of the psychoanalytic enterprise, on the other.

In arguing this, I leave aside the possibility, exploited by some,
that this principle permits or implies the reduction of the psycho-

---

[27] C. Brenner, *An Elementary Textbook of Psychoanalysis* (New York:
International Universities Press, 1957), p. 12. It should be noted that
some such assumption is implicitly or explicitly operative in *any* scientific
psychology.

logical to the strictly biological and this in turn to the physical or mechanical.[28] For we have seen that, in Freud's mind, psycho-analysis is irreducibly a psychology of mental processes,[29] and that this, according to our view, necessarily implies a psychology of meaning in the fullest sense of that term. Now to suggest that a meaning can "cause," that is, act upon and determine, another meaning and the consequent behavior which is by its very nature expressive of that meaning, as a thing acts upon another thing and mechanically causes or determines the actions of that thing, this to my mind is unintelligible, a simple *non sens*. A meaning, however corporally embedded, is simply not a thing. Hence we are dealing, not with the necessities and determinations of impersonal, third person forces operating upon and within me, but with con-nections of meaning.[30]

Only by understanding the determinations of behavior within the framework of "necessities of meaning" [31] then can the true problem of "psychic determinism" be properly posed. It is within this same context that a full philosophical analysis of the nature of and conditions of possibility for freedom of choice would be of immense value and relevance. Obviously no such analysis can be given here. Suffice it to indicate that such freedom does not mean capriciousness or lack of determination. On the contrary (and this is the profundity, one might even say mystery, of genuine freedom) its full elucidation reveals that the most fully free act is precisely the one which is most fully actual and hence most fully determined.[32] But it is a determination which the self imposes upon itself, a determination which the self, in full and conscious recogni-

---

[28] Cf. for example, T. French, *The Integration of Behavior,* Vol. 1 (Chicago: University of Chicago Press, 1952): ". . . most of us expect that a neuro-physiological explanation of behavior will ultimately be found" (p. 11). And Ernst Kris, "Psychoanalytic Propositions," *Psychological Theory,* M. Marx, ed. (New York: Macmillan, 1951): ". . . the time will come when psychological constructs will be replaced by physiological and biological constructs" (p. 336).

[29] N. 12, above.

[30] Cf. Alden Fisher, "Psychology or Psychologies — A Study in Method-ology," *Proceedings of the American Catholic Philosophical Association* (Washington: Catholic University Press, 1957), pp. 153-157.

[31] De Waelhens, "Sciences humaines," p. 236.

[32] A. Vergote, "L'intéret philosophique de la psychanalyse freudienne," *Archives de philosophie* 21 (1958), pp. 26-59.

tion of the necessities imposed by inner and outer reality, deliberately establishes by an act flowing from its own creative sources.[33] Thus, what is "freely" established now, after the fact takes its place among the "necessities of meaning."

It should cause no surprise then that the analyst, starting with present behavior and searching, in order to understand it, for its present and past determinations, will find, and can only expect to find, full determination in terms of meaning. The following quotation from Freud is illuminating on this point. He writes:

> But at this point we become aware of a state of things which also confronts us in many instances in which light has been thrown by psychoanalysis on a mental process. So long as we trace the development from its final outcome backwards, the chain of events appears continuous, and we feel we have gained an *insight* which is completely satisfactory or even exhaustive. But if we proceed the reverse way, if we start from the premises inferred from analysis and try to follow these up to the final result, then we no longer get the impression of an inevitable sequence of events which could not have been otherwise determined. We notice at once that there might have been another result, and that we might have been just as well able to understand and explain the latter. The synthesis is thus not so satisfactory as the analysis; in other words, from a knowledge of the premises we could not have foretold the nature of the result . . . Hence the chain of causation can always be recognized with certainty if we follow the line of analysis, whereas to predict it along the line of synthesis is impossible.[34]

We would be hard put to argue or illustrate our interpretation of psychoanalysis in this regard more effectively than Freud has done himself.

---

[33] It is also within this context that clarification of the real metaphysical meaning of efficient causality in, for example, St. Thomas would be illuminating. But, without such clarification, the use of the term "cause" in the framework of contemporary psychological discussions of this problem is frequently more misleading than helpful.

[34] S. Freud, "A Case of Homosexuality in a Woman," *Standard Edition,* Vol. 18, pp. 167-168.

The question then becomes, not whether behavior is fully motivated, but whether there exists within the psychoanalytic perspective the possibility of full and deliberate self-determination or whether behavior must be considered exhaustively and in all cases determined by motives and goals not open to rational inspection and control.

Whatever the exaggerations found in Freud and psychoanalytic literature generally, and they are many, it seems evident that some degree of self-determination has always been implicit in psychoanalysis and occasionally more or less explicitly recognized. Freud's statements concerning the aims of psychoanalytic therapy make this abundantly clear at the level of praxis.[35] On this plane Freud seems to concede to consciousness an autonomy of right and assigns to analytic therapy the task, where necessary, of restablishing its autonomy of fact, for he affirms that the aim of psychoanalytic therapy is precisely that of restoring to the ego its proper and rightful place as the director and guide of human action.[36]

Recognition of a certain freedom of the ego or self at the level of theory is likewise implicit in the incipient ego psychology of the later Freud.[37] It is this dimension which has been so fruitfully developed and exploited by the contemporary ego psychology. Hartmann's formulations of primary and secondary ego-autonomy, including the notion of an independent source of energy (energy, that is, not derived from and constituted by transformations of instinctual drive energy) available to the ego, the exploration of the conflict-free sphere of ego-functioning, the more precise delineations of all the functions of the ego including that of rational

---

[35] Cf. for example, *Collected Papers,* Vol. 2 (London: Hogarth Press, 1950), pp. 392-395.

[36] Vergote, *art. cit.,* p. 32; Freud, *New Introductory Lectures on Psychoanalysis* (London: Hogarth Press, 1949): ". . . the ego controls the paths of access to motility, but it interpolates between desire and action the procrastinating factor of thought, during which it makes use of the residues of experience stored up in memory. In this way it dethrones the pleasure-principle, which exerts undisputed sway over the processes in the id, and substitutes for it the reality-principle, which promises greater security and greater success" (p. 101).

[37] *New Introductory Lectures,* p. 106; *The Future of an Illusion* (Garden City, N. Y.: Doubleday, 1957), p. 93. On this point cf. E. E. Krapf, "Psychoanalysis and the Self Understanding of Man," *Acta Psychotherapeutica, Psychosomatica et Orthopaedagogica,* Vol. 6 (1958).

thought, and especially the renewed interest in the relations of ego to reality (included in Hartmann's notion of adaptiveness) — all of these show promise of even greater theoretical recognition and exploitation of the concrete workings of genuine human freedom.[38] This more explicit recognition of human freedom in action, however, will be possible for psychoanalysis only within the framework of the kind of enlarged perspective we have been trying to sketch here.[39] On the other hand, it would be unfortunate indeed if these wholesome and necessary developments carried with them a kind of regression to an exaggerated and rationalistic notion of freedom or led us to forget its precarious nature. As another philosopher has put it, in a formulation consonant not only with contemporary Freudian thought but also, it seems to me, with the best in contemporary philosophy and with the traditional views of classical realism:

Man is free when his choices are the product of full awareness of operative needs and actual constraints. Such needs and constraints, so far as they lie in the self, owe their being to a history of fulfillments and frustrations. But it is a history buried in the unconscious, and what irrationalities it engenders remain invulnerable behind masks of rationality. To remove their masks is not thereby to destroy them but only to reveal them for what they are. To know what he truly wants and what he can truly have — this truth does not make man free, but makes freedom possible. Self-mastery is not antecedently guaranteed, but is something to be achieved.[40]

This leads us directly to a consideration of the second postulate of Freudian psychoanalysis, that of the existence of unconscious

---

[38] Hartmann's pioneer work here is *Ego Psychology and the Problem of Adaptation* (now in English: New York: International Universities Press, 1958), appearing first in 1939.

[39] This is not to suggest that psychoanalysis can or should establish the essential fact of, nor the metaphysical conditions for freedom but only that it should contribute to our understanding of the concrete conditions within which freedom *de facto* expresses itself.

[40] Kaplan, "Freud and Modern Philosophy," in *Freud and the 20th Century*, p. 219.

mental processes. In its current acceptation it states that "in fact the majority of mental functioning goes on without consciousness and that consciousness is an unusual rather than usual attribute of mental functioning." [41] At first a startling idea to Freud, it has come to be an absolutely essential working hypothesis of psychoanalysis with an immense amount of confirming evidence. Moreover, much of this evidence is available upon a little reflection to anyone and not dependent upon the special techniques of analytic investigation.[42] In some ways it is surprising that this postulate should cause so much difficulty, at least at the descriptive level. For it has always been the insight of poets and dramatists that one may live out a "meaning" without explicitly knowing it, that one's actions may carry an intrinsic significance of which we are totally unaware, or only dimly so, later to be startled by the real, sometimes shocking, discovery that this *is* what we intended and that this *was* the intrinsic significance which found expression in our concrete actions. That this should have been at first glance such a disturbing notion to Freud's early contemporaries and even now to many of us is perhaps evidence of the extraordinary extent to which our thinking at the unreflective level is imbued with a Cartesian view of man.[43]

This is not to suggest, however, that there are no difficulties attached to this postulate. On the contrary, there are, and for the philosopher they are major. For what can it mean in philosophic terms to say that there are mental processes which operate outside the sphere of conscious awareness, that somehow the mind, the psychic, the non-physical, is, in some cases at least, deprived of

---

[41] Brenner, *Elementary Textbook of Psychoanalysis*, p. 24.

[42] Cf. Freud, *The Psychopathology of Everyday Life*, Standard Ed., Vol. 6, and *A General Introduction to Psychoanalysis*, (Garden City, N.Y.: Garden City Publishing Company, 1943). For an interesting account of the notion of "unconscious mental processes" before Freud, cf. L. L. Whyte, *The Unconscious before Freud* (New York: Basic Books, 1960). On this precise point cf. De Waelhens, "Réflexions sur une problématique husserlienne," in *Edmund Husserl 1859-1959* (The Hague: Nijhoff, 1959), p. 224.

[43] Contemporary studies in Descartes would indicate that however much it is a genuine fact in terms of historical influence, this "Cartesian view" of man is not wholly consonant with the actual thought of Descartes; cf. Geneviève Lewis (Rodis-Lewis), *Le problème de l'inconscient et le cartésianism* (Paris: Presses universitaires, 1950).

that very quality — consciousness — which seems its most appropriate if not most essential differentiating and defining characteristic? In other words, if unconscious mental processes exist, how are they possible and what kind of reality must be ascribed them? That this is not, at least in principle, so difficult a problem in the context of a venerable realism seems evident.[44] It is not our intention for the moment, however, to analyze within a Thomistic framework the conditions of possibility necessary to account for the psychoanalytic evidence in this regard.[45] Rather, I would like to sketch, however briefly, the way in which this aspect of psychoanalysis joins another dimension of contemporary thought, phenomenology, and thus, perhaps, show the underlying affinities of both with important elements of perennial philosophy.[46]

The central contribution of phenomenology for our present purpose, as for so many others, is its doctrine of intentionality. Here I must presuppose a general knowledge of this fundamental phenomenological theme and only indicate in passing certain relevant aspects.[47] Briefly and with regrettable simplification, this doctrine holds that every act of the mind is the act of a "subject" which in its essential structure is directed toward, aimed at, oriented to, an "other." This holds true not only of all cognitive acts such as perceiving, imagining, and judging, but of all affective acts such as longing, desiring, and willing. Thus, *every* act of the

---

[44] Cf. R. Dalbiez, *La Méthode psychanalytique et la doctrine freudienne* (Paris: Desclée de Brouwer, 1936); J. Maritain, "Freudianism and Psychoanalysis — A Thomist View," *Freud and the 20th Century;* and others.

[45] I am convinced this is possible and that it has been done in the past. Moreover, I think it will continue to be a fruitful area of reflection for Thomists and that its execution will be helpful not only to psychoanalysis but also in leading to a more thorough understanding of the strength and subtlety of a fully articulated Thomistic anthropology.

[46] I am referring strictly to the phenomenology of Husserl as developed and extended by such contemporary thinkers as Maurice Merleau-Ponty, Paul Ricoeur, and Alphonse De Waelhens.

[47] For amplification of this doctrine, cf., for example, Q. Lauer, S.J., *Phénoménologie de Husserl: Essai sùr la genése de l'intentionnalité* (Paris: Presses universitaires, 1955); M. Natanson, "Phenomenology: A Viewing" (*Methodos,* Vol. 10, 1959); and especially A. De Waelhens, "L' idée phénoménologique d'intentionnalité," *Husserl et la Pensée moderne,* H. L. Van Breda and J. Taminiaux, eds. (The Hague: Nijhoff, 1959).

mind *intends* an "object." It is in virtue of this act of intending that "objects" are rendered present to me, on the one hand, and, on the other, that precisely in virtue of which they take on meaning for me. Thus, every act of intending is at the same time a "conferral of meaning" on that "object" (a *Sinngebung*).[48]

For Husserl, reflection upon the structure of the mind and reflection upon the structure of its intentional acts become synonymous, for the mind comes to be defined essentially in terms of intentionality. This reflection — the intentional analysis of phenomenology — is usually carried out at the level of our conscious acts (evidently this is absolutely necessary as a point of departure). But the "theory of intentional analysis" is itself based upon and necessarily presupposes a crucial distinction between "explicit or thematic intentionality" and non-thematic but actually exercised intentionality, that is, an intentionality which is lived but not explicitated.[49] The former is based upon and grows out of the latter as its fundamental ground and necessary condition of possibility. Moreover, the latter is inexhaustible in principle, and a basic task of reflection in phenomenology is to render explicit and thematic that which was only implicit and lived.[50] The parallel here between phenomenology and psychoanalysis is, I think, obvious, but its fruitfulness is only beginning to be recognized.[51]

It is out of this Husserlian doctrine, developed and made more concrete by contemporary phenomenologists, that has come to be elaborated the view of man which we have already found particularly apt in the philosophical expression of psychoanalytic findings. This is the view which considers man as a being, the meaning of whose existence is determined by and expressive of the significant relations he establishes with himself, others — including God — and the world.

It is precisely at this point where I think our previous analysis, guided as it was by perspectives of phenomenology and the pres-

---

48 De Waelhens, "L'idée," p. 117.
49 De Waelhens, "Réflexions," pp. 222-223.
50 De Waelhens, "Réflexions," pp. 222-223.
51 In the article just cited De Waelhens exploits it extensively on the side of philosophy in his reflections on this problematic in Husserl and Hegel, and goes far beyond anything mentioned here.

ent discussion of the doctrine of intentionality, may be helpful in throwing some light on the question before us, the ontological status to be attributed to the reality of unconscious mental processes. To join the two themes and to demonstrate their deep affinity and capacity for reciprocal clarification, I quote a passage from a contemporary phenomenologist, Alphonse De Waelhens, which bears directly on the present point. He writes concerning the psychoanalytic notion of the unconscious:

It is clear that if the unconscious must be [considered] as made up of an agglomeration of contents — dynamic or not — shot through and manipulated by biological forces radically heterogenous to consciousness, we end up with the exact contrary of what psychoanalytic experience — obstinately and for more than a half century — proves with an evidence as blinding as the light of the sun: that is, that our actions, beneath their manifest meaning, have a meaning, and one which it is possible to elucidate, *even at the level of the consciousness of the one who poses them.* But it is precisely this which becomes absurd if the unconscious is defined as that which is radically other than the conscious and meaningful or — it comes to the same thing — if one holds consciousness and life to be "realities" of simply different kinds.[52]

The crux of the problem and the way to its solution are simultaneously revealed in this statement. In the first place, as in our earlier discussion of mental structures and processes at the level of psychoanalytic theory, we see exposed an implicit ontology which is not only unintelligible in itself but wholly inconsistent with the actual meaning of psychoanalysis in practice. Furthermore, there is implied here a radical reversal of a widely held interpretation of the psychoanalytic dichotomy between conscious and unconscious mental processes, that is, that the unconscious is the "true" reality and that conscious acts must be explained by, understood in terms of, and reduced to unconscious ones.[53] But it is precisely

---

52 De Waelhens, "Réflexions," p. 222.
53 De Waelhens, "Réflexions," p. 223.

this view which now becomes meaningless, for they are both seen to be of the *same* order of reality. Moreover, and in line with the thesis of the primacy of perception, it becomes clear that in principle as well as in psychoanalytic fact the unconscious can be grasped only from the point of view of conscious awareness and that its ontological status must be understood in terms of the structures of intentionality discovered first at this same level.[54] It is not consciousness, then, but intentionality that becomes the defining characteristic of psychic life and mental processes. And the distinction between intentionality as first lived and then explicitly thematized allows us to view consciousness, or the lack of it, as something of a continuum, perhaps wholly characteristic of some mental processes and shading off to a total absence in others. Thus we are led to affirm the *necessary* and *fundamental intentionality* of the whole of psychic life.

Once again this seems not only compatible with the actual exercise of psychoanalysis but also consonant with many of Freud's explicit views. This may be verified in his statements concerning the aims of therapy,[55] concerning the nature of certain typical mental disorders,[56] concerning the nature of dreaming,[57] and by almost any discussion at the level of the "special theory" of psychoanalysis. One of its strongest confirmations comes surpris-

---

[54] Occasionally Freud recognizes this explicitly; cf. *New Introductory Lectures,* p. 94. On the other hand, against the naive view that the essential structures of our conscious acts are immediately given, cf. De Waelhens, "Réflexions".

[55] Cf. n. 42; also, Freud, "The Claims of Psychoanalysis to Scientific Interests," *Standard Edition,* Vol. 13, pp. 167 and 171.

[56] "It was a triumph of the interpretive art of psychoanalysis when it succeeded in demonstrating that certain common mental acts of normal people, for which no one had hitherto attempted to put forward a psychological explanation, were to be regarded in the same light as the symptoms of neurotics: that is to say, they have a meaning" (*Collected Papers,* Vol. 5, p. 113).

[57] "In the pages that follow I shall bring forward proof that there is a psychological technique which makes it possible to interpret dreams, and that, if that procedure is employed, every dream reveals itself as a psychical structure which has meaning . . ." (*The Interpretation of Dreams, Standard Edition,* 4, p. 1). "The aim which I have set before myself is to show that dreams are capable of being interpreted . . . 'Interpreting' a dream implies assigning a 'meaning' to it . . ." (p. 5).

ingly enough, however, from his general theory of instinctual drives, which at first glance seems to be the point at which Freud became most biologically reductionist. Concerning them he writes:

> . . . an "instinct" appears to us as a borderland concept between the mental and the physical, being both the mental representative of the stimuli emanating from within the organism and penetrating to the mind, and at the same time a measure of the demand made upon the energy of the latter in consequence of its connection with the body.[58]

Thus, according to Freud's view the instinctual drives have their origin in the body but are translated into the psychological order in the form of strongly felt impulses or needs with a certain direction or orientation and certain goals. Hence, they too can only be understood in terms of purposes or goals, in short, in terms of a certain finality.[59] Moreover, as one writer has indicated, the concept of instinctual drives translates a fundamental fact of the human condition, that man is driven before he is self-directing, that he is subject to powerful forces before he can assume them and use them for his own ends. "These drives are characterized by their quantitative aspect and by their psychic intentionality. By these two components they participate in the united duality of the animated and lived body. . . . For [Freud] the dynamic is energy which has been transformed into a signification." [60]

The epigenetic theory of the ego so carefully articulated by Erikson provides another dimension and strong confirmation of this perspective.[61] What was once conscious at the level of lived

58 "Instincts and Their Vicissitudes," *Collected Papers,* Vol. 4, p. 64.
59 Cf. also *New Introductory Lectures,* p. 125. The notion of finality is itself subject to serious misunderstanding and in need of careful reworking.
60 Vergote, *art. cit.,* pp. 52-53. Moreover, it should be clear from this discussion that the present perspective involves no attempt to minimize the "biological" in Freud, i.e., man's profound "bodyliness"; its only quarrel is with biological reductionism. On this point, see the article just cited; for the treatment of this question in phenomenology cf. especially the cited writings of A. De Waelhens and "La Phénoménologie du corps," *Revue philosophique de Louvain* 48 (1950), pp. 371-397.
61 Cf. E. Erikson's *Identity and the Life Cycle* (New York: International Universities Press, 1959).

experience (exercised intentionality) has ceased to be so. But this does not mean that it has lost its character of intentionality nor its capacity to influence my life. In a Freudian perspective my lived past results in a solidification, a sedimentation of meaning, the locus of which is the animated body. This, and the insight of phenomenology that it is through man's body that he is inserted into and exists in the "world," establishes the fact of and provides the ground of possibility for the profound historicity of human existence. Moreover, it is in this context that the whole range of Freudian mechanisms can be seen in full and proper perspective. For Freud has done nothing if he has not given us a means of tracing the concrete structurations and vicissitudes of man's individual history, his life in the world — in phenomenological terms, the means of gaining insight into man's lived and exercised intentionality.[62]

The real discovery, then, of both Husserl and phenomenology and of Freud and psychoanalysis, each in their respective ways, is the proper and specific ontological character of psychic life and activity: its essential intentionality and its penetration with meaning. For both, "the mental must be defined in terms of meaning and this meaning is dynamic and historic." [63] Within this framework the doctrine of unconscious mental activity, far from being a stumbling block, is seen to be of central and capital importance to one whole dimension of contemporary thought, as well as, I am convinced, to traditional philosophy.

This leaves us with much unfinished business. From philosophy, for example, psychoanalysis could gain much from a more adequate epistemology, especially in the area of the relations between the ego and reality where contemporary theoretical discussions have bogged down somewhat for want of a sound theory of knowledge. On the other hand, the philosophical anthropologist and the moralist, for example, could gain a deepened insight into the concrete workings of the life of sense and the life of reason from such themes as sublimation in its full contemporary meaning. This dialogue could and undoubtedly will go on indefinitely.

---

[62] On these points, cf. particularly Vergote, *art. cit.*, and articles of De Waelhens, especially "Husserl et l'inconscient."
[63] Vergote, p. 38.

These are a few, if only a few, of the dimensions of a philosophical image of man emerging from the encounter of philosophy
and psychoanalysis. In closing, perhaps I may be permitted some
broad and sweeping statements. In the area of philosophical anthropology we are left with a renewed conviction of the unity of
man, a confirmation that the soul is truly the form of the body,
and that the subject of human acts is truly the composite, to use
the language of St. Thomas. Moreover, we see that the organic and
sensitive in man are truly integral parts of the whole, the human
existent, that if they can trouble and render difficult the life of
reason and will, they are also transformed by it and make an indispensable contribution to it. If I may be permitted the comparison: just as the life of grace presupposes nature, so the
rational in man presupposes the body, for it is through the latter
that man exists in the world and can do his *proper work*. And in
both cases, just as the higher transforms the lower, so the lower is
the indispensable ground and fundamental condition for the higher.

For the moralist psychoanalysis demonstrates again the complexity of man, the fact that, just as in the order of grace, progress
in perfection is the result of long and arduous effort, so at the level
of the natural good, man's progress toward the realization of his
potentialities as a fully human person living the good life of authentic values, is something not easily achieved but the result of
many twistings and turnings, to be won finally, if at all, only by
serious endeavor. But the end is good and it is worth the lifetime
which is required to achieve it.

If this is an image of man which deals a death blow to the pre-
tensions of an optimistic or Cartesian rationalism, it is not an
image which gives comfort to a pessimistic naturalism. In this respect Freud joins the great tradition of philosophical realism in
providing man with a balanced insight into the true human
condition. . . .

C. Commentary and Analysis

The concept of determination, as Fisher views it, undercuts, it
seems to me, the older schema of argument over psychic determi-

nation. This not only sheds considerable light on the relation between psychoanalysis and other disciplines, but it has profound implications for the development of psychoanalysis itself.[64]

One must hasten to add, however, that there is no consensus. In fact, as one reads the psychoanalytic literature, one has the feeling that many psychoanalysts are beguiled by the rigorous methodologies of more "scientific" approaches. On this basic issue, however, turns the availability of psychoanalytic theory to the understanding of the action of grace. Psychoanalysis can be reductionistic and operational, but it need not be so, as Erikson and others have demonstrated.[65] One can point to the whole area of the development of psychoanalytic ego psychology as a case in point. As Fisher points out, the rudiments of an understanding of the ego were present already in Freud. The post-Freudian development of psychoanalysis put heavy emphasis on the libido theory. Libido theory was a significant contribution of Freud's, but it lent itself to reductive interpretations and it lacked the qualifications that marked Freud's own use of it. Greater experience and realization of the inadequacies of a strict libido theory led to a reevaluation of the ego. The theoretical stature of the ego has grown ever since, so that the ego stands forth as a major element in the organization of behavior along with the libido and its determinants.

This development is particularly interesting, since it involved a reconsideration of evidences having to do with ego-functioning and brings into focus certain aspects of human activity which previously had been passed over or rejected. The issue of meaning is one of these aspects; the issue of freedom is another. Related to the whole problem is the question of whether the ego possesses independent energies which it originates and directs, or whether the energies of the ego are actually derived from the libido. There is a growing body of metatheory in psychoanalysis which endorses the former position.[66] From the point of view of a psychology of

---

[64] W. W. Meissner, "Operations and Meaning in Psychoanalysis," *Psychoanalytic Quarterly* (to be published).

[65] See especially E. Erikson, *Insight and Responsibility* (New York: Norton, 1964), pp. 47-80.

[66] R. W. White, "Ego and Reality in Psychoanalytic Theory," *Psychological Issues* 3:3 (1963), Monograph 11.

grace (which demands a capacity within the ego of independent self-determination) independent ego energies are essential. Fisher makes it clear that psychoanalytic theory is consonant with the demands of a psychology of grace, as long as that theory is understood in a sense which gives full play to the activity of the ego.

A very significant question, in terms of our inquiry, is the unconscious. The distinction between conscious and unconscious cuts across the distinction of ego and non-ego as components of psychic structure. The parallel distinction between explicit or thematic intentionality and nonthematic or lived intentionality has a descriptive validity which establishes the relevance of meaning at all levels of psychic life. Whether such meaning is experienced or not becomes then a secondary issue. The determination of meaning is a question of central importance to the understanding of human behavior.

Awareness at any moment is determined by conscious and unconscious elements. Cognitive functions belong to the ego but their operation is subject to determination from other parts of the psychic structure. These determinations are by and large unconscious. They serve to distort or color the reality-oriented intentionality of the ego. The degree to which the ego is able to function on the basis of its inherent reality-orientation is the measure of the extent to which the ego is functioning in fully autonomous fashion. Reality here represents the entire spectrum of reality, internal as well as external, natural as well as supernatural. As long as grace is operating in and through the functioning of the ego, it must be counted among the unconscious determinants of ego-functioning. Unlike determinants stemming from the id, however, grace is ordered to the more adequate functioning of the ego. There is implicit in this formulation a presumption that the results of mature ego-functioning are congruent with the results of grace in the well-disposed soul. As long as the reality of a supernatural order of existence is included in the schema, adequate ego-functioning must be measured to that degree against the demands imposed by that dimension of reality. Here again we are dependent on theology, since it makes explicit what revelation tells us about the character of the supernatural. From a psychological perspective, there is no reason to think that unconscious determinants need stand in opposition to the basic reality-orientation of the ego. It is customary to regard unconscious determinants stemming from the id as introducing a certain fantasy factor into the ego's relatedness to objects, but even this is by no means a necessary condition.

Consequently, the unconscious should be regarded as inherent in man's psychic structure. The effect of grace is not so much to reduce the unconscious elements as to bring them into congruence with the activity of a maturely functioning ego. If one may speak of a "Christian unconscious" in any sense it must represent the unconscious insofar as it is consonant with the functioning of the ego properly ordered toward the order of spiritual reality. This ordering is a function of the action of grace. It stands opposed to an inner disorder which derives from the uncontrolled concupiscence consequent on, and expressed in the concept of, original sin. The action of grace, at least in terms of its healing action, is directed to the integration of the disordered concupiscence within man. Concupiscence can be ordered or disordered, that is, it can be effectively integrated with man's higher faculties or it can operate with a certain autonomy and rebelliousness. Disordered concupiscence is frequently associated with the notion of temptation, but the concept of concupiscence is in fact much broader. This theological schema can be recast in part in psychological terms. The unconscious can be integrated with ego-functioning or it can be in some degree dissociated. The degree of integration is a measure of ego-strength and maturity.

Intentionality is fundamental to the whole of the psychic life. This extends, as we have seen, to the unconscious as well as the conscious aspects of psychic functioning. But intentionality should not be considered in merely cognitive terms. Rather it must be regarded as extending to all aspects of human relatedness. It is an openness or directedness toward objects, persons and things, realities. It is operative in the context of action by which the person relates himself to objects. The meaning which corresponds to such intentionality cannot be spelled out in merely logical categories, but must carry in itself some at least of the determinants of action.

Human action in relation to objects is judged to be reality-oriented by the extent to which action is consonant with the inherent valuation of the object. The development of the ego as a functioning part of the personality is tied to its gradual adaptation to the inherent valuation in things and to the emergence in the ego of a functioning value-system. The value-system develops in function of a hierarchy of values inherent in real objects. When the value-system corresponds to the real hierarchy of values in objects, the value-system can be described as reality-oriented. The degree and extent of reality-orientation in the value-system of the ego is a measure of the maturity and integration within the ego.

The value-system is an important part of the total intentionality by which the ego is related to the world of objects, personal and impersonal, in which it moves. The formation of the value-system is of course a function of the ego. If the ego is to derive a value-system which is fully oriented to reality, it requires a high degree of autonomous function and reality contact. It is a simple step from what we have already discussed to suggest that the value-system is particularly sensitive or susceptible to the influence of grace. Insofar as the effects of grace can be defined in terms of increased effectiveness of ego-functioning, better reality-contact and increased freedom, the development within the ego should issue in a more adequate and profound set of values.

Values as envisioned here are both objective and subjective. Objectively, they are the aspects of things which determine their usefulness or significance as objects of human activity rather than thought. Subjectively, they are the more or less internalized norms of behavior by which man in his action respects the real order of things. Not only has Christian revelation brought with it a hierarchy of objective values, but it strives to inculcate a corresponding system of subjective values in the Christian conscience. Such values serve as determinants of behavior only to the extent that they have been internalized. That is to say, objective values can be recognized as such, but they do not become operative in determining behavior until the ego has accepted them and integrated them with the subjective value-system that serves as a functioning part of the ego structure.

We are moving here into a metapsychology of the ego vis-à-vis the action of grace. I wish only to indicate at this point that such an integration of the action of grace with the structure and dynamics of the ego is quite feasible. The merit of Fisher's essay for our concern is that it offers a recasting of the problem of determinism and freedom, and opens a fruitful path for the development of a meaningful ego psychology consonant with the demands of a psychology of grace. The key question we have tried to face here is the relation between grace and the unconscious. We have suggested that the ego is the proper locus of the action of grace and have indicated some of the areas of ego-functioning which manifest the effects of the action of grace. We particularly noted the reality-orientation of the ego, especially as regards spiritual realities, and the value-system. The value-system is a function of reality-orientation in a sense, but the spectrum of values derived from the spiritual order and the revealed terms of God's intervention in salvation history are especially sensitive to the impact of grace.

Within this framework it is impossible to single out specific ego-functions as "target-functions." The total functioning of the ego seems to be involved. There must be awareness of a revelation and its implications, an acceptance of the revelation through faith, an understanding of the content of the revelation and (to some degree) its explicitation through theology, a recognition of the values inherent in the spiritual order, and, perhaps most crucially, an internalization and acceptance of the schema through faith, trust, and hope. This complex of operations involves the full complement of ego-functions. It is important to stress, however, that these are proper functions of the *ego* and that the ego is capable of performing these functions regardless of the action of grace. This does not mean that the ego is equally capable of performing such operations without grace, but the functions remain the same with or without grace.

It must further be emphasized that these are ego-functions also in the sense that the active agency is the ego itself. This is a crucial point both for the metapsychology of the action of grace and in its own terms for the ontology of grace in relation to human activity. Grace produces no action that is not the action of the ego itself. The action of grace is realized in and through the activity of the ego, and not otherwise. The action of grace is a concurrent activity on the part of God. This implies that the action of grace, whether sufficient or efficacious in theological perspective, demands ego-activity as part of the condition for its actuality. On other grounds we have seen that the ego-activity which serves as the ground in possibility for the realization of the action of grace must be a free act of self-determination on the part of the ego. Consequently, the action of grace is, to this extent, dependent on the free cooperation of the human agent. At the same time, the giving of grace is an entirely gratuitous act of divinely inspired love, depending on nothing but the divine initiative.

Questions for Discussion

1. Two values of Fisher's article are indicated by the author in his prenote. What are they?

2. What three views indicate the range of responses to the question of the relation between sciences and philosophical anthropology? What is the basis for the third view? Why is this view untenable? How is this view manifest in psychology?

3. What further point is illustrated in the intellectual development of Freud? Illustrate and explain.

4. What fourth type of interpretation of the relation between science and philosophical anthropology is advanced by Fisher? What is the basis of this view? What does it say about the starting point of psychology?

5. How does the author explain this view through examination of Freudian psychoanalytic theory? How does the admission of "necessities of meaning" affect the Freudian theory of "psychic determinism"? Discuss. How does Fisher explain the objections to the idea that unconscious mental processes exist? Discuss his treatment of objections made a) at the descriptive level; b) by the philosopher. How is phenomenology helpful here? How does the long citation from De Waelhens bear on the problem at issue? How do Freud's views confirm the conclusion? What further confirmation does Fisher find in Erikson's epigenetic theory of the ego?

6. What areas of "unfinished business" are indicated by Fisher? What is Fisher's final word to the philosophical anthropologist? To the moralist?

7. Is the view represented by Fisher the prevailing view in psychoanalytic literature today? Explain. Why is the issue a crucial one for the psychology of grace?
8. How have the libido theory and the ego fared in the growth of psychoanalytic theory? Why is this development important in our study?
9. Why is the question of conscious and unconscious intentionality important? Explain in detail. In what ways is grace related to unconscious intentionality? To conscious intentionality? What is the scope of intentionality? When can the ego be said to be mature and integrated? Indicate reasons why the ego's value system is especially important for the psychology of grace. Define objective values; subjective values. What is the special importance of subjective values?
10. Discuss the author's statement: "We are moving here into a metapsychology of the ego vis-à-vis the action of grace." How does he sum up the value of Fisher's essay? How does the author sum up his own analysis? Why cannot specific "thought-functions" of the ego be singled out? What is it of crucial importance to realize that grace acts in and through the ego.

IX
ERIK ERIKSON ON
HUMAN STRENGTHS

A. Prenote

We are deeply indebted to Erik Erikson — more perhaps than
to any other contemporary psychoanalyst, with the possible exception of Heinz Hartmann — for our understanding of the functioning of the ego. It will become clear that Erikson's contributions
come as close as anything in psychological thought to what we
have been calling a psychology of grace. Obviously Erikson is not
formulating such a psychology. He is constructing a psychological
understanding of the ego. But, as we observed earlier, the success
of this very effort is fundamental to the understanding of the action
of grace. The fragment of Erikson's work presented here represents
a direct contribution to a psychology of grace. As such, it is a
living model of the availability of psychoanalytic theory suggested
in the previous selection by Fisher. Erikson effectively subsumes
many of the specific issues already raised in this inquiry and fuses
them into a consideration of human virtues. We see in this the
continuity of Erikson's thought with that of William James. And
he places himself firmly in association with those who accept the
nonreductive, open, active, self-determining image of man that has
been taking shape in these pages.

The following excerpts are taken from Erikson's *Insight and
Responsibility* (New York: Norton, 1964), pp. 111-113, and
146-150.

B. Selection: Human Strengths

The psychoanalyst has good reason to show restraint in speaking about human virtue. For in doing so lightly he could be suspected of ignoring the evidential burden of his daily observations which acquaints him with the "much furrowed ground from which our virtues proudly spring." And he may be accused of abandoning the direction of Freudian thought in which conscious values can find a responsible re-evaluation only when the appreciation of the unconscious and of the irrational forces in man is firmly established.

Yet the very development of psychoanalytic thought, and its present preoccupation with "ego-strength," suggests that human strength be reconsidered, not in the sense of nobility and rectitude as cultivated by moralities, but in the sense of "inherent strength." For I believe that psychoanalysts, in listening to life-histories for more than half a century, have developed an "unofficial" image of the strengths inherent in the individual life cycle and in the sequence of generations. I think here of those most enjoyable occasions when we can agree that a patient has really improved — not, as the questionnaires try to make us say, markedly improved, or partially improved — but essentially so. Here, the loss of symptoms is mentioned only in passing, while the decisive criterion is an increase in the strength and staying power of the patient's concentration on pursuits which are somehow right, whether it is in love or in work, in home life, friendship, or citizenship. Yet, we truly shy away from any systematic discussion of human strength. We recognize, for example, an inner affinity between the earliest and deepest mental disturbances and a radical loss of a basic kind of hope; or between the relation of compulsive and impulsive symptoms and a basic weakness in will. Yet, we are not curious to know what the genetic or dynamic determinants of a state of hope or of a state of controlled will power really are. In fact, we do our tortured best to express what we value in terms of double negatives; a person whom we would declare reasonably well is relatively resistant to regression, or somewhat freer from repression, or less given to ambivalence than might be expected. And yet we know that in a state of health or of mental and affective clarity, a process of order takes over which is not and cannot be subsumed under the most complete list of negatives. Some of this process we call "ego-synthesis," and we gradually accumulate new observations under this heading. But we know that this process too, in some men in some moments and on some occasions, is endowed with a total quality which we might term "animated" or "spirited." This I certainly will not try to classify. But I will submit that, without acknowledging its existence, we cannot maintain any true perspective regarding the best moments of man's balance — nor the deepest of his tragedy.

In what follows I intend to investigate, then, first the developmental roots and later the revolutionary rationale of certain basic human qualities which I will call virtues. I do so, partially because I find the plural "strengths" awkward, but most of all because the word "virtue" serves to make a point. In Latin, "virtue" meant virility, which at least suggests the combination of *strength, restraint* and *courage* to be conveyed here, although we would, of course, hesitate to consider manliness the official virtue of the universe, especially since it dawns on us that womanhood may be forced to bear the larger share in saving humanity from man's climactic and catastrophic aspirations. But old English gave a special meaning to the word "virtue" which does admirably. It meant *inherent strength* or *active quality,* and was used, for example, for the undiminished potency of well-preserved medicines and liquors. Virtue and spirit once had interchangeable meanings — and not only in the virtue that endowed liquid spirits. Our question, then, is: What "virtue goes out" of a human being when he loses the strength we have in mind, and "by virtue of" what strength does man acquire that animated or spirited quality without which his moralities become mere moralism and his ethics feeble goodness?

Freud's concept of the ego is as old as psychoanalysis itself, and was in fact brought along from Freud's physiologic days. Freud first, then Anna Freud, and finally Heinz Hartmann have worked consistently on the refinement of the concept. Yet, this "structural" part of Freud's work seems to have less appeal. Psychologists have continued to refer to the field of psychoanalysis as primarily concerned with the "affective," and biologists prefer to think of psychoanalysis as covering the sexual, or, at best, the "emotional" only. It is obvious, I think, that the shock caused by Freud's earlier systematizations of the dichotomy of instinct and super-ego has been absorbed so slowly, and with so much emotional ambivalence, that Freud's later thoughts have simply not reached the attention of the majority of scientific workers. And even where the psycho-analytic concept of the ego has permeated, it has been immediately drawn into the imagery of man's "lower nature," and into the popular meaning of ego, namely, an inflated self. Thus a church-historian, in one of the best of our academic journals, could suggest that a psychoanalytic study of Luther's identity crisis was meant to show that Luther started the Reformation merely "for the satis-faction of his ego." To that extent has the popular "ego" as a designation of modern man's vain sense of a self-made Self (a precarious sense, subject to sudden deflation by the pricks of fate — and of gossip) penetrated the vocabulary even of the learned. But it happens to designate the opposite of the psychoanalytic meaning; therefore in all but the most specialized circles, it is still necessary to say what the ego is not.

The psychoanalytic meaning of ego designates it as an inner-psychic regulator which organizes experience and guards such organizations *both* against the untimely impact of *drives* and the undue pressure of an overweening *conscience*. Actually, ego is an age-old term which in scholastics stood for the *unity* of body and soul and in philosophy in general for the *permanency* of conscious experience. Psychoanalysis, of course, has not concerned itself with matters of soul and has assigned to consciousness a limited role in mental life by demonstrating that man's thought and acts are co-determined by unconscious motives which, upon analysis, prove him to be both worse and better than he thinks he is. But this also means that his motives, as well as his feelings, thoughts and acts, often "hang together" much better than he could (or should) be conscious of. The ego in psychoanalysis, then, is analogous to what it was in philosophy in earlier usage: a selective, integrating, coherent and persistent agency central to personality formation. William James still used the term in this sense. In his letters, he speaks not only of "the ego's active tension," but also of the "enveloping ego to make continuous the times and spaces not necessarily coincident of the partial egos." But then, his self-observation had brought him close to the study of impaired states in which the ego was first revealed in its weakness, and then recognized as a control regulator of remarkable endurance and power.

Psychoanalysis, then, while first concentrating on the vicissitudes of instinctual forces in man (as recognizable in clinical symptoms and universal symbolisms, in dreams and in myths, in the stages of ontogeny and the evolution of the species), never ceased its work in the second area of inquiry, namely, on that "coherent organization of mental processes" which, in this cauldron of forces and drives, assures a measure of individuality, intelligence and integrity. Only the measure of the measure varied. The original awe of the inner conflicts which motivate man made his ego seem to be a pathetic compromiser between the id, which had a monopoly on all instinctual fuel of man's "animal-nature" and the superego, which could claim the support of all-knowing priests, all-powerful parents, and all-embracing institutions. No wonder that, at the time, the ego seemed to Freud like a rider who is "obliged to guide [his horse] where it wants to go." Gradually, however, the study of the human ego, the guardian of individuality, revealed it to be the inner "organ" which makes it possible for man to bind together the two great evolutionary developments, his *inner life* and his *social planning.*

The ego was gradually seen to be an organ of active mastery, not only in defending the inviolacy of the person against excessive stimulation from within the organism or from the environment, but also in integrating the individual's adaptive powers with the expanding opportunities of the "expectable" environment. The ego thus is the guardian of *meaningful experience,* that is, of experience individual enough to guard the unity of the person; and it is adaptable enough to master a significant portion of reality with a sense, in this world of blind and unpredictable forces, of being in an *active* state. This means that a "strong ego" is the psychological precondition for that freedom which has alternately been specified as the effort through which the inevitable comes to pass — or the will to choose what is necessary.

But I must say in passing that over the years I have become less intolerant of the popular misunderstanding of the term "ego," for it covers, as folklore often does, a deeper truth. Up to a point, the ego can be understood as a guardian of man's individuality, that is, his indivisibility. But in the midst of other individualities, equally indivisible, the ego must guard and does guard certain prerogatives which man cannot afford to be without and which he therefore will maintain both with secret delusions (such as are revealed in his dreams and daydreams) and in those collective illusions which often guide his history. Some of these prerogatives are a sense of *wholeness,* a sense of *centrality* in time and space, and a sense of freedom of choice. Man cannot tolerate to have these questioned beyond a certain point, either as an individual among his fellow men, or as a member of a group among other groups. It is for this reason that in individual memories and in collective history man rearranges experience in order to restore himself as the cognitive center and the source of events. He has crowned all-powerful kings and created all-knowing gods, endowing them with all the ego-ism the individual cannot do without: a central position in violent events; a sense of having willed and created fate itself; a certainty of being eternal and immortal; a conviction of being able to know the secret of life; the ability of being totally aware of goings-on everywhere and of influencing whatever one wishes to change. To restore this necessity of ego-ism in his own little self, man has also found means (inspirational, artistic, toxic) to be "beside himself" in order to feel himself to be more than himself. With all due respect, I see the latest version of this inexorable inner need in these post-Darwinians who insist that man, now that he recognizes himself as a part of evolution, and may learn to steer some of it by dint of this recognition, becomes the crown and the goal of it instead of a creature who does well if he manages to restore or undo what he has unset and wrought in the tiny and dark corner that he, at best, can know. When faced with one of the customary apotheoses of man by an otherwise strict scientist, I am apt to remember the remark of a coed who expressed the depth of our darkness in the direct way reserved to women. Her escort had just mused aloud that life was a strange thing, indeed. There was a silence which he took for inspired consent. But she asked quietly: " . . . as compared with what?"

If the superego, then, has guarded man's morality but also has made him its slave, the ego, more adaptively, permits him a measure of human balance, yet not without dangerous illusions—dangerous, I should add, because of the destructive rage which accompanies their failure. In this sense, the basic virtues enumerated here have their illusory side which can develop into grand delusions of vain virtuousness, and lead to specific rages of disillusionment. Yet each is indispensable, and each is necessary for that ensemble which is man at his most balanced; while all in moments of humor and wisdom, in prayer, meditation, and self-analysis, can be charitably transcended [146-150].

C. Commentary and Analysis

There are several reasons for our having included this selection. Erikson presents a sensitive analysis of the drift in psychoanalytic thinking toward an ego psychology. At the same time, he distinguishes between what the ego is and what it is not. This is crucial to our inquiry, since the entire question of what the ego is and what it does is extraordinarily susceptible to misunderstanding and misinterpretation. This alone would be a significant contribution, but in addition, Erikson has set up a bridging notion in his idea of "ego-strengths." This notion is both a revivification of the scholastic concept of *virtus* and a prolongation and explicitation of the psychoanalytic concept of "ego-strengths." One must be careful, however, of oversimplification. Erikson has done much more than adopt an older usage. The traditional notion of the virtues owing to its development from the Stoic schema, is philosophically oriented. Traditional analysis did not press its inquiry much beyond the limits of classification and ontological definition. Erikson, however, is suggesting that the virtues have a psychological relevance. They represent the strengths of the ego and offer a basic scheme in terms of which a richer understanding of ego-functioning can be developed. Consequently, the "virtues" may be regarded as denominatively the same as the classic *virtutes,* but the formality of understanding is quite different. Erikson offers us the

possibility of integrating the notion of the virtues with an understanding of the psychological functioning of the ego. This is a distinct advance.

It is immediately obvious, in terms of our inquiry, that the virtues
are directly related to the action of grace. The effect of grace can
be spelled out in terms of the mobilization or intensification of ego-
strengths. It is important to specify what is meant by "ego-strength"
in this context. White recounts Fenichel's attempt to spell out the
implication of ego-strength: "Fenichel enumerated the ability to
tolerate tension or excitation; the ability to judge validly and to
carry out intentions despite hindrances; strength in controlling and
channeling the instincts; ability to modulate the more archaic manifestations of the superego; and power to reconcile conflicting elements within the ego itself." White himself prefers to formulate
the concept in these terms "A strong ego, let us say, is one which
has developed substantial competence in dealing with impulse and
with environment. A weak ego is one which, lacking this development, has had to make heavy use of defensive measures of the an-
ticathectic type, thus sacrificing further flexible learning." [1] The
key concept in White's usage is that of competence. The strong
ego has developed a capacity to manage and control instinctual
energies and impulses and to deal effectively with the environment.
The weak ego, on the other hand, has failed to develop this capacity and is forced to divert a large portion of its available energies to the effort of resisting instinctive impulses. This diversion
minimizes the ego's capacity to deal effectively with environmental
demands because the major share of ego-energies are not available.

It seems, therefore, that at least two of the major constituents
of ego-strength are the available ego-energies and the degree of
ego-autonomy. One should not think of ego-energy as a fixed
quantity, as though the ego were constituted with a fixed amount
of energy subject to the laws of conservation of energy and thermodynamics. Ego-energy is, at least in part, a developmental property.
The total quantity of energy is probably subject to genetic influences, but it is also influenced by developmental history. The available energies are also determined in part by a certain economy

---

[1] R. W. White, *art. cit.,* p. 137.

of distribution. Energies diverted into one channel are not available for utilization in other channels. Energies consumed in establishing ego-control over id-derived impulses and sugerego-derived demands are diverted, to that extent, from the adaptive and constructive concerns of the ego. It also seems true, in some degree, that the less control the ego has to begin with, the more of its energies are required to establish and maintain a given degree of control. This can be translated into terms of autonomy. Autonomy and ego-control are directly proportional. The autonomous ego enjoys a degree of mastery over inner impulses that requires very little energy to maintain its control. Its energies are maximally available for dealing with external demands adaptively and for further constructive and synthetic efforts within itself.

Such strengths are developed within the ego. In the traditional analysis, the virtues were regarded as acquired perfections or habits. This concept is equally applicable in relation to ego psychology. Ego-strengths are in a sense produced by ego-activity. For the ego is in fact the only available agency capable of setting up within itself the conditions which we describe in terms of "strength." The disposition of ego-energies is a proper activity of the ego. The establishment of ego-control is an ego-function. The process of ego-synthesis depends entirely on the efforts of the ego directed to its own internal organization and synthesis. There is, therefore, a reciprocity between ego-strength and ego-activity. The stronger the ego is, the more capable it is of such dispositional and synthetic activities. Conversely, the more capable it is of such activities, the greater its strength and the more effective its ability to build that strength.

What, then, is the role of grace within this framework? The function of grace is, in the first instance, to increase ego-strength. This function is accomplished by increasing the available independent ego-energies. Grace is, therefore, a dynamic and energizing principle of activity. This energizing effect is implemented within the ego. Consequently, the phenomenological prolongations of the action of grace appear both under the aspect of and in terms of ego-energies. They appear under the aspect of ego-energies in so far as the action of grace itself is completely unconscious. They appear in terms of ego-energies in so far as they exercise themselves within the ego, and do so concurrently with the very activity of the ego itself.

The action of grace, therefore, is directed to the increase in ego-strength and ego-strengths. The measure to which this is possible is generally a function of available strengths and the level of current autonomy achieved by the ego. But the impact of such an energizing impact on the ego need not be limited by current weakness of the ego. We are faced with a complex of influences within the psychic structure which are involved in interdependence and interaction. It is possible that the well known conversion experience, commonly attributed to the influence of grace, represents an energization of the fragile ego which overcomes existing resistances or obstacles to effective ego-activity. But such instances seem to be the exceptions that prove the rule.

If we accept the proposition that the action of grace is realized in and through the activities of the ego, we are constrained to recognize that the action of grace becomes subject to the terms of development of the ego. The action of grace, therefore, is subject to developmental laws and psychological analysis. It should be noted that the action of grace is being considered here in its specifically psychological dimension. The developmental principle is inherent in the traditional analysis of the virtues, and it is equally, if not more, relevant to the psychological analysis we are proposing here.

It is important in this context to clear up one possible source of confusion. In common parlance, one often speaks of "willpower" in association with the strength of character related to ego-strength. Willpower represents a kind of ego-strength, but ego-strength must not be identified with willpower. Nor must it be assumed that weakness of the ego is simply a matter of lack of willpower, as though to say that if an individual really wanted to, he could pull himself together and function effectively. The major lesson of modern psychiatry is that this choice is often not a possibility. Herein rises the central problem of modern psychotherapy.

We have not attempted to reproduce here Erikson's analysis of the inherent strengths of the ego. This would be part of the elaboration of an ego-psychology and a psychology of grace. But such an elaboration is beyond the scope of our present inquiry.

However, the way is open for a fruitful and meaningful analysis which provides a channel for a deeper understanding of the action of grace in the human soul.

Questions for Discussion

1. Indicate some of the specific reasons for Erikson's inclusion in this book?
2. Why, according to Erikson, should a psychoanalyst show restraint in speaking about human strengths? Why and on what terms does he want to discuss them?
3. In general, what happened to Freud's concept of the ego at the hands of later psychologists? Of popularists?
4. What is the psychoanalytic meaning of the ego? What does Erikson say about the relation between this meaning and earlier uses of the term? How did James use it?
5. How does Erikson describe the emergence of the ego as an "organ" of active inner mastery? What elements does he point to in showing its mastering function?
6. What is the deeper truth covered by the folklore about the ego? How does this "deeper truth" apply to "ego-strengths" — i.e., to virtues?
7. Does Erikson's understanding of "virtues" correspond exactly to the traditional classic *"virtutes"*?
8. How is the inquiry into a psychology of grace affected by Erikson's understanding of virtues as "ego-strengths"? What precisely is meant by "ego-strengths" here?
9. What two major constituents of ego-strength are discussed by the author? Explain the interrelationship of these two constituents. Does the traditional view that virtues are acquired perfections or habits apply to virtues as ego-strengths? Why?
10. The author summarizes the role of grace within the framework of ego-strength. What is this role? How might the effects of grace in conversion be interpreted from this point of view? Finally, can ego-strength be identified with "willpower"?

X

GERALD McCOOL ON RAHNER'S PHILOSOPHY OF THE HUMAN PERSON

A. Prenote

One of the foundation stones for the elaboration of a meaningful psychology of grace must be the image of man advanced by theological analysis. To speak of an image of man is equivalent to speaking of a conception of human nature which underlies a theological anthropology. If the effort to formulate a psychology of the life of grace is to come to any fruition, it is clear that the image of man which springs from the wisdom of theology and revelation ought to be congruent, in some degree, with the image of man as seen from the viewpoint of scientific psychology. Our main effort at this point has been to bring into focus that psychological image.

As one turns to the theological dimension, one is immediately overwhelmed by the richness of the Church's teaching about man and his nature. The treasures extend from the primitive insights of the salvation history recorded in the Old Testament, through the rich theological anthropology developed by Paul, through the developments of patristic thought in men like Augustine, through the intellectual convulsions of the scholastic age and the incredible synthesis of Aquinas, through the post-scholastic era and on into the post-modern and existentialist revitalization of contemporary theology and thought. At every stage of this rich history, theological inquiry has been concerned with the agonizing question: "What is man? Who is he that the infinite God should have such exquisite concern for him, and even take to himself a human nature in the incarnate Word?" The *fides quaerens intellectum* has sought not only understanding of God, but also of the relationship between God and man; not only understanding of the mysteries of salvation, but also of the mystery of man himself.

There is little wonder in this. If one seeks to understand a relation, one must first understand the terms of the relation. If one seeks to find some understanding of the relation between God and man, one must search out an understanding of both the nature of God and the nature of man. Like the inquiry after God, the inquiry into man has been renewed in each new age. Each generation of theological inquiry distills the richness of its tradition into a new synthesis. The formulation of the image of man is always incomplete because man himself is changing and evolving. The image needs continual renovation because man needs to understand himself as a contemporary reality. There is a danger of deception in this, however. Our times are not so much subject to the error of archaism as they are to the seduction of modernism. By modernism is meant a tendency to reject the old as somehow useless and irrelevant and to accept only the new and shiny. One must remember that the contemporary reality of man is a historical reality. Man himself is a historical existence, and his evolution is betrayed if its historicity is denied. Evolution is not metamorphosis.

In our own day, no theologian has had a more influential role in the reformulation of the image of man than Karl Rahner. The central core of his reflections has been directed toward a metaphysics of man's existence and his relatedness to a revelation. There are Catholic thinkers and others who believe that this attempt has not been altogether successful. Many Catholic thinkers have grave reservations about his acceptance of a Maréchalian metaphysics and others find difficulties with his theological analyses. These are important objections and they are the stuff out of which theological progress is made. But the fact remains that Rahner has made a wide-ranging and consistent attempt to shape an image of man, which reveals man as by his nature open to the hearing of God's revealed Word, and open also to the concrete operation of the Word through grace. Unfortunately Rahner's thought is complex and involved. But we have included the selection below because it presents clearly and concisely some of the aspects of Rahner's thought relevant to our present inquiry.

The article from which these excerpts are taken is by Gerald A. McCool, S. J., and was published in *Theological Studies* 22 (1961), pp. 539-552.

B. Selection: The Philosophy of the Human Person in Karl Rahner's Theology

In *Geist in Welt* Rahner accepts as the starting point for his reflection on the possibility of metaphysics the starting point proposed by Heidegger: the consciousness of man as he raises the most fundamental of all questions, that of the significance of being. As a Maréchalian Thomist, however, it is his aim in reflecting upon this fundamental question to lay bare the a priori conditions of possibility for its appearance in human consciousness. The absolutely unconditional Pure Act of being, after all, is not one of the material objects of the spatiotemporal world made present to the human subject through the data of sensation; and experience supports St. Thomas' insistence on the fact that man has no direct and proper objective knowledge of entities other than those found in the material, sensible world with which the philosophy of nature concerns itself. Indeed, man is capable of the implicit self-reflection in which he knows himself as a spiritual subject only through the act of affirmation in which he predicates a universal quiddity of a material object given to him in sensible intuition. If, then, the human subject is essentially a "spirit in the world" (*Geist in Welt*), if the human subject is essentially a knower whose conscious possession of himself cannot be achieved in isolation from the act of affirmation through which he distinguishes himself as subject from the material objects of his judgment, how can he become aware of that unconditioned Absolute whose significance is at stake in the most fundamental of all questions, which is, as Heidegger has so well said, the conscious act in which man's authentic structure reveals itself? Since this infinite Absolute cannot enter human consciousness as the content of objective knowledge given in sensible intuition or in the concept, it can only be present to man "unobjectively," as a reality which, although it cannot be represented in objective, conceptual knowledge, is nonetheless grasped by the intellect as the real term of its a priori drive to self-perfection through intentional assimilation of realities other than itself.

Objective judgments would be impossible if the infinite Absolute of being were not present to consciousness in this unobjective manner. For it is its reference to this absolutely unconditioned "horizon" which confers upon the "is" of every judgment the metaphysical necessity which places its affirmation under the laws of being; and it is against the same "horizon," the infinite term of the a priori drive of the agent intellect, that the form of the sensible singular seen in the phantasm appears to the intellect as limited, and hence capable of indefinite repetition in other sensible singulars. For its unobjective grasp of the infinite Pure Act of being enables the intellect to see by contrast the limited character of the sensible form which grounds the capacity of the specific form to repeat itself indefinitely in other individuals; and thus the intellect is enabled to grasp the universal form in the sensible singular presented by the phantasm through a single operation which is at once its abstraction of the universal species and its conversion to the phantasm.[1]

If, then, through its objective judgments the human spirit is implicitly aware of itself as a being which is both intelligent and intelligible, it grasps in the same act the real Infinite which is the fullness of being, and therefore the fullness of intelligence and intelligibility as well. Metaphysics is seen then to be both possible and necessary, even for an intellect whose proper concepts are confined to the essences of sensible objects, because in every judgment the intellect transcends the world of space and time to touch at the term of its a priori drive the infinite unity, truth,

---

[1] The theory of abstraction through a single operation of the intellect which is at once the abstraction of the species and the conversion to the phantasm is one of Rahner's contributions to the metaphysics of knowledge. It has now been incorporated into at least one manual published by a leading German faculty of philosophy. Cf. Walter Brugger, S.J., *De Anima Humana* (Pullach, 1958), pp. 135-39.

and goodness of the unconditioned Absolute, in whose reality every finite object of its affirmation must participate. God, then, as the infinite, intelligent, and consequently free, creative source of all finite reality, is the transcendental condition of possibility for the self-fulfillment of the human spirit through its knowledge of the world.

From this it follows that between God and the human spirit personal relations are possible. Man's will is free because, as an appetite specified by his intellect, it is in its turn a drive toward the infinite Absolute; and so none of the finite participants of God's reality which are the objective terms of its desire can satiate it. God then appears once more as the "horizon," the transcendental condition of possibility, of the free acts in which the human spirit, precisely as free person, tends to self-fulfillment. A free act of the will, however, is more than just a tendency toward an object. An act of the will is free because, unlike the act of an appetite which is wholly determined by the structure of a nature, it is always a self-determination of the spiritual agent, a free stand taken up by him before the objects of his act of acceptance or rejection. What is most precious and important in a free act is not what the agent brings into being in the external world by means of it. Rather it is the attitude which the agent imprints on his own spirit in its fulfillment. For, at its core, each free act consists in an opening or closing of the agent's spirit to an object in the whole context of its presentation, a spiritual attitude of acceptance or rejection whose ground and source cannot be found in the determinism of his nature but only in the positive capacity to say "yes" or "no" to being which is rooted in the dynamic *esse* of a spiritual form intrinsically independent of matter. In the dynamism of every free act, therefore, the human agent, as self-determining person, takes up an attitude to the world of objects which forms the field of exercise for his free decision. More than that, he takes up an attitude toward the absolute Person, the free, creative source of all reality, whose existence as the real term of the a priori dynamism of his will is the transcendental ground of possibility for every free choice. The free, spiritual agent is, according to his essential structure, a finite person taking a stand before the infinite absolute Person.

PHILOSOPHY OF RELIGION

Furthermore, if the Absolute of being, truth, and goodness is personal, the innermost depths of that supreme reality can be known by others only in the measure in which he chooses to reveal them in some form of free communication, and in the measure in which a knowing subject can receive and understand the revelation communicated to it by this personal God. Thus, the results of Rahner's transcendental reflection on the conditions of possibility for human knowledge and volition make it evident that the relations between the human person and the absolute divine Person are of such a nature that a free revelation of God's inner personal depths to man is possible, should God decide to give it. Nor is there any reason to place limits on the possible content of such a revelation, since an intellect which is an a priori drive to the infinite Absolute excludes no possible object from the analogous knowledge which it can have of the infinite term of its spiritual a priori by employing concepts whose content of representation has been derived from the objects of man's sense experience.

Man's metaphysical structure, therefore, Rahner tells us in *Hörer des Wortes,* makes him essentially the recipient of a possible divine revelation whose content must be determined by the divine will. Consequently, the function of a philosophy of religion can never be the a priori determination of the content of revelation; it can only be to determine the conditions of possibility for the communication to man of a revelation whose objective content can be known only a posteriori, since it depends on a free decree of God. Its task, therefore, will be to bring these conditions of possibility to light by a closer study of the metaphysical structure of the human subject to whom any possible revelation must be communicated. *Hörer des Wortes*, accordingly, is a continuation of the transcendental reflection on the a priori conditions of possibility for man's conscious activity begun in *Geist in Welt*. In his first book Rahner had already shown that the knowledge of the subject which becomes aware of itself only through affirming a quidditative predicate of a sensible singular is possible only if both the affirming subject and the object of its affirmation are beings whose hylomorphic essence is composed with the accidents of quantity and quality. To become aware of oneself as a subject affirming a sensible object is to become aware of oneself as a being which has become intentionally another being, and one could have become intentionally another being only through becoming the patient in which its transient activity is received. In a reflection which we have not space to follow here, Rahner discovers that such transient activity demands in both agent and patient a hylomorphic essence modified by the accidents of quantity and quality. This enables him in *Hörer des Wortes* to uncover two further essential structures of the human subject. Man is essentially social and essentially historical.

As a form received in matter, the human spirit is by its nature the limited essential act of one of the many individuals who constitute the human species, and who must communicate with each other through the material symbols of speech and cultural artifacts; for these are the signs which carry the personal revelation of their authors through the spatiotemporal world of sensible experience to the intellects of other incarnate persons. The necessity of society, language, and culture has as its ground, therefore, the essential structure which determines the nature of an incarnate person's self-perfection through conscious activity. Furthermore, again as a form received in matter, the self-determining, free human subject must work out his self-perfection through acts of knowledge and free decision which, because of their extrinsic dependence on matter, share the successive character of events in the spatiotemporal world; while, at the same time, the intrinsic independence of matter enjoyed by the self-determining spirit gives to his choices their character of personal uniqueness and unpredictability. Man is not only a temporal and social being; he is essentially historical.

If, then, God should determine to communicate his personal revelation to man, he would be compelled to do so by means of some sensible symbol, a "word," a spatiotemporal perceptible event, which will carry God's message to man. If there is to be a revelation, it must be a unique, historical event. Thus philosophy brings man to the threshold of theology. For if man, by his essential structure, is potentially a "hearer of the word" of God, it is his duty to study his history attentively to see whether in fact God has spoken such a word.

IMPORTANCE OF TRANSCENDENTAL ANTHROPOLOGY

Even in a rapid and perforce superficial sketch of Rahner's metaphysics of knowledge and volition, such as the one given in the preceding paragraphs, the methodological importance of transcendental anthropology in his whole system is very evident. The immutable metaphysical characteristics of man, material reality, and God cannot be determined by a facile process of abstraction, which can do little more than schematize the general characteristics of empirical data. It is very dangerous simply to assume, as too many scholastics are inclined to do, that such a process of abstraction can be taken without more ado as a valid source of evidence concerning the necessary connection between empirically observed characteristics and the necessary and immutable essences of the sensible singulars of which they are affirmed. Immutable metaphysical characteristics are revealed by a transcendental reflection which discloses their existence as a priori conditions without which experience itself would be metaphysically impossible. The absolute universality of such characteristics has its ground in their unconditioned necessity for the conscious activity of the human spirit as such. There can be no doubt, then, that the structure of man and of the world disclosed in the reflections of transcendental anthropology is the structure of the necessary and changeless essences of things themselves. This epistemological principle, as we shall see, has a decisive influence on the method of inquiry pursued in Rahner's theological studies.

Of great importance, too, for the conduct of Rahner's theological investigations has been the analysis of human experience derived from the transcendental anthropology of *Geist in Welt* and *Hörer des Wortes*. Human experience contains far more than the objective judgment in which the human knower affirms a quidditative predicate of a material sensible object; it contains man's unobjective knowledge of his own personal reality and of the personal reality of the infinite creative source of being. Universal ideas make up an important element of the experience of the reflecting human subject. Sometimes they are mere schematizations of empirical data, but, if they are the result of a transcendental reflection on experience, they can manifest the necessary structure of finite and infinite reality. In the experience of an incarnate person, however, there are also found realities whose fullness eludes expression in the concept and the universal statement. None of the abstract formulations found in universal judgments exhausts the concrete reality of the sensible singular presented to the intellect by the phantasm and in which it sees the universal form. Furthermore, since man is a free spirit whose reality cannot be absorbed into the impersonal determinism of matter, the human subject is capable of experiencing a free encounter with God and finite persons, the fullness of whose concrete content cannot be captured in abstract, general formulas. One of the most important elements in the constitution of man's total experience of reality is, as we have already seen, the unique free attitude which he adopts toward the universe and its creative source in the dynamism of every free decision concerning the objects of the spatiotemporal world. In his considerations on the supernatural, on the natural law, on existential ethics, and on the role of the free individual in the hierarchical society of the Church, Rahner systematically exploits these different levels of human experience, whose full significance could not come to light in a theology dependent on an objectivistic Thomism whose epistemology and metaphysics were derived from a study of inanimate nature rather than from a prolonged reflection on the consciousness of the human subject.

INTELLECTUAL DYNAMISM AND THE SUPERNATURAL EXISTENTIAL

Rahner's philosophy of religion culminated, as we have seen, in his conception of the human spirit as a dynamic reality which can be called, by virtue of its essential structure, an obediential potency for the reception of a divine revealing word. It depends on God, however, whether the word is spoken or whether man is given no further knowledge of the personal Absolute beyond what is contained implicitly in the exigencies of the human intellect and will. The whole development of *Hörer des Wortes* is ordered to the delineation of the metaphysical structure which makes the human spirit an obediential potency for revelation; it is never suggested that man, in virtue of his created nature alone, has an exigence or right to receive a manifestation of God's innermost personal life. There is no reason to be surprised, therefore, that even before the unequivocal statements on the subject by Pius XII in *Humani generis,* Rahner took issue with the theologians of the Maréchalian or Augustinian schools who interpreted the a priori dynamism of the human spirit as a natural desire for the beatific vision. [2] In doing so, however, he saw no necessity to abandon the Maréchalian metaphysics of the human person which had formed the core of his philosophical reflections. He did, however, see the need to broaden his philosophical anthropology into a theological anthropology whose speculations would take into account the data of revelation.

Transcendental reflection can distinguish between the merely contingent, empirical characteristics perceived by man in his experience of his own person and the essential structure of his human nature which is the a priori condition of possibility for that experience itself. It is true that a yearning for an immediate encounter with the fullness of infinite personal being has been so interwoven with the experience of man's drive to self-fulfillment in all ages and in all places that philosophers and theologians have identified this longing for a personal vision of God with the essential dynamism of created human nature. Since man is open to a revealing word from God, it would be well, however, to look and see whether revelation has anything to say about the subject. Revelation does have a word to say. It tells us that the beatific vision belongs to that supernatural order which is the effect of a special elevation of human nature to an end essentially beyond its created powers and exigencies. The word of God, accordingly, enables us to acquire an accurate awareness of the limitations of our human nature which man could not obtain by the workings of unaided human reason. The distinction between the essential dynamism of pure

---

2 "Über das Verhältnis von Natur und Gnade," *Schriften zur Theologie* 1, 325-45; *Theological Investigations* 1, pp. 297-317. For a discussion of Rahner's theology of the supernatural order, see J. P. Kenny, S.J., "Reflections on Human Nature and the Supernatural," *Theological Studies* 14 (1953), pp. 280-287. See also L. Malevez, S.J., "La gratuité du surnaturel," *Nouvelle revue théologique* 75 (1953), pp. 561–86, 673–89.

human nature and a desire for the beatific vision is a task for theological, not purely philosophical, anthropology.

In the construction of his theological explanation of man's elevation to the supernatural order, Rahner has drawn on the resources of Maréchalian and Heideggerian philosophy. As a true Maréchalian, convinced of the reality of intentional being, he is certain that God's decree elevating man to a supernatural order would be a chimera and not a real decree, if it did not have as its effect the production of a corresponding ontological reality in the human spirit. No purely extrinsic theory of man's elevation, which would leave man's nature metaphysically unaltered by God's positive decree ordering him to a supernatural end, will explain the supernatural satisfactorily. Because of God's decree calling man to a supernatural end, therefore, even before the reception of the first elevating grace, a supernatural reality has been produced in the human soul. Due to that new reality, man's whole spiritual dynamism is now ordered with all its energy to the beatific vision. What name is to be given to this supernatural entity? It is not elevating grace, since it is possessed by every soul, even those of the damned in hell, for it is the metaphysical ground of their searing pain of loss. As an essential structure determining the meaning-giving end of man's most authentic personal activity, it deserves the name Heidegger reserves for the fundamental structures of human consciousness: an existential. Due to God's positive decree, every human soul, before the reception of sanctifying grace, is elevated to the supernatural order by the reception of a supernatural existential, an entity for which it has no exigency, but for which, as spirit, it is an obediential potency.

His theory of the supernatural existential enables Rahner to preserve a great deal of Blondel's fruitful insight that a study of the exigencies of human action must ultimately confront the philosopher with the possibility of an encounter with the God of revelation without compromising the gratuity of the supernatural order as other Maréchalian theologians had seemed to do. In the dynamism of historical human nature, even though it be deprived of grace, there is always a longing for God which has its metaphysical ground in the supernatural existential. Experience presents the philosopher with a drive which is supernatural; only a theological anthropology, with its more accurate awareness of the limits of human nature, can recognize that drive *as* supernatural.

THEOLOGICAL ANTHROPOLOGY AND THE NATURAL LAW

Rahner is thus able to draw a distinction between a philosophical concept of human nature and a metaphysical one. In a philosophical concept those essential characteristics of man would be represented which human reason can discover without employing the resources of revelation. The metaphysical concept would contain only those characteristics which are essential elements of human nature. Both the contingent and the supernatural would be rigorously excluded. In the light of Rahner's theory of the supernatural existential, it is clear that, in his opinion, a theological anthropology alone can furnish such a metaphysical concept of human nature. The exact determination of the content of this metaphysical concept of human nature, moveover, is a task of no small moment for the Christian moralist and for the Christian theologian, for it is the metaphysical essence of man which is the ground of the rights and obligations of the natural law.[3] Unhappily, the facile generalization of experience indulged in all too frequently by our Christian moralists can never result in the abstraction of a truly metaphysical concept of human nature. In experience there is much that is contingent and much that is conditioned by the historical state in which man finds himself. Because a characteristic has been associated with man up to the present, it does not follow that this characteristic is part of his changeless essence. The Christian moralist has the lesson of history to teach him that. It is part of the task of the Christian philosopher and theologian, therefore, to continue the transcendental reflections on the necessary a priori conditions of human experience as such which were initiated in *Geist in Welt* and *Hörer des Wortes*. It is not enough to know that man is necessarily and changelessly a being who is spiritual, social, and historical. Much more must be learned about his metaphysical essence, if we are to ground the

---

[3] "Bemerkung über das Naturgesetz und seine Erkennbarkeit," *Orientierung* 19 (1955), pp. 239-43.

demands of natural-law morality. As a sign of what he hopes may be accomplished, Rahner himself attempts to establish by such a transcendental reflection on human experience that it belongs to the metaphysical essence of man to be a member of a species whose origin must be found in a single wedded pair.[4] Yet he is not entirely convinced that the method of transcendental reflection by itself will be able to constitute a metaphysical concept of human nature whose comprehension is wide enough to ground in man's absolutely changeless essence all the propositions of natural-law morality. Some way must be found, he believes, of joining empirical observation to the transcendental reflection on the conditions of possibility of human experience. It must be one of the chief preoccupations of scholastic philosophers to discover whether in this way the results of empirical observation can share to some degree in the necessity which up to the present has been the exclusive property of propositions derived by the method of transcendental reflection.[5]

THEOLOGY OF CONCUPISCENCE

The metaphysics of human knowledge which he worked out in *Geist in Welt* and the metaphysics of human freedom developed in *Hörer des Wortes* made it possible for Rahner to provide an original and very satisfying answer to another problem connected with the relations between nature and grace: the content of the dogmatic concept of concupiscence.[6] The Platonic type of thinking which would identify concupiscence with the sensible appetite whose drive to the things of earth resists the pull of a spiritual

----

[4] "Theologisches zum Monogenismus," *Schriften zur Theologie* 1, pp. 253-322, esp. 311-22; *Theological Investigations* 1, pp. 229-96, esp. 289-96.

[5] "Bemerkung über das Naturgesetz und seine Erkennbarkeit," pp. 242-43.

[6] "Zum theologischen Begriff der Konkupiszenz," *Schriften zur Theologie* 1, pp. 377-413; *Theological Investigations* 1, pp. 347-82. For an excellent discussion of Rahner's theology of concupiscence, see J. P. Kenny, S.J., "The Problem of Concupiscence: A Recent Theory of Professor Karl Rahner," *Australasian Catholic Record* 29 (1952), pp. 290-304; 30 (1953), pp. 23-32.

appetite which is by its nature a drive toward the things of heaven cannot be squared with the metaphysics of human knowledge and desire. The human spirit is not only a subsistent act; it is also the form of a body-soul composite. From the soul, as the radical specifying principle of being and activity, emanate both the sensible and intellectual faculties through which the total man comes into contact with his world. In the experience of the body-soul composite, therefore, there can be no such thing as purely sensible knowledge in which the intellect plays no part at all; in a knower who cannot think without conversion to the phantasm, and whose intellect has as its proper object the essences of material beings, there can be no such thing as purely spiritual knowledge. If man's knowledge is never purely spiritual, it follows that his tendency toward the goods he knows can never be a purely spiritual desire. Sensible objects, therefore, are known and desired in a sensory-spiritual fashion; and spiritual objects are known and desired in a spiritual-sensory way.

Nor can one square with the metaphysics of the will the theory which would identify concupiscence with the spontaneous desires of the will which in man's present state necessarily precede the act of free election. Each free act of the will, as we have already seen, has as its essential core the act of self-determination by which the agent takes up a position toward a finite exterior object presented to him for his acceptance or rejection. In the finite agent, the taking up of such an attitude necessarily involves a transition from potency to act. Such a transition, however, in order to be possible, presupposes that the faculty through which such an attitude is taken up was not always in possession of the object. The object, therefore, must have been presented to the will itself, and not just to the intellect; otherwise the will, which is an essentially different faculty, could not have made the transition from potency to act in relation to it. In a faculty, however, which is by its nature an active tendency toward an object (not just a faculty of passive receptivity like the intellect), the presentation of an object can only take place through a spontaneous movement of the faculty toward it. From this analysis it follows that the indeliberate acts which precede the act of free election belong to the necessary nature of the human will. They are an indispensable condition of possibility for any deliberate act of that faculty. Consequently, the essence of concupiscence cannot consist in the presence of these spontaneous motions of the will without which even Adam before his fall would have been incapable of eliciting a free act.

The metaphysics of human freedom developed in *Hörer des Wortes* does more, however, than simply bring to light the inadequacy of these erroneous theories concerning the comprehension of the dogmatic concept of concupiscence. It enables the theologian to determine accurately what the positive content of that concept must be. In the dynamism of every free act, as we have already seen, the agent takes up a free attitude toward the absolute Person, since no human good can be accepted or rejected except in virtue of the dynamism of the will toward this infinite fullness of goodness. Furthermore, from the analysis of the human person carried out in *Geist in Welt* and *Hörer des Wortes* it is clear that the fundamental characteristic activity of the human person is self-possession through spiritual activity. Through his intellect the person possesses himself by means of the perfect reflection which in the judgment enables the subject to distinguish himself from the object of his affirmation. Through his will the subject possesses himself in the autodetermination of his own self contained in the free disposition of his person, the adoption of an attitude, in relation to the finite objects of the world and to God, the ultimate "horizon" made present to him through the dynamism of every choice. But just as there are many elements of the body-soul composite which cannot be captured in the person's self-possession by means of his intellect, so too a large part of man's affective dynamism, his sense desires and the spontaneous motions of his will which have their roots in his nature and in his acquired virtues and vices, refuse to be taken into the personal disposition of the agent, the free attitude adopted by him toward an object in a single act of free decision. This resistance of man's spontaneous affectivity (which Rahner in this context calls his "nature") to his "person" in his endeavor to dispose of himself completely in the engagement to an object or a person effected through his free decision is the reality designated by the term "dogmatic concupiscence." Dogmatic concupiscence is not necessarily an evil thing. It prevents a human being from making the total, irrevocable commitment of his whole being to evil of which the pure angelic spirit is capable; and it is the source of the instinctive resistance to an evil choice offered by the spontaneous movements of the will which check a virtuous man on his course toward sin and summon him to repentance after he has fallen. In Adam, then, the gift of integrity consisted, not in the absence of the spontaneous movements of his affectivity, but rather in the lack of any resistance on their part to his total disposition of himself in an act of free decision. Its purpose was not to make sin less difficult; for it actually carried with it the peril of a graver and more fully deliberate offense to God than the sin of which a man is capable when the force of his choice is weakened by the movements of concupiscence. Rather, its aim was to make Adam more fully that free, self-possessing source of action which is the human person, and to include the driving energy of his whole being in the unimpeded commitment for or against the absolute Person involved in his free choice of good or evil. If integrity, therefore, was the reason for the gravity of Adam's sin, the concupiscence which followed it was the ground of possibility for his repentance. Its spontaneous resistance to his choice against his Creator deprived his will of that fixity in evil which is the mark of the fallen spirit. Offering an opening for the grace of contrition, the motions of concupiscence explain why Adam's fallen nature was an obediential potency for redemption. . . .

C. Commentary and Analysis

It is clear that man's basic capacity to transcend the limitations of the sensible reality through abstraction and affirmation is an essential theological starting point. In the affirmation of a universal and abstract *quiddity* (essence) there is involved an implicit moment of self-reflection in which the human subject is concurrently aware of his own existence as spiritual subject. In this implicit consciousness, the infinite absolute is "unobjectively" present to the intellect as the real term of its a priori drive to self-perfection through the assimilation of realities other than itself. The scholastics had a way of saying that the knowing subject "became the other." This fundamental capacity of the human intellect to assimilate the reality of what is not itself, and in this very act to determine its own reality as subject, is made possible by the implicit presence to consciousness of the absolute Infinite. The hypothesis is daring and debatable. But it brings into focus an essential point. Man's intellect endows him with a capacity which places him in a specific cognitive relatedness to God. The dynamism of intellect is inherently open and self-perfective and the real term of this a priori drive is God.

This inherent openness to being and self-perfective dynamism is found also in man's capacity for freedom of will. The act of self-determination involved in human freedom is self-perfective insofar as it involves an imprinting of an attitude of acceptance or rejection of an object. It is also an implicit taking up of an attitude toward the absolute Person, whose existence is the real term of the a priori dynamism of the will. The human person in free self-determination is a finite person taking a stand before the infinite Person. Here we should stress the aspects of openness, self-perfective dynamism and personality which form the under-lying currents of this analysis. Insofar as they represent the dis-tillation of the essential elements of a theological anthropology, they are immediately relevant to the image of man we are trying to bring into focus. The reality of man's existence as person is subject to an inner becoming. It is a dynamic process spelled out in terms of the dynamism of intellective confrontation and free decision implemented in the context of human relations, culture, social organization, economic involvements and the whole world of objects.

In all of this, however, there is an implicit relatedness to God as a real term. The human person becomes more of a person and, therefore, more human, in the degree to which he approximates the real term of the a priori dynamisms which constitute the essen-tial aspects of his nature. The reality of these dynamisms lays the foundation for and gives essential meaning to Rahner's concept of the supernatural existential. For man's essential relatedness to

God is equivalently a relatedness in being to the supernatural order. The problem in conceptualizing these inner dynamisms of man's nature is that the concrete fulfillment of these dynamisms is ultimately beyond the capacity of man's nature and in the hands of God. The utter gratuity of that fulfillment as a gift of love is inviolate, regardless of the inherent dynamisms of man's nature. This is not a problem for man's existence, since the gratuity of the gift does not override the love of the giver. It is rather a problem in the theological understanding of man's relatedness to God and its implications.

The supernatural existential, then, is the point of confluence between grace and nature. Moreover, it is through grace that the inherent dynamisms of nature are activated and energized in one perspective and fulfilled in another. The degree to which such dynamisms operate is a function of the extent to which implicit self-awareness and free self-determination are realized in the individual acts of intellection and decision. The greater the degree of implicit self-awareness, the greater the degree to which the absolute Infinite is "unobjectively" present; the greater the degree of freedom in an act of decision, the more intensely is the implicit attitude of acceptance before the person of God realized. The function of grace in this context is to maximize these inherent dynamisms and, in vitalizing them, to bring to fruition the compelling self-perfective drive which they embody. There is implicit, then, in the very notion of the supernatural existential, a dynamic image of man's nature. Likewise there is implicit in the notion of grace a self-perfective dynamism which works within and through man's natural capacities. Thus, grace, while it is gratuitously supernaturalizing, is *ipso facto* perfective of man's nature and personality.

Questions for Discussion

1. What shift in the focus of the inquiry takes place in Chapter 10? Why is the theological dimension important here? Why is

a presentation of Rahner's anthropology included here?

2. What are the conditions for a human knowledge of God, according to Rahner? Why is man's will free? Why is it that, in his free choice, man "takes a stand" before God?

3. What makes a divine revelation possible? Why is man essentially social and essentially historical? Explain. How does this bear on the question of a divine revelation? What scholastic tendency is rejected by Rahner in favor of transcendental anthropology? Why? What is the view of human experience derived from Rahner's transcendental anthropology? To what extent are universal ideas applicable? To what extent are they inapplicable? Explain.

4. What does revelation have to say about the fulfillment of man through a personal vision of God? Define and explain Rahner's "supernatural existential."

5. Why is theological anthropology alone able to determine the content of a metaphysical concept of human nature? Why is precision here important to the theologian and the moralist? Rahner feels the theologian needs help in making the concept precise. From what source? Discuss.

6. What is the Platonic view of concupiscence rejected here? Why is it rejected? Why does Rahner reject the theory that concupiscence is found in the spontaneous motions of the will? What is Rahner's positive view of concupiscence? How does this apply to the case of Adam?

7. What essential theological starting point emerges from McCool's discussion of Rahner's theological anthropology? What "daring and debatable" hypothesis does the author discuss?

8. What is the real term of the a priori dynamism of the will? What relevance does this have to man's personal freedom?

9. In what does Rahner's concept of the supernatural existential find its essential meaning? Explain. Is the gratuity of God's love a problem here?

10. What is the function of grace in regard to the inherent dynamism of nature?

XI
GUSTAVE WEIGEL ON THEOLOGY AND FREEDOM

A. Prenote

The concept of freedom has always held a central position in Christian theological consideration. It is central because so much depends on it, and because the very notion carries within it a residual mystery that defies definition. One might say that the concept of human freedom is the most significant element in the image of man provided by a theological anthropology.

This essay by the late Fr. Gustave Weigel has the merit of offering a clear, yet highly synthetic appraisal of the meaning of freedom in theological perspective. There is probably no more necessary concept in the reconstruction of a psychology of grace than the concept of freedom. Yet it is the one concept that is most easily misunderstood and abused. Christian theology, from the time of Paul until now, has been preoccupied with the problem of freedom, because, it seems to me, human freedom is the essential element without which religious existence becomes an impossibility. In some fundamental sense, the very acceptance of a revelation depends on man's free decision. The participation in a supernatural order, as Rahner has suggested, demands a free response, such that participation on any other grounds would constitute a violation of the structure and dynamisms not only of man's nature, but of the supernatural.

The excerpts which follow are taken from *Thought* 35 (1960), pp. 165-178.

B. Selection: Theology and Freedom

Thirty years ago when a young collegian manifested his intention to dedicate his life to theology, eyebrows rose. In the second and third decades of this century, the thinking world of the West put theology on a par with phrenology and astrology. No serious man would have anything to do with such occult arts. They were supposed to be based on false assumptions and, practically, they had nothing to give to man.

All that has changed. Theology has once more achieved respectability, while astrology has only acquired popularity and phrenology has withered away. The reason for this change is manifold, but one reason is certainly the collapse of the optimistic naturalism which flourished at the end of the nineteenth century and through the first two decades of the twentieth. It was not the naturalism which annoyed the men of the late twenties and middle thirties. It was the optimism.

By strictly empirical tests there was no ground for optimism. Things were getting different but not better nor was there any visible hope for improvement. Insecurity and threat faced men all over the world. The United States had its economic depression. Europe had the turmoil of naziism, fascism and Stalinism. Imperialism agitated the East not so much because of western action, which was bad enough, but because of the ambition of Japan. Technology indeed was advancing in gigantic strides. Aviation, radio and electronics shrunk distances and there were machines for every human effort. But all this evident progress did not make the lot of the earth-dweller any more tranquil. In some respects the machines were a cause of the trouble. The leisurely production of the ancient craftsman who adjusted his instruments to his own needs and temper was gone. The new machines worked at a fixed tempo to which man had to adjust and when he used his new tools as perforce he had to, he was under tension. It was not now the eagle eye of the foreman which had caused him nervousness in the past, but rather his mechanical tool which was next to him and in accelerated operation every minute of his working day. Technology was seen as absolutely necessary but it alone was not going to solve the problems of the human situation.

Things were certainly not getting better of themselves. You had to put your collective mind to it. When the collective mind did go to work in the League of Nations and in the Rooseveltian braintrust, it was suddenly discovered that "the best laid schemes o' mice and men gang aft a-gley an' lea'e us nought but grief and pain for promis'd joy." The reason why they often "gang a-gley" is because there is an uncontrollable factor in human action which for ages had been called man's freedom. In other words, the heart of the human situation was the problem of human liberty. No matter how you treated man, this stubborn indeterminism showed its ugly head. Force and coercion were applied to men; persuasion most skillfully employed was directed toward him; knowledge was deluged over him; but there was no known medium which could infallibly control that freedom. The existentialist philosophers who were coming to the fore in that time invented the phrase, "Man is condemned to freedom."

Freedom was not a new word in the twenties and thirties. It had come down to us from the past and there was a glorious ring to it. In fact we had the Liberty Bell as one of its most revered symbols. It was the mark of the United States that culturally it was a champion of freedom, while other western communities had lost their faith in it: Italy, Germany and Russia, for example.

Yet freedom was on trial. It was universally recognized that it was not true that its only possible fruit was good. It was evident that it could also bring forth much evil. In man freedom produced the problem of evil. Evil had not been the object of man's contemplation for many decades, and the men who spoke of evil did not explain it. They only explained it away. Their usual solution was that evil was only a manifestation of bad organization, which through education would automatically evolve into good organization. Evil in this view was only the birth pain of the better. This was consoling doctrine but it was not satisfactory to a world which experienced evil and saw no great good burgeoning out of it.

It was here that theology suddenly took on a new significance. This discipline had for millennia dealt with the problem of freedom and evil. It was the only discipline around with something profound to say about the matter. In consequence Cinderella suddenly became a princess. Karl Barth, Emil Brunner, Reinhold Niebuhr and

Paul Tillich, theologians all, talked to our time about the concerns of the age. And they were heard. The dignity of theology was recognized again and this dignity has survived to our day. It is not the majestic eminence once enjoyed by theology in the distant past but at least the theologian no longer has to apologize for his presence among the molders of ideas.

What has the theologian to say about freedom? Very much, and he has been doing it for many centuries. As Mortimer Adler in his *The Idea of Freedom* (New York: Doubleday, 1958) has pointed out, most theologians have seen that freedom is a complex notion having as many as four or five levels of meaning. Political freedom is hardly the heart of the matter and even the psychic capacity for choice is a superficial aspect of liberty.

Theologians of the Catholic tradition have without exception taken the human capacity of choosing for granted. They never went into great investigations of this obvious phenomenon, which even determinists freely admit. As a phenomenon, the choice of alternatives is evident in all conceivable agents when they are thrust into situations which permit a variety of reactions. Even the dog must choose which of two chewable bones he will chew on. But the Catholic theologians felt that the problem of choice of future lines of activity took on a peculiar freedom when the different possibilities of reaction were previously contemplated. In such an event, and only a contemplating agent is capable of it, we have deliberate choice, and this is free in a sense higher than mere contingency. Granted indeed that the resulting action was contingent, its contingency was in function of the deliberation, decision and responsibility of the agent. Catholic theologians never bothered to prove that man acted in this way. They simply considered it to be an existential datum and as a datum it presented man with problems. They wisely refused to solve the problems by denying that the ground of the problematic was real.

This is the first contribution of theology, the serene and unbefuddled admission of man's freedom as an experienced datum. In this admission theology did not confuse contingency and liberty. Liberty is a quality peculiar to rational action. It says more than the truism that all things are possible; it affirms that man can comprehend possibility and control its actualization. Liberty is, therefore, a dignity and a sign of human worth. What is more, liberty does not make man worthy but man is free because he is antecedently worthy.

This first theological affirmation concerning liberty is of immense consequence. To suppress a man's liberty by coercion, duress or meddling with his being is to treat man in disaccord with his worth. He is being unworthily treated and if the man himself succumbs to such interference, he is conducting himself unworthily. There is in this position the firm basis for an effective humanism. Man becomes an agent of peculiar value for no other reason than that he is a man. Christianity's approach to slavery ended slavery not by banning the institution but by removing the postulate which justified the system. If any man is by his very being free, then he cannot because of his essence be a slave, and accidental slavery is only an economic arrangement agreed upon by those concerned with economic ends. The pagan's contempt for the slave always rested on the supposition of the unworthiness of the slave, a notion patent in the writings of such men as Plato and Aristotle, though attacked by Stoics like Epictetus, Seneca and Marcus Aurelius. But even the Stoics considered the slave's worth as something he could achieve by asceticism and not as something antecedent to his own behavior. The Christian theologians went beyond both the Academy and the Stoa by insisting that man was worthy before he acted. In this situation master and slave were really equals, and in consequence the system lost any advantages it may have had. When it lost its advantages, it lost its reason to exist, and in Christianity the system could only wither away and finally disappear. We have here an eloquent instance of the way theology works. It does not necessarily attack objectives by direct assault; it simply floods them with light under which the objectives melt away.

The mere recognition of the fact of human liberty is not of itself a superlative achievement. As it is a datum, it really is not denied by anyone, if we limit liberty to its phenomenological level, namely, deliberate, responsible decision. Every man knows that he posits such acts and there is no use telling him that he does not do so. The problems of liberty arise when we go beyond the mere experimental fact and relate it to the whole framework of universal meaning. What are the metaphysical implications of freedom? What does it tell us about the world and its structure? What does it tell us about the ground of being? What does it suggest as a decent pattern for human coexistence? There are the real questions which are brought to man's attention because he is involved in deliberate, responsible decisions. In answering these questions only theology is competent to give ultimate answers, and every ultimate answer will be theological, even though it may be a very bad theology.

From the very phenomenon of choice we know that freedom is self-affirmation. The question immediately arises whether it is only self-affirmation, or to put it in its ultimate form, what is the self who affirms? Is the self an isolated, unrelated consciousness, floating without orientation or direction on the mysterious sea of existence, itself selfless? There are those in the past and present who have answered affirmatively. Of course, this answer supposes that history is a seething mass of maggots in an opaque puddle, unlovely, without pattern and beyond judgment. This answer is reckless and has only the glory of wildly manifesting freedom, which as we have seen is a noble thing. When man is confronted with the real, he inevitably looks for its meaning, so that the meaningless and nothing are synonyms. The fury of chaos is unthinkable. The self is somehow definable; it is not a mere splutter in an ooze.

From this basic insight Catholic theology has had much to say about freedom and self-affirmation. It begins with the supposition that the self is structured and its affirmations must be related to that structure. Any affirmation inconsistent with such structure is not a self-affirmation, but a self-denial, and by that very fact treason to the self. Such a preposterous affirmation is indeed a manifestation of freedom but it is not its proper fruit; not its use but its abuse. This was basic to the Christian theologian's conception of freedom. Liberty does not mean absolute indifference to either of two alternatives, though it did in finite agents suppose that physically either alternative could be chosen. But only one *should* be chosen, that which accorded better with the structure of the human self. Freedom was conceived as an instrumentality for perfection, not as an expression of unconditioned autonomy. In this conception freedom is a responsibility rather than an absence of law. Freedom is not man's possession in order to enable him to do what is good or evil; it is an enablement to do the good in a rational way.

It is at this point that Catholic theology takes a stand on freedom which opposes it to almost all other forms of visions of liberty. Theology sees three dimensions in the self. First of all, it is an agent rooted in the ground of being which transcends the particular human agent but without which the agent is nothing. Man's being derives from a source distinct from himself and man's activity shows up not only the finite self but an infinite self, the last and first spring of being and action. Second, any reference to an inbuilt design in the human self is unrealistic if only constructed in the light of an atemporal idea of man achieved by abstracting from history. To understand man's true design we must study man in his historical context. Third, man's history will not be adequately achieved by consulting man alone. It will be necessary to contemplate the vision of man as possessed by the author of history. The purview of this vision is granted only by divine graciousness in a personal self-revelation inviting man to faith.

These three principles have weighty consequences. According to Catholic theology, historical man has a flaw in his structure. This flaw is labeled by the term "original sin." The term affirms that the active human self is a disturbed personality and nothing which man can do can eliminate the disturbance. At most he can reduce the disturbance but he cannot get rid of it. As a consequence man will freely express his own split self by split action, which will be simultaneously self-realizing and self-defeating. He cannot by himself reach the goal of liberty which is perfect self-affirmation, for when he affirms self, he is affirming a self torn between being and non-being. Here we find theology's criticism of all optimistic naturalism which supposes that man can by education, training, guidance or asceticism achieve a totally satisfactory self-expression. There is a death or destruction impulse vitiating all human effort. This view of man and his freedom has exasperated all naturalists because it flatly denies the basis of their own philosophy. It has been a constant temptation of Catholic theology to compromise its own basic insight in its dialogue with the thinkers from beyond its own circle, but the compromise has always been resisted by the major voices of the Catholic tradition. Augustine rose to attack Pelagianism and Semi-

pelagianism and his views have prevailed. The Augustinian conception of man has often been caricatured by its own friends as a
doctrine of total depravity. But Augustine never thought that man
was a monster; he only denied he was a balanced agent.

What makes Augustinian anthropology most distasteful to naturalists is the doctrine held by all Catholic theologians that man's
self-affirmation, to be adequate, must ultimately be an affirmation
of God in the self. This demands a consciousness of God derived
from the self's returning to the ground of its being. Such a state is
not natural because in it man leaves the order of nature and only
beyond nature can he truly realize himself. To make such a goal
the dynamism of man, irritates the secularist because he wants man
to occupy himself only with secular goods. But Catholic theology
has always denied that such an orientation can have ultimate meaning for mankind. All being is divine in its ground and the elimination of the ground of being from the consideration of man directs
him not to what absolutely is but to what is absolutely not, and this
is a frustrating activity. From the point of view of the Catholic
theologian, secularism and naturalism are self-defeating and therefore are lamentable programs of human action rather than liberating saviors. In the bitter dialogue between the theologian and the
secularist, the secularist has one defense: he does not believe that
God has made any revelation concerning the destiny of man. Here
he stands impregnable and that is why he glories in his unbelief and
exalts the fact of freedom. It never dawns on him that he is not
defending freedom but only using it, for to believe is as free as
unbelief. To say that there is a revelation is just as much a manifestation of freedom as to say that there is not. The only difference
is that, if there is a revelation, to reject it freely is an abuse of
liberty and not its proper function. Freedom gives man no grounds
for rejecting the real, though it does make it possible.

For the Catholic theologian, then, absolute freedom, the freedom
of the unconditioned creator, is not and cannot be the freedom of
man. To treat human freedom as if it were divine is nonsense in any
hypothesis, but it is tragic nonsense if we consider man as he historically exists, since this man is prone to abuse freedom in every instance. Yet Catholic theology is not a despairing pessimism. It has

an optimism of its own which stands up better than the naive optimism of the naturalist and secularist.

Man indeed is a split personality; he will always abuse his own freedom, and this abuse will bring suffering to individual man and to the human community. However, man operates in function of an original divine will and God is good, kind, wise and all-powerful. His beneficent design cannot be thwarted by human willfulness for he uses even the wrath of man to praise him. What is more, he can overcome the schizophrenia of men by interiorly inspiring and gently moving them to proper choices in their freedom. This action is called grace, the gracious sanating intervention of God in a bent world, whereby the kind designs of the Creator become real. The weakness of man and the limits of human freedom need not depress the human agent. In his weakness the power and majesty of God are at work, and human history, produced by human agents, will bring glory to God and peace to men of good will.

On hearing this gospel, one might think of Leibniz who considered ours the best of all possible worlds, a theory which was savagely ridiculed by Voltaire in *Candide*. Others may see in it the Stoic principle of detached resignation. Actually the doctrine neither rests on delusion nor leads to passivity. Suffering and disappointment are not denied nor is it pretended that they can be transmogrified into pleasures. It is not suggested that we have no part in the formation of the destiny of the self or history. Above all it is affirmed that history is a divine comedy and not a Greek tragedy.

What is demanded by the Catholic theology of freedom is intense activity and, as far as possible, the elimination of all obstacles to free choice deriving from human duress or neurotic compulsions. The capacity for free choice must be heightened to the degree compatible with the limiting situation of original sin. Action is called for in the framework of my little world with its stimuli and challenge. The man envisaged by Catholic theology does not retire from the external world into the cave of his isolated self, not even when he becomes a hermit. He is always open to the world and its impinging action. In the light of his faith, and of reason enriched by faith, he tries to solve the problems, individual and social, which come his way. He makes the most of his being, which is active and creative, nor is he afraid to trust his understanding of things, extremely fallible as it is. However, he is under no illusions. He knows that whatever is ultimately valuable in his contribution comes not from him, but from the good God working in him in a way he does not understand. The evil which results even from his best-intentioned efforts will not dismay him, because he knows that he is a faulty organism, and the very evils will set the stage for something extremely good when seen from the viewpoint of eternity, which he now can only grasp by faith, not by vision. Wisely he will not expect paradise in the secular order nor is his eye fixed on such a goal for his actions. Yet nonetheless he will with wisdom fight injustice and unrighteousness and strive to acquire more knowledge wherever it may lie, always remembering that his wisdom is shot through with folly and his projects of amelioration fraught with strains of old and new injustice. He can do this because in the long run, in the moment beyond time, it will work out unto definitive good. In defective freedom he creates his world because the free Creator is using him as he is for the awesome glory of total creation. In part he understands, and this partial understanding is buttressed by faith, but much he does not understand and he accepts on trust the meaningfulness of it all. He may be weak, perverse and purblind, but God writes straight with crooked lines.

I submit that this man is free in the fullest sense of human freedom. It is not here a question of the physical possibility of choosing this or that, but the capacity for action, creativity and insight for the fullest liberation of human potential. We are not dealing with mere freedom *from* something as if that were all of the question, but we are proposing freedom *for* something, rendering freedom dynamic, liberating and creative. . . .

C. Commentary and Analysis

The notion of freedom, then, is a complex intelligibility which cannot be restrained within the limits of any simple set of formulae. We are forced to view it from many perspectives. That is why the

Christian reflection on freedom is open-ended and must be renewed continually.

Fundamental to the notion of freedom is a second notion, that of self-affirmation. Freedom is an act of self-affirmation. The description of freedom as choice between certain limited and non-necessary goods is an analysis of freedom at its most superficial and meaningless level. Much more profoundly, freedom involves an affirmation of self. Self-affirmation is essential to integral human existence. The self needs affirmation or else it withers, withdraws, becomes less and less self. It is necessary to the growth and maintenance of the Christian life.

One can carry this notion a step further. The self, as Weigel indicates, is a structured reality. It makes no difference how the terms of that structure are defined. We have been attempting to indicate some of the psychological aspects of that structure, but this is only one dimension. The essential note is that self-affirmation is, *eo ipso,* self-construction. The structure of the self is an evolving structure, always in the process of attainment. The affirmation of self in and through freedom is equivalently definable in terms of organization of structure. Freedom is thereby the *via regia* for self-organization, self-structuration, self-perfection. We can crystallize the psychological dimension of this aspect of freedom under the term "ego-synthesis." The free act, therefore, is an act of self-definition by which the ego elaborates and shapes the reality of the structure of the self. There is a transition from potency to actuality, from imperfection to perfection, from indetermination to determination. It is important, of course, to realize that human freedom from another point of view is a limping, fragile affair. The affirmation or structuration of self is never complete and is always tenuous. It achieves its objectives, if ever, in a painfully partial and piecemeal fashion. Perhaps the hardest thing for man to achieve is to become a fully autonomous and total self. The most difficult task is to become oneself.

Yet this is precisely what man is called to by the inherent dynamisms of his own nature. In fact, as Weigel points out so clearly, the goal of liberty, which is perfect self-affirmation, is beyond man's capability. Herein lies the most perplexing, the most mysterious, and yet the most essential facet of human existence: that man, who is compelled by the most profound dynamisms of his nature to seek the perfection of his own self-affirmation, carries within himself the obstacles to that achievement. His very affirmation is an affirmation of a torn and divided reality. The situation is not desperate, however, as we well know. The self-affirming and creative aspects of human freedom are an integral and most significant part of the divine plan. The dynamisms inherent in man's freedom are contiguous with the dynamisms operative through the salvific intervention of God. The completion of man's self-affirmation becomes possible only through the action of grace. What is important here is that one cannot say that man's self-affirmation is completed by grace. This is an impossible statement because it destroys the reality of man's self-affirmation and distorts the nature of grace. Affirmation of self must remain an active process carried out through the agency of man himself, or else it is no longer self-affirmation. Further, it is essential to the nature of grace that it exercise no effect independently of the agency of man himself. Rather, we must say that man's self-affirmation becomes more perfectly affirmation of self through the action of grace.

Weigel sums this up in the formula: Man's affirmation of self must ultimately be an affirmation of God in the self. The turn of phrase catches the intricacies of the life of grace. The inner dynamisms of man's existence find the fullness of their realization in man's inner relatedness to God. In Rahner's terms, the supernatural existential finds its proper and proportionate response in the dynamism of the action of grace. It is important, I think, to make it clear that the basic supposition in such a formulation is that man's nature is capable of affirmation and progressive perfection and that the agency of such affirmation is man himself. Without this realization, the whole import of the action of grace and the centrality of human freedom in the life of grace can be missed. Man's intrinsic perfection is the culmination of man's inherent relatedness to God, and conversely, the full realization of man's relatedness to God is dependent on and reflective of man's intrinsic perfection.

In a theological perspective, then, freedom is not so much a property as it is an enterprise. It is an enterprise demanding intense activity, and an enterprise whose objectives are as severe as any man proposes to himself. The enterprise is to become fully oneself. But the vision of what one is to become is itself beyond man's capacity. The goal of man's self-affirmation must be seen in the perspective of revelation. It is there that the more complete vision of man and his nature is embedded. It is the work of theological reflection to bring that vision into focus. It is interesting, therefore, that Christian theology stresses the profound reality of freedom and emphasizes its significance in the Christian life. In so doing, it gives to human freedom a most important role as an integral part of the image of man consonant with a theological anthropology.

Questions for Discussion

1. What factors make freedom so centrally important to theology?
2. To what root cause does Weigel ascribe the newly realized significance of theology?
3. What is "the first contribution of theology" to the discussion of freedom? Illustrate the significance of this contribution in the case of slavery.
4. Theology "begins with the supposition that the self is structured and that its affirmations must be related to that structure." Explain how this statement applies to freedom.
5. What are the three dimensions theology sees in the self? How does original sin fit into this perspective? Why is Augustine's anthropology very distasteful to naturalists?
6. Can the theologian admit an unconditional freedom in man? How does Catholic theology's optimism differ from Leibnizian optimism and Stoic resignation, according to Weigel? Discuss.
7. Why does the author say self-affirmation is essential to freedom?
8. Explain the meaning of "ego-synthesis."
9. What are the consequences of the fact that perfect self-affirmation is beyond man's capability?
10. "Freedom is not so much a property as it is an enterprise." Explain.

XII
PETER FRANSEN AND
THE PSYCHOLOGY OF GRACE

A. Prenote

The following essay represents in many ways a reaffirmation and resume of many of the points that have already been made in the course of our inquiry. However, Fransen also adds some considerations which further our inquiry into the life of grace.

Grace is, of course, opposed to sin. And the core of sin is denominated here as egoism. We should recall in this context the comments of Erikson on the opposition of the authentic ego and egoism. Egoism is a reflection of man's lower nature, of that vain sense of pride which magnifies the importance of the self-made and distorts the best instincts of man's real ego. It seems evident that the authentically functioning ego, in the most complete and irrevocable sense, stands in opposition to the disorientation we call egoism. If the staple of egoism is pride, the staple of the ego is humility. Humility must be included among the ego-strengths of which Erikson speaks.

It may seem strange that traditional Christian spirituality has always regarded humility as a *virtus*. One is prone to associate this "strength" with weakness — as though one could presume that only the weak would be humble and they only because they are weak. This is not Christian humility. Humility is related to that secure sense of self-possession which we speak of as a "sense of identity." The person who has achieved this sense is secure in the realization of his own antecedent worth and has no need to remind himself or others of it. At the same time, he is in a position to recognize and accept the worth and dignity of others. He respects that dignity and in so doing honors the inherent freedom and right of every man to that which is his due. Humility is often spoken of in terms of self-knowledge. It is more than that; it is self-acceptance. Total self-acceptance is impossible without a complementary acceptance of others and a regard for the autonomy of the other. In a Christian context, self-acceptance likewise requires a recognition and acceptance of one's essential creaturehood, an awareness of who and what one is as he stands in relation to the creating and loving God.

In the personality possessing a secure sense of identity and humility, there is not only no place for pride, but there is no need for it. It seems likely that pride itself is a psychological reaction to the lack of identity. Erikson speaks of the lack of identity under the rubric of "identity diffusion." The term is a good one, for the lack of definition of self, the lack of affirmation of self, is a kind of diffusion compounded by confusion. This is a threatening state, one which is permeated with the anxiety born of self-doubt and insecurity. This threat and this anxiety must be defended against. Pride is undoubtedly a form of defense in which the anxiety resulting from diffusion of the self is warded off by an urgent casting-up of a pseudo-self. Thus egoism is in reality a pseudo-egoism and the ego which is thus wrought is a fragile structure built upon the sands of insecurity. It must be bolstered continually with the treacherous bulwarks of an overweening self-confidence and the superficial trappings of self-esteem.

This is an important point, I think, for it highlights the action of grace, in its psychological influence and in its opposition to human sinfulness. The opposition between grace and pride would suggest that the operation of grace is localized at that segment of the psychic structure in which pride takes its origin. The operation of grace within the ego, then, strikes not at pride itself, but at the root of pride, the deficiencies of the ego which give rise to the defense of pride. Moreover, human sinfulness is a form of disorientation and defective valuation. Grace works not so much against sinful acts as against the basic disorientation or defect in the ego which gives rise to that disordered behavior we call sinful.

We have here before us the beginnings of a program of psycho-

logical reflection and study which extends the psychology of grace
to the limits of the Christian experience. The Belgian theologian
Peter Fransen sketches some of the lines of that immense program
in the following excerpts from an article published in *Lumen Vitae*
12:2 (1957), pp. 203-232.

B. Selection: Toward a Psychology of Grace

Introduction

Our period is partial to totality. We do not like conceptual dis-
section; sciences in watertight compartments annoy us and prevent
us from reaching the moving, living and integral reality. This passion for the totality of reality ought not to make us forget the ac-
quisitions of past centuries. Each science, in fact, possesses its
own method, imposed by its subject. And in its turn, this subject
only attains one very definite aspect of the reality which corresponds strictly to the point of view proper to the science. Medicine was only able really to develop when it was freed from
Aristotelian philosophy. It is indubitable that the secret of the
immense success of modern positive sciences lies in this emancipa-
tion and specialization.

This desire for unity which is the note of our period may give
rise to the illusory dream of a unique science, which would
threaten the integrity and the wealth of our scientific effort. In this
connection we may be reminded of the naive enthusiasm of the
first humanists in the fifteenth century. It is fair to admit, however,
that it expresses a very profound truth. Reality is one, truth is one,
and the man who thinks and seeks is one. But confusion never can
breed unity. Every man for himself, and the whole of mankind,
journeying throughout history, has the intellectual, moral and religious task of elaborating a coherent view of the totality of reality.
This work, which appeals intensely to the men of any period who
have not lost the strength and courage to be human, will only be accomplished in the scrupulous respect of the subject and methods
proper to each science.

The unity and integrity of our vision of reality cannot be limited to a special science or faculty, even to our understanding. It is our personal affair; it depends on an existential and personal choice which appropriates to itself and integrates the multiple data of the different sciences. This fundamental option is sovereign, because responsible; it is not however either independent or blind, because at the same time it is an act of humble submission to reality in its amplitude, but also in its depth. For a believer it will end in an act of faith and adoration.

Whatever may be thought in certain quarters, this anxious search for the unity of knowledge affects the believer above all, not of course him for whom the faith is a comfortable excuse dispensing him from thought, but the true believer who, like Jacob, wrestles with his God. It is one of the chief reasons which have led us to seek for the implications of the divine mystery of grace on the human plane.

Grace is before all a divine act. This act is not at all foreign to our life; on the contrary! By that very fact grace becomes a very complex reality. We cannot here refer to the theology of the Christian East, a theology of participation, divinization, image and light. Even in the West many were the ways followed by Christian thought concerning this fact of faith and, what is more, through their different point of view, they do not entirely coincide. One theology can be studied without having to think of the other. But by the very fact of their unique subject they are truly complementary and mutually correct each other.

If we consider the history of western theology on grace, we first discover a method which is descriptive by means of symbols, images or reasoning, especially attentive to the *psychological and moral* fact. Next comes the *scholastic* method, familiar to theologians, a strictly scientific, reflective, objective and conceptual method. Starting from a revealed truth, this method searches for the necessary and universal a priori conditions of the metaphysical possibility of this subject of faith. Our period regards this method with a certain disfavor, but easily forgets its qualities of clarity, precision and depth.

It also has its limits. And so we find, starting from the philosophy implied in sacred scripture, in the great mystical schools of the middle ages and down to our own times, a third way which today we may call *existential, personalist* and *dialectical*. It is inspired by a great phenomenology of the personality and may develop in the direction of a true metaphysic of Christian existence.

In this article we shall be dealing chiefly with the psychology of grace. But a purely descriptive psychology would, in that case, be very difficult and open to suspicion. We deliberately outline this psychology as a Christian philosopher and a believer. We shall then complete it by a philosophy which is chiefly personalist, inspired by the work of Karl Rahner, S.J., and the dialectical and mystical anthropology of the Blessed John Ruusbroec, one of the most remarkable thinkers of our country. . . .

1. Nature and Liberty

The first point of our article introduces the *fundamental consideration of man and his liberty*. For it is with man above all that we are concerned.

Man is not a soul lost as though by accident in a vile and weighty body, a spirit imprisoned in foreign matter, hostile to his highest aspirations. Those are gnostic, Platonian and Manichaean errors which have not yet been entirely exorcized. *Man is intrinsically one:* a spiritualized body, or, more correctly, a corporal person.

On the other hand, the soul is not the body. Soul and body are like two poles in a unique magnetic field, in which the lines of force cross each other and continually interpenetrate one another. In no way can the actions, states, even the most subtle or the most material, which belong uniquely and exclusively to the soul or body, be disassociated. The psychology of man and child leads to this conclusion and it is therefore unnecessary to dwell upon it.

It would, however, be an error to imagine that we look upon body and soul as two opposing forces, practically equivalent, different, but purely complementary. It is still more important for our viewpoint to perceive that in this profound unity the spirit still keeps an *inalienable initiative*. The image of God which he in his creative action has implanted in my whole being is most deeply imprinted in this spiritual center of my being, that center of personal density in which I am most myself, and by reason of that, most in God. It is from this center of existential density that these features of the divine image are diffused through all the levels of my existence, always further penetrating into my intellect and my will, my imagination and my sensibility, all my psychism of heredity and behavior, my habits and my daily actions, to bestow even on my body an aura of nobility and beauty.

Here a Christian theology of the creation and the divine image and a sane personalist philosophy should complete, correct and develop what there is of imprecision and indistinctness in the conclusions of psychology, however just they may be.

God is love. The image of God in us will therefore also be love, the force of love of God, of others and of myself in God. This fundamental power of love constitutes my person. I am in fact a person because I am spirit. Because I am spirit, I am liberty and therefore love. For liberty is above all a power of spontaneous gift from one person to another, before being choice, election, judgment and free will.

In fact, there is in us as it were a double liberty, precisely because we are corporal spirits, bodies with a depth of life which far exceeds the requirements of our material and even our earthly life. There is naturally the liberty which we all know from experience, what is commonly known as *free will*. There is further down in us a *fundamental liberty of existential and totalizing option*.

This distinction is of capital importance in order to understand human behavior in general, and especially to detect the incidence of divine grace in us.

We know by experience what I have called free will, that liberty by means of which man can to a certain degree order his life. He gets up, he eats, he reads a book rather than go for a walk, he refuses an invitation, he is obstinate, persistent, or accepts an excuse. Even children very early possess this possibility of choice. It is freedom in the usual sense of the word. All the same, it may be asked whether *as such* it merits the name of liberty. Animals have it also, if we can judge by their behavior, and children who, whether they profit by it, or abuse it, do not by that prove themselves already capable of true liberty.

If it is to become truly human, this early form of liberty must

be directed by something deeper, more stable also and more complete. It must be supported and directed by a profound and total
commitment, by a fundamental option in which *I express myself
wholly* with all that I wish to be in this world and before God.
The fragmentary variety of daily options is therefore unthinkable
— I might say, inhuman and therefore animal — without a totalizing, profound, stable and spontaneous orientation of my life, of the
whole of myself before the totality of the reality which I either
accept or refuse.

Note well: These two forms of liberty *have no separate existence.*
We have often noticed that we are not understood on this point.
The fundamental option is not one particular action, more important than others, following or preceding the more specialized choice
of some concrete action. It is not a matter of determining in the
first instant a "fundamental option," and then freely to develop
all the concrete implications, as does an architect who first designs
the sketch of the house to be built, chooses one or another kind
of villa, in order to finally carry out the plan in its least details in
the course of several months' work.

For this fundamental option, this existential and total engagement is also impossble if it is not *at the same time* actualized in a
series of particular actions, forming the visible woof of our life. It
is not therefore a concrete action; it is an orientation freely imposed
on our whole life. It is *implied* in every truly human and free action,
for each concrete and determined action in so far as it is truly free
is caught in the free and spontaneous movement toward the final
goal of my life. . . .

In order clearly to establish the essential, we have had to sim-
plify the problem a little. The human situation is rather more deli-
cate and it is here that the psychologists come in. Man is spirit and
person in this temporal and material world. That is to say that my
fundamental option cannot emerge to the surface of my daily activity except by a *long process of maturation in time.* Neither can it
incarnate itself in a series of precise and concrete actions except
by *traversing a thick layer of humanity,* in which spirit and body
intimately interpenetrate and in which man is no longer alone in
bearing the responsibility of his life.

1. *The fundamental option is only expressed in time.* Liberty is

not bestowed upon us like a beautiful Minerva, rising whole out of the head of Jupiter. We have to conquer it freely, to deserve to be free. We are not yet speaking of grace, which according to the ancient councils restores to us our lost liberty. We are speaking of that human condition, situated in time, borne by the flux of history. Every action which is truly free, every good action, fully responding to the truth of what we are and should be, frees us further. Every bad action, that is to say, false and deceitful, freely degrades that same liberty. In a certain sense, *we are not free; we freely become so.* That is our vocation as men, which has to be fulfilled in the totality of each life.

To be a person, to be free, is the task of a whole life. It is a true creation — in the artistic sense — irksome, arduous, prolonged. It is a long process of maturation, appertaining to all living things. It is true that man can distort this process of growth, can interrupt it, turn it away from its true end, and empty it of meaning by a kind of spiritual atrophy, freely accepted under the disillusions of life.[1]

2. *Our fundamental option is psychologically conditioned by the influence of others.* It would here be opportune to glance at a communal philosophy of the person, but it would take us too far and some psychological considerations will suffice for the moment.

By the very fact that the spirit plunges and sends its roots into this psycho-somatic humus of humanity, it can no longer be sovereignly alone. Man is linked to others by his body and his whole psychism, he receives as much as he gives. In his youth, he does almost nothing but receive. He receives his body, and with his body many other things which are largely determinant for him: his heredity, his temperament and character to a great extent preformed in his race, his people, his family and national culture, the atmosphere of his native land.

In order to act he has to reason, which implies a certain intelligence, received at birth, later formed in a family, school and cultural milieu. He has to will. It is therefore important that he should

---

[1] This spiritual atrophy may find its source in certain forms of illness or senility. It is then involuntary and pathological. But it may also be freely willed as a form of personal suicide. See on this subject the remarkable article by J. De Guibert, "La médiocrité spirituelle," *Revue d'ascétique et de mystique,* 16 (1926), pp. 113-131.

possess a certain force of character, stability in his intentions, an amount of endurance in difficulties. A spoiled child inherits, by his sentimental and imprudent parents, a softness which will not affect the child in a numerous family whom his parents have educated with a virile and strong love. All this therefore does not depend only on his liberty.

Man also needs an atmosphere of optimism, confidence, a nervous and affective equilibrium. To express himself in a fundamental option which is rich and integral he has to dispose of several faculties (intellect, memory, will) and certain spiritual organs with a psychic basis, such as the sense of the beautiful, the real, others, the sense of values, and even the moral sense. He also must be able to count on a sane and stable equilibrium of his instincts. Finally, even the health of his body is of importance in this total exercise of his liberty.

This total liberty is therefore expressed through a dense network of determinisms, influences foreign to my own will. The success of my life will depend on the art with which I learn to use to the fullest extent everything at my disposal, everything which has been given to me. That is the meaning of the parable of the talents, what is nowadays called the *situation* in which I find myself, from the beginning of my life. The object of all education is to render this situation of departure as favorable as possible.

Man is therefore placed by God in a determined situation of which the multiple incidences are far beyond his personal initiative. But these determinisms, these foreign influences, good or bad, cannot raise him to the level of a truly human life unless he possesses in the depths of himself a divine source of life, a force of activity, a creative and fundamental power of love. God is love. Man created in the image of God is love above all, the reflection of the first Love, as Dante said in the last verse of his work: *L'amor che muove il sole e l'altre stelle!*

In this depth of himself, man reposes in the hands of God and God sustains him in existence. In these depths reposes what the bible calls the "heart" of man, the center of all his activity. The mystics have called it the "interior flame," or with St. Francis de Sales, "the fine point of the soul." This "metaphysic of depth" owes nothing to the researches of psychoanalysis. It is part of the

Christian philosophy, especially experienced by the greatest mystics. In writing these pages we desire nothing more than to express in modern language one of the most profound thoughts of the anthropology of Blessed John Ruusbroec.[2]

2. Theology of Grace

Man's situation, as taught us by Christ and scripture, is still more complicated by the fact of sin. Man is no longer whole. He is born a sinner. What does that mean? I have just described that fundamental and total option of an entire life: the spiritual and spontaneous engagement of a free person, which takes place in those mysterious depths of personal liberty, but which is incarnated and actualized in my daily actions. It is at that level that the problem of sin is most acute.

That option is situated, in fact, before an essential alternative. St. Augustine's lapidary expression is well known: There are only two possible loves for us, the love of God to the forgetfulness of self, or the love of self to the forgetfulness and denial of God. At first sight this alternative might seem simplistic and foreign to the variety and multiplicity of choices offered to man. But on the level of our fundamental option, St. Augustine could not have expressed himself more correctly. On that level there is only one possible alternative: love of God through love of others, for that is our human condition, or else love of self, the voluntary inclusion in oneself under all the forms of vanity, brutal and even sensual egoism, pride, or simply in the form of spiritual atrophy by a drawing into oneself, a slackening of our activity, a kind of flight from reality and others into a minute world of imagination or bourgeois comfort. This self-love is sin, the only definitive evil for man.

We must insist in respect of this on the fact that sin always has a core of pride, or simply egoism, the petty vanity of the bourgeois. There is often to be found among certain educators or preachers,

---

[2] The best introduction which we know of, to the anthropology and theology of Ruusbroec, is that by P. Henry, "La mystique trinitaire du Bienheureux Jean Ruusbroec," in *Recherches de Science religieuse,* 40 (1951-1952), pp. 335-368 and 41 (1953), pp. 51-75.

even among scholarly theologians, an obsession with sins of the flesh. Obviously, sexual sin is a sin, and even a grave one, but it is grave because of a spiritual reason. If it is a grave sin it is because it is, for men, the most absorbing occasion for incarnating and actualizing a fundamental egoism and love of pleasure. From the specific point of view of passionate or instinctive disorder, it is above all a human weakness.

This definition enables us to determine more exactly the nature of that malice which we all have inherited from our parents and which we call original sin. I have neither the intention nor the opportunity of expounding here the whole theology of original sin, above all the nature of the consequences of that state of perdition and separation from God, called in technical language *concupiscence*. It has been stated quite often that the consequences of original sin are to be found in a disequilibrium between the tendencies of the body and those of the soul. This explanation is insufficient. There is something deeper and more essential than that. This seed of iniquity which infects our life possesses, like everything else in man, *a spiritual root*. Original sin as a sore in human nature is a latent love of self, a fundamental individualism which dwells in man and which causes him to make use of everything which comes into his hands for his own petty and immediate purposes. It is besides because my spirit is "curved in on itself" that my sexual instincts have such a strong hold on my life, are so often a cause of sin and that there is an unstable balance between the aspirations of my body and my soul.

Thus, from the psychological point of view, the task of an educator will necessarily be the creation of an atmosphere of devotion, of service, self-forgetfulness, and even, simply, interest in others. Everything that detaches the child and man from himself, which opens windows on reality, nature, his fellows, has a real religious significance. Man has to be saved from himself, gently and adroitly extracted from that circle in which the hardness and clumsiness of adults, as well as his own sinful tendencies, have enclosed him.

Let us now turn our attention to grace. It is love above all. It is again St. Augustine who gives us this happy definition of grace: *Quia amasti me, fecisti me amabilem.* "Because you loved me first, Lord, you have made me lovable": in the double sense of "worthy of love" and "capable of love." In these words is summed up the whole mystery of divine grace. In grace, it is God who begins, God who works, God who finishes: this divine primacy of grace is often neglected by our western Semipelagianism.

Grace has been defined as a divine force, a divine movement in me, a divine gift, supernatural wealth, a merit carefully inscribed in the book of life. That is all true. But grace is much more. It is above all the communication of the divine life to me, as the Greek fathers have said: God became man so that men might become God. But what does that mean? Grace is, fundamentally, the fact that by the divine love of the Father I have become his child; I have become like his own Son, not obviously by identity of nature, but an adopted son by divine gift. I truly share through grace, although in a human degree, in that immense reality which is the love of the Son for his Father. I therefore love the Father through grace in a certain way as he is loved by his Son. I also love other men a little bit as the Son himself loved them and still loves them. And as it was through the strength of the Spirit that Christ on earth — Ruusbroec would add, and also in heaven — loved his Father above all in the execution of his work of redemption, so our love of the Father, in the image of that of the Son, is borne and sustained by that mysterious force, so gentle in its divine violence, which is the Holy Spirit.

That love which descended into me by baptism is a new "filial" love in the most profound sense. By baptism we became, as Fr. Emile Mersch writes, *filii in Filio;* adopted children in and through the only Son. This love is nothing else than a participation in the love which the Son has for the Father. The Father loved me first from all eternity as his child in and by his only Son. And, by the creative and saving force of this first eternal and personal love, I can in future love the Father with the Son, like the Son, because of the Son and by the Son, all by the strength of the Holy Spirit.

This love, therefore, does not possess its explanation and root in the fact and experience of human love, but in the revealed mystery of the divine love of the Son for his Father. It is important here to note that being essentially a divine reality which by participation descends into our life, this love, as such, cannot be the subject of psychological experiments or studies. It is supernatural, for it raises us to the level of the divine life in the intimacy of the blessed Trinity. Moreover, it is given us during this life as "seed," a vocation to be realized in the course of our existence on earth. It is only in heaven that what we are will appear. As such it is the object of faith.

We now can understand how grace really destroys sin in us. It is not a juridical affair, as one might think from reading some theological treatises. Grace truly destroys, burns up in us every trace of sin, because it is an appeal to filial love: precisely the opposite to sin. Fundamentally, there is only grace which can deliver us from self-obsession. This is one of its most profound effects, because grace is love, love of others, and by this sacrament of fraternal charity, love of God. It is true that this warfare against sin in us and around us will last our whole life long. The primordial fact remains that only grace is able to break that magic circle, that solitude of sin.

There is nothing clearer than this vision of our faith. We are born sinners, or more exactly, in a state of loss, distance and solitude, with that self-approbation which is the immediate consequence. We are the more confirmed sinners the more we continue to actualize this fundamental egoism; we settle down more firmly in our pride. Only the grace of Christ can save us from ourselves, and therefore give us back to ourselves. This grace of Christ restores to us that liberty of which we wrote in the first part of this article.

We must consider in what way this divine life operates in us. This life affects us, in fact, chiefly *in the heart of our free being,* where our existence is and continually flows from the creative hands of God.

This divine love comes to me first as a call from God, an exigence from above, a creative ascendancy which penetrates into the deepest part of my being and invites me, draws me, attracts me, as St. John says, to the total and loving acceptance of God in faith, hope and charity. Grace is a reality which, while impregnating the very center of my personality, this existential density of which we spoke above, gently urges me, *from inside,* to a fundamental option, this time a supernatural one, because divine, struck in the image of the Son by the seal of the Holy Spirit. It is therefore an existential engagement of the Christian, an engagement of grace: inasmuch as I am, in the depths of myself and in my totality, borne and penetrated by the aspiring force of divine love to the constant realization in the development of my life of this profound and total gift of my "heart."

Grace is therefore united to this fundamental liberty of my person in order to metamorphose slowly, but from the interior, in a lengthy maturation and spiritual growth, my intellect, will and sensibility and even my body. If these effects of grace are often so little perceptible in our lives, it is precisely because we are so slow to welcome this divine call. Only the saints witness clearly by their lives the earthly triumphs of grace.

Blessed John Ruusbroec has defined in a few words the supernatural process of this growth in grace in his book on spiritual marriage. God, he says, acts from the interior to the exterior; man, on the contrary, from the exterior (words, examples, acquired habits, etc.) to the interior. Thus God acts in every man from the interior, the center of his existence, to penetrate him slowly by an extension and an infiltration of his gracious influence out to the peripheral regions of his humanity.

3. Psychology of Grace

Let us first consider the question of the possibility of a psychology of grace, for the answer is not an obvious one. It is not even uniform in Catholic theology. We shall then venture to make some general suggestions for the elaboration of a psychology and phenomenology of grace as foundations for a Christian humanism.

At first sight it appears as though any psychology of grace is an impossibility. There are various theological and philosophical reasons for this. The mystery of grace is a divine mystery. It entirely transcends the powers of our created and sinful humanity. Grace is a participation of the divine life in us. God does not allow himself to be the subject of experiment.

The fundamental option of grace is, moreover, said to be supernatural both by its source, which is divine, and its object, which also is God, the revealed God of our salvation. These two aspects of our supernatural commitment necessarily elude our psychological experience. Besides, the supernatural influence which raises this option to the level of participation in the divine life does not penetrate it from the outside like a foreign body, or a coercive force which would break and interrupt the spontaneous evolution of our liberty. In this case it would impose itself upon our attention, if only in a negative way, by the force of its impact, leaving a kind of subconscious trauma in the soul.

No one shows more respect for our liberty than God himself. It is the very imprint of his eternal liberty, the image of his love in us. That is why we think the dialectical anthropology of Blessed John Ruusbroec so important on this point. Grace penetrates us in the depths of our being, the point at which we are continually proceeding from the creative hands of God. It is therefore truly "from the inside" that God acts on our liberty, from that connecting point, if one may so call it, where that liberty is continually engendered by God and rests in his conservative action. So this divine influx leads us freely "from inside to outside" ourselves, by the inwardness of our liberty. Starting from this existential and total center, the divine influx adapts itself perfectly, without check or break, to the evolution of our free spontaneity. This is the only possible explanation, the place where Creator and creature meet, absolute existence and shared existence. . . .

We do not in any way agree with the opinion which was very widespread during the last centuries in theological treatises on grace. Their objections allow us, however, to make certain important concessions, which will influence our final reply. Human and Christian experience does in fact appear to support them. Grace does not change anything in physical laws. It changes nothing in the historical laws which rule our human condition, in the social, psychological and biological laws. The fact that I am in a state of grace does not save me from bankruptcy if I am imprudent in business; from beng killed in a motor accident; from becoming ill, from letting my mental equilibrium be affected by an unfortunate heredity, or drink, or sorrow, or overwork. . . .

It is thus that the world always keeps its own earthly laws open to human sciences. These laws ensure to human sciences, psychology, sociology and even pedagogy, theoretical and practical, the autonomy to which they have a right, not an absolute autonomy, proper to what would then be a unique science, yet a complete autonomy in their own sphere. This sphere is clearly limited by their subjects and methods. . . .

In these preliminary considerations we have left free to speak all those who for theological, philosophical or psychological reasons are opposed to the possibility of a psychology of grace. Their objections demonstrate that the problem is not a simple one. They free us from any naiveté or undue enthusiasm. What is more, they allow us to outline certain distinctions, very important in practice.

We have an unquestionable preference for the ancient doctrine: the doctrine of the fathers, especially of St. Augustine, the pre-scholastics and the great theologians of the thirteenth century.

After an eclipse of several centuries, this doctrine has in our time acquired a preponderant position in Catholic theology. We therefore accept without hesitation the thesis called Thomist, according to which there really exists a psychology of grace. The reasons are given above. We are even so convinced that we think that a philosophy of man, even if pretending to be a philosophy of pure nature, in other words, of man without grace and delivered over to himself alone, even if it is an atheistic philosophy, will be influenced and conditioned, often unconsciously, by this primordial reality of our existence.

All philosophy, even objective, as it is called now, and conceptual, must inevitably start from man's concrete experience, the experience of departure, also controlled experience. This experience cannot but be influenced by this primordial reality: *the fact that God calls every man to a supernatural intimacy with the blessed Trinity.* It is true that only believers possess a definite consciousness of this, received through revelation. That does not alter the fact that since the promise on the threshold of our history, mankind has lived in what is called in theology the *status hominis lapsi et reparati;* every man lives under *the concrete and creative will* of God, who wills to save us in Christ. This divine will *has radically changed the very basis* of our existential and concrete dynamism. Karl Rahner has called this obscure aspiration of every man toward the God of salvation a supernatural "existential," that is to say an a priori constituent of our historical and concrete existence.

If every man is fundamentally oriented toward God from birth, what of the man who freely lets himself be urged by this supernatural impulse, and accepts by a fundamental option this interior vocation of divine grace? What was at first only an obscure urge, an implicit tendency, a fundamental orientation, "offered grace," as Karl Rahner says, becomes under divine influence "grace accepted existentially." We thereafter act under the impulse of a fundamental option of grace, supernaturally; we are really in a state of grace, really justified and sanctified. We have already dealt at length with this state of grace under the divine influence and in the fundamental consent of our liberty.

We should like to touch on another aspect, which is not sufficiently taken into account in the western theology of grace, which is often somewhat Manichaean. Grace can in a certain measure, as we see in the life of St. Teresa of Avila, become a *force of spiritual and psychic health.* Grace, in fact, tends to heal us completely, certainly after this life, but to a certain extent already on earth. It depends among other things on the will of God and also on the fullness of our submission to the call of grace. This theology is to be found among the Greek fathers, who often describe grace by its *corporeal* aspect as the seed of incorruptibility and immortality. Grace possesses already and now a real sway over the whole of our humanity. It thus prepares our body for the final resurrection and can heal our psychic weaknesses. It remains a fact that for most men a defective psychism may continue, as we have seen, to hinder to a large degree and to inhibit the development of their moral personality, even with grace. Grace is not yet heaven. But it effectively guides us to heaven and because of that, as the seed of eternity, prepares us and predisposes us to the resurrection and eternal beatitude. . . .

If what we have stated so far is true, grace and the life of grace are of paramount interest to the psychologist. There is only one condition for success. He must at least accept as a real possibility the existence of a personal God of love who interests himself in man. It is obvious that faith and charity will greatly sharpen his spiritual sense. One can only understand a life by living it oneself. That is the meaning of the words of that great psychologist of grace,

Augustine, so often repeated by the mystics: "Give me one who loves and he will understand what I say; give me one who desires, who is hungry, who feels the nostalgia of solitude in this exile, and who is thirsty and sighs after the living waters of the eternal fatherland; give me such a one, and he understands what I say. But if I must explain myself to a frosty indifference, he will not understand." This psychology remains a closed book to the man who has chosen an atheistic or vaguely pantheist materialism. . . .

Psychology is mainly a science of observation. It must observe, consider, describe, individual or collective religious experience. Here there is an immense field of study open to the psychology of grace.

The Christian psychologist will however feel specially drawn to certain experiences, the freshness, authenticity and inner intensity of which attract his attention. The difficulties of which we have spoken above, which make it so hard to discern the fundamental inspiration of a concrete life, inevitably bring out favorable examples. We are thinking of the testimony of converts, or the long story of eternal pilgrims like Péguy or Simone Weil. Their youth and their intellectual, sentimental and spiritual formation has often been deprived of typically religious or theological influences. They do not know the religious clichés, the pious reflexes, the "suitable words," which so often disguise the sincerity or real fervor of the believer coming from old Christian stock. The conventional language of certain nuns is of little use in these psychological studies! Take for example the discussions concerning the manuscript of the *Story of a Soul* of little St. Thérèse!

There are also moments of intense or prolonged religious life which force us to a greater nudity in our gestures, attitudes and words. They recur at times of bitter trial or great joy, in the story of a vocation or a great love. All true love purifies, in marriage as well.

These different advantages are all to be found in the lives of the great mystics. They have all been the privileged subjects of religious and Christian psychology. We are still too easily distracted by the study of the extraordinary phenomena which belong to psycho-pathology or para-psychology. These studies have their own importance but the inner life must exert an irresistible attraction for any psychologist who is really fascinated by the problem of man and his destiny. In the mystics we shall discover that only the true act of virtue is really free, the secret and the originality of true liberty. There is nothing more fascinating than this infinite originality of the saints, compared with the monotony of sin, the mechanical and empty automatism of evil.

To these central themes we could add tributary subjects for study, which may be of great utility when treated with prudence and discernment. First, there is artistic religious expression. The artist who treats a religious subject is not always a believer. Aestheticism, as we know, floats in the space between dream and reality. On the other hand, true artists have a power of introspection and especially of suggestive expression which not all the saints possess.

There is also the comparative study of other religions. And in this connection, it is not primarily a matter of demonstrating what they lack. According to our faith every man is called by God and every sincere man will find God in the intimacy of his heart and by means of the traditions, doctrines and authentically religious actions of his beliefs. We can therefore discern in these other religions those fundamental attitudes which already foreshadow the actions of the Christian. For instance, it is remarkable to note how the great Chinese convert, John Wu, distinguished jurist and politician, former Chinese ambassador to the Holy See, confesses that he rediscovered, enriched and unified in Catholicism, the noblest aspirations that he had nourished in Confucianism, Taoism and Buddhism.

We have always been struck by the difference between the "great converts" and those whose sincere conversion leaves something to be desired on the human and religious plane. The former have perhaps struggled and suffered much before taking the decisive step, but after having found peace they never refuse to witness to their profound gratitude for the most authentic teachings of their ancient beliefs. The converts whom I may shortly describe as poor and pitiful can never rid themselves of a certain "renegade" complex. They have a quite useless desire to attack and deride their former coreligionists, showing thereby that their conversion is not yet complete, but remains impure, stained by an aggressiveness which is not religion.

Finally, collective religious phenomena cannot be set aside.

There is naturally the folklore and religious symbolism to which Jung has drawn attention, and which so easily deteriorates by the weight of the human masses into superstitions and magical practices. But there is more than that. It is false to think that people as a whole are exclusively inclined to materialize religious sentiment. In this connection we think that we ought to provide a special place for the study of prayer, its fundamental attitudes, its universal structures, its privileged positions, its great themes and its communal expression in liturgy. Those who have followed closely the revival of the celebration of the Paschal Vigil know that people are capable of an authentic religious life if they are initiated into religious mysteries by an enlightened preparation and a liturgical symbolism which touches their own lives. It is true that sentimentality is the poetry of the masses, but they are able to go beyond it when invited to an active and intelligent participation.

The psychologist has not only to observe, but must try to understand. Every science of observation understands by unifying, discovering under the multiplicity of phenomena what is their deep-lying meaning, their identical structure. It is here that psychology can develop into phenomenology. . . .

As we said at the beginning of this article, we do not want to linger on questions of technical methodology. It is enough to describe it in these terms. We here mean by *phenomenology* any psychological description of the fundamental and concrete attitudes of man, in a particular experiment aiming at the discovery of those structures and forms which by their uniformity, intensity and depth give a meaning to and explain the foregoing experiment. Religious phenomenology will therefore attempt to discover by successive reductions the concrete, existential and personalist structure of religious experience, that is, the fundamental experience in its pure state.

We are here confronted by an extensive and little explored region. We have chiefly been speaking of grace and we now propose to suggest some chapters for a phenomenology of grace. This example will go further than our description to explain what we mean by these words.

The life of grace, especially if it is intense, always implies *a sentiment of the divine presence* from the objective point of view.

I find myself entirely absorbed by an invisible personal mystery. It is a total, living presence, a divine activity, more real than my surroundings. Visible things both hide and display it. This divine mystery is in things and beyond them. It is silent and speaks to me, signs to me, through this created world which separates me from and unites me to my Lord.

It is moreover a *holy* presence. It fills me with fear, with an immense respect, a religious terror. At the same time I feel drawn to it, warmed, followed by a loving gaze, in intimate union with this mystery which surrounds and penetrates me.

When I now turn my attention to the subjective aspects of this experience as far as it seems to appear at the surface from the depths of my consciousness, I am aware of a deep tearing away, an inner suffering, an inexpressible *solitude*. I feel myself alone before my God, misunderstood by others, but also far from God himself, because totally unworthy of his presence. The better I know myself, the more the distance between the divine sanctity and my unworthiness increases like an unbridgeable chasm. The more I allow myself to be penetrated by the sanctity of his presence, the further I descend, the further I am from my Love. It is the night of the mystics, the wounding of the soul experienced by every man who has to lose himself to find himself by finding God. It is also the anguish of risking all, of the leap into the invisible. One perceives with ever increasing clarity that one must truly leave all to find all, to lose everything which supports my human certainty.

And yet this suffering is accompanied by a profound *joy,* an ineffable accomplishment. Even in physical sufferings, in the sorrows of life, this peace and intimate sweetness never leaves me. It is such a sweet joy, which seems hardly perceptible, and yet I feel it in me strong and unbreakable, able to change me entirely, to carry me along above the worst trials. It is known that this joy can sometimes become so intense that it has to express itself by gestures, song, cries and tears of joy. It is a sweetness which brings us also *near to others:* we can no longer keep it jealously for ourselves. Others also, our brethren, must know and share it.

It might be thought that an experience such as this appears to be disconnected, unbalanced and torn by contrary sentiments. But the contrary is true. If there is anything certain it is that this religious experience exerts a wonderful power of interiorization. It is supremely unifying, totalizing. A man may lead a life torn by multiple responsibilities, destroyed by terrible trials, but nothing escapes this aspiring power of spiritual integration which rises from his heart. Nothing surprises him, nothing dismays him, nothing discourages him. Everything takes on a meaning and becomes possible, for he is possessed by love. We have said above that this unifying presence can also attain to the integration of physical forces and even cure a mental lack of balance from the inside. . . .

We have made a few suggestions for a psychology and phenomenology of grace. The importance of such studies will be realized by all. They save the theologian from his abstractions, present the philosopher with the description of a vital, concrete and rich experience which is able to control his systematic analyses. For the psychologist by nature and vocation they seem to me to be of most superior and absorbing interest.

We would like to end this article by drawing attention to the practical utility of these studies for a sane and normal religious life. The psychologist indeed is almost the only one, if he remains truly faithful to his Christian sense, to be able to unmask with authority all the manifestations of a sickly and false religiosity. There is nothing more harmful to the life of grace than that hysteria or paranoia which apes religion. On the other hand, nothing so attracts unhealthy minds as the mysteries of our faith. It happens that priests and often even religious or ecclesiastical superiors are easily deceived. An eminent superior of a religious order confessed one day that it had taken him ten years of experience to realize that most of his subjects who had laid before him vast plans of reforms or activities were psychically unstable. This hidden disease, which is moreover terribly infectious, is a real menace to any life of grace. It distorts that maturation in grace of which we have spoken, and also creates unhealthy and fallacious illusions, which spoil many lives. Vanity and pride soon take their part in it, for these forms of unhealthy religiosity are so much easier, so much more alluring, because more obvious and exciting. With a defective theology of the supernatural and a propensity for the extraordinary, one soon arrives at despising the humble work of every day and exalting all forms of activity or apostleship which are in any way out of the ordinary. An incessant disquiet urges these injurious minds to continual reforms which, scarcely outlined, give way to other manifestations, each more striking and unexpected than the last. This disease is a threat to religious orders, schools of spirituality, youth movements, and many other institutions in the Church which could be so useful without it.

It is the task of the Christian psychologist to educate his contemporaries and demonstrate to them the ways of a real mental hygiene and frankly to draw their attention to the many dangers of deviation.

Humanism and Christian humanism is much talked about. The Greco-Roman humanism has exhausted its resources. Confronted by this new world opening before us, with its technology, its totalitarian spirit, its mixture of races and civilizations, we need a humanism more conscious of itself, more conscious also of its possibilities and its limits. We think that the Christian psychologist has a very special vocation in the world of today. He is able to collaborate in the evolution of a true Christian humanism, wiser because more universal, in depth as in breadth. Humanism is not of course grace. But the Church has very rightly always believed that it was indispensable for the normal development of the interior and divine life in this earthly society, the rough draft of the future city.

C. Commentary and Analysis

While the resources of the Christian tradition are immense, the reality of grace is complex. It influences the Christian life at the most profound and meaningful levels. Yet historical riches do not constitute a psychology of grace. The Christian psychologist must make a needed reformulation, a resynthesis in terms which have psychological relevance and significance. We have felt that the essential first step in such a reformulation was to bring to focus an image of Christian man which would provide a common ground for a sound psychology and a theological anthropology. From the basic image, the psychology of grace can proceed on its own terms, guided by the riches of tradition which are cast in terms made relevant through a common image. For there is little question that the psychological inquiry cannot go very far on its own. Ultimately our knowledge of the reality of grace, and the nature of its effects, rests on the revealed word of God and the continuing inquiry of the Church into its theological significance. Psychology, then, functions here as the handmaid of theology, bringing theological understanding to bear on the problems and concerns of the contemporary world. The work of the Christian psychologist, then, has special relevance, because there is no place where the Church's teaching touches modern man more intimately and more profoundly than in his search for self-understanding.

One can turn, therefore, to the vast wealth of patristic teaching, to the rich implications of religious symbolism, to the sublime and tormented experience of chosen souls, to the acutely analytic reflections of the theological tradition, and to the phenomenology of the Christian life as it is lived in our day. In all of these we find substance for psychological reflection on the life of grace. But from the point of view of psychological inquiry, one cannot work in a vacuum. One must choose a point of view, a systematic organization of ideas, to serve as a guide for one's thinking and theoretical formulations. Although our consideration thus far has suggested that psychoanalytic theory is the one current reconstruction which bests suits our purpose, this is an arbitrary choice, and may not suit others as well. I find it useful insofar as it touches the reality of man's psychic complexity and profundity at a level which seems to me most relevant to the understanding of the action of grace.

It should be said immediately (and perhaps quite unnecessarily) that to adopt such a systematic orientation does not mean and cannot mean that the psychology of grace is no more than a translation of the relevant insights of the Christian tradition into psychoanalytic terms. This may be feasible at some points, but at many points a rethinking and a resynthesis of both theological conceptions and psychological formulations are required. This, in fact, seems to me to present the real challenge of a meaningful and realistic psychology of grace. The mere parroting of phrases will never substitute for the understanding a true psychological inquiry seeks. One might even hope that such an inquiry, carried out with sincere Christian conviction, might share some small portion of the inspiration and vitality of grace, so that it would share that freedom from the preconceptions and restraints which so often burden merely human efforts at self-understanding.

Questions for Discussion

1. How are egoism and the ego opposed? What is Christian humility, as related to psychological theory? Discuss.
2. Is a unified vision of reality possible or not? Explain. What are the three general approaches of western theology to grace? What approach is Fransen following?
3. How does Fransen explain man's double liberty? How are the two forms unified? Under what conditions is the liberty of fundamental option exercised?
4. Fransen speaks in his discussion of the theology of grace of two fundamental alternatives. What are they? What are the consequences of original sin? How is grace related to love? To egoism? Where does grace chiefly affect man? Explain. What does Ruusbroec say about the direction of the movement of God's grace.
5. Why does a psychology of grace seem impossible, according to Fransen? Why does he accept the idea that there is a theology of grace? What contributions of Rahner and the Greek fathers are mentioned here? What are some of the religious phenomena Fransen finds psychologically interesting? Discuss.
6. How does Fransen define phenomenology? What are some of the elements of a phenomenology of grace, as Fransen conceives it? What two special tasks does Fransen suggest for the Christian psychologist?
7. Is psychology capable by itself of advancing the inquiry into grace?
8. How does psychology function here? What is the special relevance of the Christian psychologist today?

9. What does the author say about the religious *content* Fransen has discussed in his article? What does the author say about the method of inquiry?

10. Why does the author prefer the psychoanalytic construction? Is it enough to recast the relevant insights of Christian tradition in psychoanalytic terms? Explain and discuss.

XIII
PIERRE TEILHARD DE CHARDIN
ON CHRISTIAN PERFECTION

A. Prenote

In bringing this part of the inquiry into the life of grace to a resolution, it is necessary to reaffirm some important reflections which serve as a bridge to the working through of a Christian spirituality. There are several essentials of the life of grace which deserve particular emphasis at this point. No one in contemporary Catholic thought has better grasped and better expressed the realities of the Christian life than Pierre Teilhard de Chardin. He has understood the significance of the revelation and reality of the incarnate Word in all its unique relevance to the concerns of our day.

The passage which follows is taken from Teilhard's *The Divine Milieu* (New York: Harper, 1960), pp. 64-70.

B. Selection: The Christian Perfection of Human Endeavor

There was reason to fear, as we have said, that the introduction of Christian perspectives might seriously upset the ordering of human action; that the seeking after, and waiting for, the kingdom of heaven might deflect human activity from its natural tasks, or at least entirely eclipse any interest in them. Now we see why this cannot and must not be so. The knitting together of God and the world has just taken place under our eyes in the domain of action. No, God does not deflect our gaze prematurely from the work he himself has given us, since he presents himself to us as attainable through that very work. Nor does he blot out, in his intense light, the detail of our earthly aims, since the closeness of our union with him is in fact determined by the exact fulfillment of the least of our tasks. We ought to accustom ourselves to this basic truth till we are steeped in it, until it becomes as familiar to us as the perception of shape or the reading of words. God, in all that is most living and incarnate in him, is not far away from us, altogether apart from the world we see, touch, hear, smell and taste about us. Rather he awaits us every instant in our action, in the work of the moment. There is a sense in which he is at the tip of my pen, my spade, my brush, my needle — of my heart and of my thought. By pressing the stroke, the line, or the stitch, on which I am engaged, to its ultimate natural finish, I shall lay hold of that last end toward which my innermost will tends. Like those formidable physical forces which man contrives to discipline so as to make them perform operations of prodigious delicacy, so the tremendous power of the divine attraction is focused on our frail desires and microscopic intents without breaking their point. It sur-animates; hence it neither disturbs anything nor stifles anything. It sur-animates; hence it introduces a higher principle of unity into our spiritual life, the specific effect of which is — depending upon the point of view one adopts — either to make man's endeavor holy, or to give the Christian life the full flavor of humanity.

1. The Sanctification of Human Endeavor

I do not think I am exaggerating when I say that nine out of ten practicing Christians feel that man's work is always at the level of a "spiritual encumbrance." In spite of the practice of right intentions, and the day offered every morning to God, the general run of the faithful dimly feel that time spent at the office or the studio, in the fields or in the factory, is time taken away from prayer and adoration. It is impossible not to work — that is taken for granted. Then it is impossible, too, to aim at the deep religious life reserved for those who have the leisure to pray or preach all day long. A few moments of the day can be salvaged for God, yes, but the best hours are absorbed, or at any rate cheapened, by material cares. Under the sway of this feeling, large numbers of Catholics lead a double or crippled life in practice: They have to step out of their human dress so as to have faith in themselves as Christians — and inferior Christians at that.

What has been said above of the divine extensions and God-given demands of the mystical or universal Christ, should be enough to demonstrate both the emptiness of these impressions and the validity of the thesis (so dear to Christianity) of sanctification through fulfilling the duties of our station. There are, of course, certain noble and cherished moments of the day — those when we pray or receive the sacraments. Were it not for those moments of more efficient or explicit commerce with God, the tide of the divine omnipresence, and our perception of it, would weaken until all that was best in our human endeavor, without being entirely lost to the world, would be for us emptied of God. But once we have jealously safeguarded our relation to God encountered, if I may dare to use the expression, "in his pure state" (that is to say, in a state of being distinct from all the constituents of the world), there is not need to fear that the most trivial or the most absorbing of occupations should force us to depart from him. To repeat: By virtue of the creation and, still more, of the incarnation, *nothing* here below *is profane* for those who know how to see. On the contrary, everything is sacred to the men who can distinguish that portion of chosen being which is subject to Christ's drawing power in the process of consummation. Try, with God's help, to perceive the connection — even physical and natural — which binds your labor with the building of the kingdom of heaven; try to realize that heaven itself smiles upon you and, through your works, draws you to itself; then, as you leave church for the noisy streets, you will remain with only one feeling, that of continuing to immerse yourself in God. If your work is dull or exhausting, take refuge in the inexhaustible and becalming interest of progressing in the divine life. If your work enthralls you, then allow the spiritual impulse which matter communicates to you to enter into your taste for God whom you know better and desire more under the veil of his works. Never, at any time, "whether eating or drinking," consent to do anything without first of all realizing its significance and constructive value *in Christo Jesu,* and pursuing it with all your might. This is not simply a commonplace precept for salvation. It is the very path to sanctity for each man according to his state and calling. For what is sanctity in a creature if not to adhere to God with the maximum of his strength? — and what does that maximum adherence to God mean if not the fulfillment — in the world organized around Christ — of the exact function, be it lowly or eminent, to which that creature is destined both by natural endowment and by supernatural gift?

Within the Church we observe all sorts of groups whose members are vowed to the perfect practice of this or that particular virtue: mercy, detachment, the splendor of the liturgy, the missions, contemplation. Why should there not be men vowed to the task of exemplifying, by their lives, the general sanctification of human endeavor — men whose common religious ideal would be to give a full and conscious explanation of the divine possibilities or demands which any worldly occupation implies — men, in a word, who would devote themselves, in the fields of thought, art, industry, commerce and politics, etc., to carrying out in the sublime spirit these demands — the basic tasks which form the very bonework of human society? Around us the "natural" progress which nourishes the sanctity of each new age is all too often left to the children of the world, that is to say, to agnostics or the irreligious. Unconsciously or involuntarily such men collaborate in the kingdom of God and in the fulfillment of the elect. Their efforts, going beyond or correcting their incomplete or bad intentions, are gathered in by him "whose energy subjects all things to itself." But that is no more than a second best, a temporary phase in the organization of human activity. Right from the hands that knead the dough, to those that consecrate it, the great and universal Host should be prepared and handled in a spirit of *adoration.*

May the time come when men, having been awakened to a sense of the close bond linking all the movements of this world in the single, all-embracing work of the incarnation, shall be unable to give themselves to any one of their tasks without illuminating it with the clear vision that their work — however elementary it may be — is received and put to good use by a Center of the universe.

When that comes to pass, there will be little to separate life in the cloister from the life of the world. And only then will the action of the children of heaven (at the same time as the action of the children of the world) have attained the intended plenitude of its humanity.

2. The Humanization of Christian Endeavor

The great objection brought against Christianity in our time, and the real source of the distrust which insulates entire blocks of humanity from the influence of the Church, has nothing to do with historical or theological difficulties. It is the suspicion that our religion makes its followers *inhuman*.

"Christianity," so some of the best of the gentiles are inclined to think, "is bad or inferior because it does not lead its followers to levels of attainment beyond ordinary human powers; rather it withdraws them from the ordinary ways of humankind and sets them on other paths. It isolates them instead of merging them with the mass. Instead of harnessing them to the common task, it causes them to lose interest in it. Hence, far from raising them to a higher level, it diminishes them and makes them false to their nature. Moreover, don't they admit as much themselves? And if one of their religious, or one of their priests, should happen to devote his life to research in one of the so-called secular disciplines, he is very careful, as a rule, to point out that he is only lending himself for a time to serve a passing whim of scholarly fashion or even something ultimately of the stuff of illusion, and that simply in order to show that Christians are not, after all, the stupidest of men. When a Catholic works with us, we invariably get the impression that he is doing so in a spirit of condescension. He appears to be interested, but in fact, because of his religion, he simply does not believe in the human effort as such. His heart is not really with us. Christianity nourishes deserters and false friends: That is what we cannot forgive."

We have placed this objection, which would be deadly if it were true, in the mouth of an unbeliever. But has it no echo, here and there, within the most faithful souls? What Christian who has become aware of a sheet of glass insulating him from his non-believing colleagues, has not asked himself uneasily whether he was not on a false tack or had not actually lost touch with the main current of mankind?

Without denying that some Christians, by their words more than their deeds, do give grounds for the reproach of being, if not the "enemies," at least the "stragglers" of the human race, we can safely assert, after what we said above concerning the supernatural value of our work on earth, that their attitude is due to an incomplete understanding and not at all to some ineradicable flaw in our religion.

How could we be deserters, or skeptical about the future of the tangible world? How could we be repelled by human labor? How little you know us! You suspect us of not sharing your concern and your hopes and your excitement as you penetrate the mysteries and conquer the forces of nature. "Feelings of this kind," you say, "can only be shared by men struggling side by side for existence; whereas you Christians profess to be saved already." As though for us as for you, indeed far more than for you, it were not a matter of life and death that the earth should flourish to the uttermost of its natural powers. As far as you are concerned (and it is here that you are not yet human enough, you do not *go to the limits* of your humanity) it is simply a matter of the success or failure of a reality which remains vague and precarious even when conceived in the form of some super-humanity. For us it is a question in a true sense of achieving the victory of no less than a God. One thing is infinitely disappointing, I grant you: Far too many Christians are insufficiently conscious of the "divine" responsibilities of their lives, and live like other men, giving only half of themselves, never experiencing the spur or the intoxication of advancing God's kingdom in every domain of mankind. But do not blame anything but our weakness: Our faith imposes on us the right and the duty to throw ourselves into the things of the earth. As much as you, and even better than you (because, of the two of us, I alone am in a position to prolong the perspectives of my endeavor to infinity, in conformity with the requirements of my present intention), I want to dedicate myself body and soul to the sacred duty of research. We must test every barrier, try every path, plumb every abyss. *Nihil intentatum* . . . God wills it, who willed that he should have need of it. You are men, you say? *Plus et ego.*

Plus et ego. There can be no doubt of it. At a time when the consciousness of its own powers and possibilities is legitimately awakening in a mankind now ready to become adult, one of the first duties of a Christian as an apologist is to show, by the logic of his religious views and still more by the logic of his action, that the incarnate God did not come to diminish in us the glorious responsibility and splendid ambition that is ours: *of fashioning our own self.* Once again, *non minuit, sed sacravit.* No, Christianity is not, as it is sometimes presented and sometimes practiced, an additional burden of observances and obligations to weigh down and increase the already heavy load, or to multiply the already paralyzing ties of our life in society. It is, in fact, a soul of immense power which bestows significance and beauty and a new lightness on what we are already doing.

C. Commentary and Analysis

Christian sanctification is both a making-holy of human endeavor and a humanization of Christian life. Humanization and sanctification ultimately come down to the same thing. Or putting it another way, man uniquely and sublimely fulfills his divine vocation when he is most completely and most specifically human. Teilhard has caught the Pauline vision of the Christification of human existence. This has never meant that the incremental incorporation of the Christian into Christ, and of Christ into the Christian, signifies a diminution of individual personality. It has meant that the degree of Christification is identical with, or proportional to, the degree of personification. Self-affirmation must ultimately be an affirmation of Christ in the self.

The Christian vocation, therefore, is a vocation to self-affirmation in the best and most authentic sense of which we have spoken. We are called, as Teilhard puts it, to the responsibility "of fashioning our own self." The self is, therefore, "fashionable," and the action of grace is intimately involved in that fashioning. And, more to the point, it is the self and no other agency that works out this fashioning.

The crucial question for Christian spirituality, then, must be how this fashioning, self-affirmation, this ego-synthesis, shall be achieved. Teilhard has an answer. It is achieved in action. It is carried forward in those actions in which man achieves his complete humanity. It is carried forward in every action by which man engages himself in the real. For it is in such engagement that man becomes most authentically himself. The Christian vocation is, therefore, a vocation to engagement in the real, to immersion in human activity. To retreat from the responsibility of human activity is to negate the Christian life and to disengage the action of grace. The Christian vocation is a commitment to man's quest for understanding — of himself and his relatedness to the whole of creation and to God. The Christian man, beyond all others, seeks self-affirmation, and the self he affirms is identified by its relations and interactions with other selves and other objects. There is no enterprise, no search, no inquiry to which modern man is called to which the Christian man is not antecedently called in virtue of his divine vocation. "Nothing . . . is profane for those who know how to see."

It is grace which unifies, intensifies, vivifies all of this. And its energy is essential. Without it the human spirit would flag in disappointment and despair. For humanity is an achievement and the effort of humanization is unending and uninterrupted. Man is a dynamic reality always in the process of becoming. Because his becoming is linked to and involved with the reality of his divine vocation, the energizing and dynamizing action of grace becomes an integral part of man's existence.

Existence and the divine vocation are identical for every human being. Therefore, Christian spirituality and the psychology of grace have no meaning unless they assert the identity of the sanctification of human endeavor and the humanization of Christian endeavor.

In the vision of Teilhard de Chardin, we can see the exigencies of the psychology of the life of grace extend themselves to the concrete realization of a Christian spirituality. There is a direct and unbroken line running from the image of man through the psychology of grace to the highest objectives of the spiritual life.

Questions for Discussion

1. What general remarks does the author make about Teilhard's importance to the study of grace?
2. In Teilhard's view, does the seeking of the kingdom of heaven blot out earthly aims? Discuss.
3. Describe work seen as a "spiritual encumbrance." What is the value of daily encounter with God "in his pure state"? Why and how can man continually be immersed in God? Supposing that the work is dull? Supposing that it is enthralling?
4. What should be the attitude of Christians toward "natural progress"? When will the action of Christians have attained the plenitude of its humanity?
5. What deficiencies do "the gentiles" find in Christianity? Do you think their indictment is too strong? Discuss.
6. Why is progress of life on earth so vitally important to Christians? Why is the Christian even more committed to human achievement than "the gentile"?
7. Explain the author's statement that "humanization and sanctification ultimately come down to the same thing."
8. Given this perspective, how can the Christian vocation be described?
9. How does Teilhard answer the question of how ego-synthesis is achieved?
10. Why is the energizing influence of grace especially essential to the Christian in the modern world?

XIV
EPILOGUE

In bringing this inquiry into the psychology of grace to a close, I would like to attempt a recapitulation of the tentative formulations previously advanced. The focus of our consideration has been on the feasibility of a psychology of grace, the clarification of its relations with theology, and the formation of an image of man incorporating the fundamental insights of the theological approach to grace with those of the psychological approach.

It is possible to take a further unsteady step. In so doing we are moving from the level of preliminaries to the psychology of grace, moving across the threshold of psychological consideration. I would like to try to formulate a more or less central concept as an initial step toward a psychological theory of the action of grace. The constructs which are to make up the theory of the psychology of grace are produced by the action of grace. In the view we have evolved in the preceding pages, these represent structural entities in the ego which function analogously to natural psychological structures, yet have their own proper specifying characteristics.

The concept I would like to advance here is that of "spiritual identity." The term will elicit immediate connotations for the contemporary psychologist. One of the most significant concepts to be advanced in recent years is Erik Erikson's notion of identity.[1]

---

[1] *Identity and the Life Cycle* (New York: International Universities Press, 1959).

I am suggesting here that, just as identity subsumes those aspects of personality development and function which characterize the successful achievement of adult personality and maturity, so spiritual identity serves to bring into focus those psychological characteristics which result from the effective operation of grace.

Several points can immediately be suggested to structure the relationship between these concepts. The sense of identity represents a level of integration within the ego. It is, therefore, a state of personality development which properly pertains to the ego. Spiritual identity is likewise a state of synthetic organization within the ego. Moreover, personal identity and spiritual identity are reciprocally related precisely because they represent states of organization of the same identical ego-structures. The difference lies in the fact that spiritual identity is due in part to the energizing influence of grace, and in the fact that spiritual identity is functioning in part on a supernatural level.

The relationship between personal and spiritual identity can perhaps best be developed by first clarifying their respective meanings and then trying to define their relationships. Personal identity, as Erikson develops the idea, is a complex notion. It represents a definitive stage of psychosocial development which characteristically takes place in the adolescent years and which normally involves the taking-shape of the adult personality. As Erikson views the process of ego-development, the infant and growing child passes through a more or less consistent sequence of developmental phases, each of which is characterized by a psychosocial crisis. The psychosocial crisis is a basic alternative in the quality of social and interpersonal relations which the child must resolve in one direction or other, in one degree or other. These stages and their respective crises develop in more or less loose association with, and in function of, the course of psychosexual development. We need only note the parallelism here to indicate that it is this parallel development which establishes the pattern of psychosocial development in the context of more basic instinctual developments.

The first stage of infancy sees the development of the initial and very fundamental crisis of trust. The infant is placed in a position of extreme dependency on his parents, particularly his mother.

The primacy of his needs is oral at this stage, and these oral needs determine the significance of his interpersonal contacts with the mother. It is she who satisfies the hunger need and it is on her that the child must uniquely depend. In this situation, then, the child develops a quality of relationship to the mother which depends in large measure on the mother's response to the child. The basic issue in this relationship is that of trust. If the mother is loving, warm and mothering, the child is able to put his trust in her, to take confidence in her responsiveness. He is thus able to become trusting toward another human being. The quality of trust is a fundamental quality of human relationships, and Erikson feels that this basic quality is established in this orally organized mother-child interaction.

There is an alternative possibility. The mothering relation from the point of view of the mother is an extremely complex one. The intimate association of mother and child in the breast-feeding relation serves as a sort of focal point for much of the mother's adult adaptation. In this relation she is functioning very specially as woman, wife, and mother. Her own mature acceptance of these roles and their implications and her adjustment to their demands become major determinants of the quality of her contact with the child. If she has successfully adjusted to the demands of these roles, if she has successfully achieved a mature acceptance of her own femininity, the feeding relation becomes a rewarding and ful-filling experience. If she has not, however — if she has rejected her own femininity and has failed to integrate her various roles into an adequate adjustment — the possibility arises that the quality of her relation to the child will suffer. Love and acceptance may be replaced by hostility and rejection. Instead of trust, there can develop a basic distrust.

For the child, the alternatives are decisive. He faces a crisis of development. The crisis will be resolved in one direction or the other — toward trust or toward distrust. The resolution will strike a balance between the polarities of trust and distrust, and this balance will set the tone for the future stages of the child's development. If the resolution of this first crisis is decisively in the direction of basic trust, then the foundation has been laid for the successful progression through succeeding crises. The successful

resolution of crises at each level of development lays the foundations for subsequent successful resolutions and forms a developmental progression toward personal maturity. In the degree to
which such sequential crises are not successfully resolved, or
are resolved in favor of the more negative alternative, the development of the maturely functioning personality is to that extent
impeded.

We can summarize some of the subsequent psychosocial crises
briefly. The stage of early childhood sees the crisis, between
autonomy and shame or doubt, taking shape around the issue of
early discipline. The struggle between the child's emerging will
and the parent's will is typified by the toilet-training situation. In
the subsequent play age, the child faces the crisis of initiative
as opposed to guilt. In the school age, it is the development of a
sense of industry as opposed to a sense of inferiority. Each of these
stages has its characteristic quality and problems. But the emerging
personality must work its way through them as it passes through
the early phases of the life cycle. Each succeeding phase builds,
therefore, on the residues of preceding phases and the resolutions
of preceding crises.[2]

The critical phase for our present consideration is that of
adolescence. For it is in adolescence that the identity crisis emerges.
As the child comes into the adolescent years, he bridges the chasm
between childhood and adulthood. There is of course the biological fact of puberty which tends to carry with it a maturation of
sexual drives and orientation. This maturation confronts the
adolescent with the necessity for regarding himself and accepting
himself in a specific sexual role. The sexual role, as male or female,
is not only biologically determined, but it carries with it a heavy
complement of social and cultural expectations which must be
integrated into a mature sexual adjustment. There is also the
necessity for defining a mature adult position and function in the
community. This also forces the adolescent to crystallize his own
concept of who and what he is. Along with these extrinsic determinant, there is an emerging awareness of the individual's own
continuity over time in the form of a sense of self-identity. There

[2] E. Erikson, *Childhood and Society* (New York: Norton, 1950).

is also involved a basic recognition on the part of others of this continuity along with an acceptance of the individual in terms of some definite set of role-relations and expectancies. The sameness of internal self-awareness and the external regard of others sets the stage for a kind of mutual reinforcement which underlies the sense of identity unique to the individual. It is in terms of this sense of identity that the previous developmental accretions receive a more or less definitive form and are integrated into a well-adapted and maturely functioning personality.

Identity, then, is an integrating concept. A mature sense of personal identity depends on the successively successful resolution of the developmental psychosocial crises. It implies a basic sense of trust in which the ego finds itself trusting and trustworthy and has therefore a degree of self-confidence which implies a secure self-possession. It implies a basic sense of autonomy which underlies a capacity for self-assertion and independence, for self-expression and self-control without the loss of self-esteem, and a capacity to respect the autonomy of others and to achieve rewarding and effective cooperation with them. A capacity for initiative, responsibility and dependability without the burden of guilt or shame is also involved, as well as a basic sense of industry and a capacity to direct and sustain one's efforts to achieve specific goals.

Identity is then a resume and recapitulation of the developmental history of the personality. But it is more than this. The specific position which an individual occupies and which determines to a large extent the identity which he assumes is not a random acquisition. In seeking to define himself as a functioning personality, the child passes through a series of identifications which structure in one degree or other his manner of adjusting and behaving. He identifies first usually with parental figures, later with teachers, older relatives, or even to some extent with admired or respected peers. Each of these identifications is in one degree or other partial, but they each leave a residue in the evolving personality. In the process of identity formation, the aggregate of these residues of identification is given a more or less definitive shape. But identity formation is not just the aggregate of previous identifications. Identity formation is an active process in which the ego injects something of its own. Thus the resultant identity is something unique and different in its own right.

Identity or the sense of identity is, therefore, a product of the synthetic activity of the ego. It is produced within the ego and by the ego. The ultimate form which this identity takes, then, is due to the ego itself, acting autonomously and independently. It is a fundamental form of self-assertion and self-realization. Moreover such ego-synthetic activity is a specific and proper activity of the ego, and only of the ego. Whatever other determinants are at work, environmental or intrapsychic, the ultimate agency of organization of the personality is the ego itself. As a corollary, then, we can say that the degree to which identity formation is defective depends in large measure on the degree to which the ego is incapable of autonomous and independent activity. To put it in the framework of Erikson's psychosocial crises, it is precisely in the degree to which the resolution of preceding crises contributes to or interferes with the basic capacity of the ego for autonomous synthetic activity that the resolution of the crisis of identity formation depends.

The notion of spiritual identity, like the notion of personal identity, is an integrative notion. Over and above the question of the individual's capacity for personal maturity, there is the fact of man's basic incapacity to lead a supernaturally oriented life without the assistance of grace. From the very first moment of spiritual rebirth in baptism, man becomes a *nova creatura*. Through the divine indwelling he assumes a new existence which is specifically supernatural. That existence is nourished and developed by the power of grace. Implicit in such a view of man's supernatural existence is the realization that such a supernatural existence is subject to development. In some sense, the life of the Spirit in man is like a seed that begins in the simplest manner and undergoes a slow and sometimes painful development.

From the point of view of psychology of grace, we are interested in the psychological aspects of this development. But the analysis of such development remains as the work of a future psychology of grace. I would merely like to suggest here that such a development must follow a specific pattern and developmental principles, and must observe certain priorities in the sequence of phases through which the development progresses. I would like to concentrate here on spiritual identity as a sort of *terminus ad quem* of this development. I would like to suggest that, just as man achieves a certain sense of identity in his development to psychological maturity, so he achieves a certain sense of spiritual identity in his development to spiritual maturity.

We can elaborate the notion of spiritual identity by turning to a more traditional analysis. There is involved an awareness and acceptance of a realm of spiritual values which are derived from a prior acceptance of a supernatural order of existence. The basic disposition to such an acceptance comes through faith. There is a maximal development of. those basic strengths of temperance, fortitude, justice and prudence. There is then the full complement of the virtues, crowned by the theological virtues of faith, hope and charity. In short, spiritual identity in the fullness of its development stands for the full flowering of Christian virtue and saintliness.

This is not the place to catalogue the elements in such a picture. But several points should be made. Spiritual identity is dependent on grace for its growth and achievement. Without grace, it is not possible. Spiritual identity is related to psychological qualities of a distinctly different order from the qualities associated with personal identity. This does not mean that there cannot be a tremendous area of overlap between these respective identities. It is difficult, if not impossible, to conceive of a man motivated by supernatural charity not being at the same time capable of trust and of intimate relations with his fellow men. But it remains true that without grace supernatural charity is not possible, and, although it presumes intimacy, it involves much more. Further, it is not enough merely to indicate that spiritual identity encompasses the Christian virtues. Our understanding of the Christian virtues must be set down in psychological terms. It is precisely on this level that the hardest work for a future psychology of grace must be done. One cannot presume that we have any meaningful psychological understanding of the Christian virtues. Erikson has opened the way for us to conceptualize the Christian virtues in psychologically relevant terms. One can presume that such a development will in time be rewarding and fruitful, both for the psychology of grace and for the understanding of the functioning of the ego. But in indicating the virtues here, we are doing no more than indicating the direction of a future program of study and understanding.

It is important to stress, from the psychological point of view, that the achievement of spiritual identity, to whatever degree this is realized in the individual person, is an achievement of the ego itself. Grace does not change man, but it gives man the power to change himself. Man grows to spiritual maturity under grace through his own activity. If the development of the virtues is to have any meaning psychologically, it must be in terms of the synthetic activity of the ego. The development of such virtues implies growth, restructuration, organization and integration within the ego.

The achievement of spiritual identity implies a right ordering of behavior and internal impulses and the integration of psychic energies under the direction and control of the ego. This is akin to what the theologians have referred to as an ordered concupiscence. The rebelliousness of man's lower nature through disordered concupiscence is one of the unfortunate consequences of original sin. But the effect of grace is to reestablish the control of man's higher nature and bring about an internal integration. This is achieved psychologically through the establishment and maintenance of ego-control over the energies of the instinctive part of man's psychic structure. Consequently, spiritual identity implies such ego-integration, but I hasten to add that personal identity implies the same thing. This, then, is to say no more than that spiritual identity builds upon personal identity.

It should be evident, from the terms of this partial analysis, that there is a kind of reciprocal relationship between personal identity on the natural level and spiritual identity on the supernatural. The reservation must constantly be advanced that we are speaking of spiritual identity as a psychological reality. Obviously the life of grace involves much more than a change in man's psychological organization. But it is precisely this latter that we are concerned with here, and not the whole gamut of theologically relevant effects which are the proper matter of a theology of grace. In psychological terms, then, spiritual identity builds upon personal identity. There are two consequences of this relationship. First, the degree of spiritual identity which a man can achieve is limited by, or related to, the degree of prior personal identity he has achieved. Second, spiritual identity is in some sense perfective of personal identity.

An explanation of these propositions will make their relationship more clear. If spiritual identity is dependent on the capacity of the ego to exercise its synthetic function autonomously, then the extent to which the ego has achieved a sense of identity is a measure of that capacity. Therefore, the more mature ego is more autonomous, more in control of the energies at its disposal, and so more capable of bringing about the self-modifications motivated through grace. Or putting it another way, the higher degree of ego-control in the mature ego permits it to utilize more effectively the energies put at its disposal through grace.

Spiritual identity is perfective of personal identity in the sense that the effect of the added energizing activity of grace is to enable the ego to function more perfectly due to the greater energy resources at its disposal. Furthermore, the structures and functions associated with spiritual identity are identical with the structures and functions associated with personal identity, but raised to a higher level of activity. This underlines the point we have already made that grace is operating in and through ego functions. The increase of energy which the ego can channel into these functions underlies the capacity of the ego to form a spiritual identity.

A more concrete example may help to clarify these relationships. We have already presented at some length an analysis of basic trust. This is the first psychosocial crisis and one of the basic qualities of the adult sense of identity. We may compare this with faith. Faith is a basic disposition for any spiritual life. One must recognize and accept the reality of God and of his governance of love before any meaningful spiritual activity is possible. What then is involved in faith? Basically faith implies a receptivity, an openness to God, a willingness to accept his Word. It involves a basic trust in God in the sense of confidence in his love and saving power. It involves a basic trust in God in the sense of confidence in oneself and one's judgment to be able to make that commitment of self which is necessary to bridge the chasm between the security and self-reliance of reason and the darkness and other-reliance of faith. The relation between faith and trust is underlined in Erikson's treatment of trust. He remarks that

> . . . the psychological observer must ask whether or not in any area under observation religion and tradition are living psychological forces creating the kind of faith or conviction which permeates a parent's personality and thus reinforces the child's basic trust . . . in the world's trustworthiness . . . All religions have in common the periodical childlike surrender to a Provider or providers who can dispense earthly fortune as well as spiritual health; the demonstration of one's small-ness and dependence through the medium of reduced posture and humble gesture; the admission in prayer and song of mis-deeds, of misthoughts, and of evil intentions; the admission of inner division and the consequent appeal for inner unifica-tion by divine guidance; the need for clearer self-delineation and self-restriction; and finally, the insight that individual trust must become a common faith, individual mistrust a commonly formulated evil, while the individual's need for res-toration must become part of the ritual practice of many, and must become a sign of the trustworthiness of the community.[3]

It seems safe to say, then, that faith is a basic quality of the spiritual identity, but that it somehow depends on the prior capacity in the individual to trust. One's ability to trust in God and to put one's reliance in him is limited by the degree to which the person has developed that basic capacity to trust others and to feel a certain confidence in the trustworthiness of one's own beliefs. Faith then builds upon trust. If an individual has achieved a sense of basic trust, the enlargement of that sense of trust into a trusting relation to God through faith is facilitated. If, however, the in-dividual has in the course of his growth to maturity failed to achieve that sense of basic trust, and has resolved the initial psy-chosocial crisis in the direction of basic mistrust, then it would seem exceedingly difficult for him to build the relationship of faith.

But this does not exhaust the possibilities. Grace, as we are considering it here, has a sanating effect. It is directed to healing

---

[3] *Identity and the Life Cycle,* pp. 64-65.

the disintegration and the wound of nature. Consequently, even when basic distrust has come to dominate the adjustment, grace can so vitalize and charge the energies of the ego that it becomes possible for the ego to overcome the defect of development and begin to function on more mature and adaptive terms. The effect, however, is not wrought by some miraculous alteration. It is wrought by the self-constructive and self-assertive capacity of the ego. I am persuaded that no circumstances could so distort the ego that it would be placed beyond all capacity to recover its loss. Yet, while grace facilitates such recovery, it does so in terms of the inner laws of the ego's functioning. The greater the degree of trust the ego can achieve, the more effective is the influence of grace.

If grace, then, can bring the ego to faith, by a kind of reciprocal interaction, faith must induce an enhancement of the degree of basic trust. So it is that grace can perfect nature, both by elevating the prior disposition of nature to a new and more intense level, and by reciprocally nourishing the dispositions of nature to draw them to their own proper function.

This kind of analysis can be extended to other aspects of spiritual identity as well.[4] However, the major point is that faith is an act proper to man's faculties insofar as it is an act of intellect and will. But it is not an act that man can make unaided by the power of grace. We have tried to formulate the effects of grace, in this instance, by suggesting that faith is indeed an act of man, using his faculties in their proper fashion. We have noted, however, that the activity of those faculties is somehow elevated or extended. We are not concerned here with the supernaturality of the objects of the act of faith, but we are saying that in faith man achieves a higher level of psychological activity. It is this higher level of activity that the energizing effect of grace makes possible.

The concept of spiritual identity, then, may serve as a kind of prototype for concepts which might be developed in a more mature psychology of grace. We have only attempted here to suggest a kind of formulation. Development of the concept of spiritual identity would in itself be a considerable undertaking; I only hope that I have been able to suggest that it would be a valuable one. Future

---

[4] W. W. Meissner, "Prolegomena to a Psychology of Grace," *Journal of Religion and Health* 3 (1964), pp. 209-240.

steps would entail the formulation of the developmental phases of spiritual identity, as well as the analysis of its relation to structures and functions within the ego.

Questions for Discussion

1. What have been the main emphases in the consideration thus far?

2. What new concept does the author advance, as the initial step toward a psychological theory of the action of grace?

3. What are the common notes of, and interrelationships between, spiritual identity and personal identity?

4. How does Erikson view the process of ego-development? Illustrate by describing the various phases. Where and how can the development be impeded? What phase is the most critical?

5. Upon what does mature personal identity depend? How does the author describe the various aspects of personal identity?

6. How does the author characterize spiritual identity? In terms of man's new life? In terms of the parallel concept of personal identity? How is spiritual identity different from personal? What interrelationships are pointed out? How does the ego fit in? Is "ordered concupiscence" achieved?

7. What are the consequences of the interrelation between spiritual and personal identity?

8. How do trust and faith fit into the picture? How does grace work its healing effects?

9. What does the author indicate are the limits of his conclusions here? What further lines of development do you see as possible?

10. What suggestions have you for formulating the developmental phases of spiritual identity, in view of the phases of personal identity discussed earlier? From further study, for example of Erikson's works, could you contribute to the analysis of the relation between spiritual identity and structures and functions within the ego?

INDEX